Royalty
IN EXILE

Charles Fenyvesi

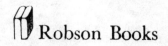 Robson Books

FIRST PUBLISHED IN 1981 BY ROBSON BOOKS
LTD., 28 POLAND STREET, LONDON W1V 3DB.
COPYRIGHT © 1981 CHARLES FENYVESI.

British Library Cataloguing in Publication Data

Fenyvesi, Charles
  Royalty in exile.
  1. Ex-kings — Europe
  I. Title
  940.55'092'2   D1073

ISBN 0-86051-131-6

The Publisher wishes to thank the following copyright holders for permission to use their photographs in this book:

The Bettmann Archive: p. 14

Photo Section

The Bettmann Archive: p. 4, top left, top right; p. 5, bottom; p. 8, bottom left, bottom right; p. 12, top left; p. 14, bottom left.

Keystone Press: p. 2, bottom; p. 6, top left, top right, bottom; p. 15, bottom right.

Magnum: p. 15, top.

Milwaukee Sentinel: p. 14, bottom right.

Monarchist Press Association: p. 2, top right.

New York Times: p. 1.

Time-Life: p. 2, top left (Herbert Gehr); p. 3, top (Loomis Dean), middle, bottom (Alfred Eisenstaedt); p. 4, bottom (David Lees); p. 5, middle (Nina Leen); p. 7 (Loomis Dean); p. 10 (David Lees); p. 11, top (Hank Walker), bottom (David Lees); p. 12, bottom (John Phillips); p. 13, top (John Phillips), bottom (Nina Leen).

UPI: p. 5, top; p. 8, top; p. 9, bottom; p. 11, middle; p. 12, top right.

Wide World: p. 9, top; p. 15, bottom left.

Printed and bound in Great Britain by R. J. Acford, Industrial Estate, Chichester, Sussex.

Pour la Reine Li Zou

ACKNOWLEDGMENTS

My first thanks go to the royal subjects of this book who graciously agreed to take part in a twentieth-century enterprise of journalistic inquiry. I will always treasure the memory of their hospitality and conversation.

Of the scores of people who helped with leads and details and suggestions, there are a few who must be mentioned: Prince David Chavchavadze, a Romanoff on his mother's side and a choice companion; Akosh Chernush of Washington and formerly of Paris and Budapest, a gourmet of words and moods; my good neighbor Charles Mayer, formerly of Vienna and Brussels, and his brother Peter, from New York; Nestor Ratesh, a skeptical journalist and his fellow Romanian, former Foreign Minister Constantin Visoianu; Aladár Szegedy-Maszák, Hungary's first postwar ambassador in Washington and a wise old friend; the witty James Symington, former congressman and State Department chief of protocol; veteran *Time* correspondent Simon Bourgin and ex-BBC man Leslie Finer; Professors David Korn and George Kousoulas of Howard University; international lawyer Vittorfranco Pisano from the Library of Congress and his father Paolo, who practices law in Rome. Special thanks are due to historian Giovanni Artieri, senator from Naples, and to Yevgeni Vagin and Géza Mihályi, both from the Italian radio. In Paris, Francis Schell of the *Reader's Digest* gave me invaluable assistance, including an introduction to Eugénie, princess of Greece, born a Bonaparte. In London, genealogist David Williamson, editor of the authoritative *Burke's Peerage*, shared his treasures with me, as did the hospitable Ivan Bilibin, head of the Imperial Chancellery of Russia, and former anti-Nazi partisan Nemanja Marcetic, originally from Yugoslavia. Poets George Faludy and Joseph Brodsky offered stories and visions.

I am grateful to Martin Peretz, editor of *The New Republic*, for the idea of the book and the assignment, as well as to editor Joan Tapper for shaping journalistic interviews into chapters. Acknowledgments are due to two other editors at New Republic Books, Marc Granetz and Fran Moshos, who curbed some of my excesses, and to the designer, Lynette Ruschak.

Finally, there is a countess, born in the last century, who did not wish to be mentioned by name or country, but whose spirit of forward-looking nostalgia surfaces many times on these pages, as does the counsel of Yemin Cohen, chief rabbi of Tangier, Morocco, a citizen of the Golden Age in Iberia and a descendant of King David of Jerusalem.

Washington, D.C.   C.F.
August 14, 1979

A Passage to
More Than an Hour Ago

Crown Prince Michael, later king of Romania, plays chess on his third birthday.

When to the sessions of sweet silent thought
I summon up remembrance of things past,
I sigh the lack of many a thing I sought,
And with old woes new wail my dear times' waste:
Then can I drown an eye, unus'd to flow,
For precious friends hid in death's dateless night.
And weep afresh love's long-since cancell'd woe,
And moan the expense of many a vanish'd sight.
Then can I grieve at grievances foregone,
And heavily from woe to woe tell o'er
The sad account of fore-bemoaned moan

Shakespeare, Sonnet XXX.

I teach chess to my seven-year-old son. He learns quickly about pieces and moves, and we are soon playing his first game. It does not take long for him to receive a check.

"Check," he cries, "that means that my king is being checked?"

"That's right."

His voice trembles. "My king is in danger. *My king!*"

Is it just the tension of playing a new, truly adult game? Or is it an emotion deeper and older—an echo? I don't know. But there is gravity in his voice, a Shakespearean tone.

He loses the game. Looking at his face, I feel guilty. I tell him, "That's chess, and that's how you learn the game."

He is close to tears. "I wish I made different moves," he says. "I wish we were back an hour ago."

If only time could be recovered! If we could go back and reason with the mob storming the Tuileries, talk sense to Kaiser Wilhelm, or stop the Greek colonels. If we could retrace our steps to our mistakes, or to our moments of glory and be valedictorians and radicals once more—instead of middle-aged men and women with narrowing horizons, Frenchmen who cannot be enthusiastic about a united Europe though they know they ought to be, Austrians bored with their prosperity, and old Bolsheviks who are absolutely sure by now that even getting rid of Stalin did not solve anything.

This book is not an attempt to recapture the time before the fall, or to redefine the sweetness of the ancien régime. Nor did I go in search of a luminous thought to redeem our century—who said it is "our worst, so far"?—now in its dying years.

This book is a report on the losers, history's dropouts. I paid visits on people whose ancestors ruled over my ancestors and whose houses and heads are haunted by rebels and emperors, by thoughts of decline and fall. I joined their resistance to forgetfulness, and I shared in some of their illusions. We revisited old battlefields, compared scars by Father Time and by the Vanguard of the Proletariat, and we talked of shoes and ships and sealing wax, of cabbages and kings.

I did not approach their majesties and highnesses worshipfully, or in a mood to challenge dragons. They are not dragons, nor creatures hiding in the peaty darkness of a Loch Ness. They are people who worry about their children's education and who look for a wife or a job. One of them uses his title to get bank loans for refugees. Another is raising an army to reconquer his homeland. Or so he says.

I am not a muckraker, and I came across no scandals. I was interested in the ways nonreigning royalty defy modernity—in character under the pressure of inherited obligation and in that separate peace that each has been obliged to sign with the egalitarian and permissive present.

I searched for their Achilles' heels; the decisions they or their ancestors reached that they now regret, friends and comforters with the wrong advice, the ambivalence of strongmen who have sought to replace them, their missed opportunities and their strategies of waiting.

I hoped to find them in a liberal mood in which royalty and reporter, sovereign and subject, patriot and alien, Gentile and Jew could reach across the table and speak as if the walls of caste and purpose did not exist—as if we carried equal burdens of the past, as if we could start anew. I dreamed of that magic hour in a tavern by the king's highway where we met centuries ago, in that faraway spring of our ancestors, when we and the world were confident that a philosopher king or a good man could resolve the great conflicts of multinational empire and local nationalism, inherited privilege and social justice, the need for unity and the urge for dissent. Or I hoped for a reunion, soft with wisdom and remorse and the tolerance of age, to compare regrets after a lost revolution and enlightened repression, to agree in our contempt for compromise and rehabilitation. Then, as now, we clinked our glasses, drank good local wine, and toasted women, projects, and, above all, life.

There may be no such tavern and no such highway and no such tolerance.

But I looked for such an illusion, as optimistic as only a father and a gardener could be, as persistent as a reporter. Much to my surprise, my best companion was Germany's Louis Ferdinand Hohenzollern. How he loves his grandfather, Kaiser Wilhelm, whose schemes unraveled the old world! My saddest meeting was with Romania's King Michael, who earned historic credit by having turned against Hitler at the age of twenty-three. His courage has led him nowhere; he was too good a man for a sorry epoch. Then there was Prince Alexander Karageorgevitch—a most likeable young man who could make a good ruler of Yugoslavia and who is waiting wisely. But should he be so wise?

The question they were all delighted to answer had to do with their favorite kings. I liked best the response by Henri, the count of Paris: "St. Louis and Henri IV," he said promptly, without hesitation. "I love them. They are intelligent, devoted, astute, capable, and pure."

The tense he used was clearly, unmistakably the present. Not past, but present perfect—as if French had such a tense.

I found Grand Duke Wladimir an autocratic Romanoff and his cousin Nicholas a choice companion on a wintry ride across birch forests. Archduke Otto is the supple, thoughtful Habsburg the Danubian basin has always needed; Dom Duarte João is steeped in the melancholy of his Portugal; Italy's Umberto plays the role of a king superbly; and Bulgaria's Czar Simeon is a composite picture of his ancestors from every dynasty in Europe.

The instinctive awe one feels when encountering royalty is the heart's fluttering testimonial to the memory of feudal thralldom. It is a primeval deference, an involuntary bow before the ultimate in class, breeding, and tradition.

Royalty—banished or reigning—are closer to the gods of Mount Olympus than to us, ordinary mortals. They stand on pedestals, frozen in poses of utmost dignity and ineffable grace. They go through life as if in a series of stage sets. They are always center stage; action revolves around them. The stories they act out are all-important; nothing incidental or trivial ever happens to them.

They partake of another reality: not merely someone born at a particular time in a particular place, they represent the timeless ambitions of a people, notions of historic continuity and legitimacy. They are heroic Latin mottos embodied, harbingers of ancient prophecies, carriers of blessings and curses. History moves through them; even those with forebears deposed generations ago cannot divest themselves of that conviction. The cities they visit were founded, conquered, and lost by their ancestors, and the highways they travel on were once invasion routes. The people who surround them—a court, inevitably—as well as paintings in national museums and equestrian statues towering over main squares all serve to remind them who they were, who they are, who they must be. Like Jews, they are people of memory; like pious Jews living outside the Holy Land, they regard their life without the throne as exile.

Royalty provide one of the grand illusions of life: that above the everyday, the ordinary, there is some higher realm of understanding and authority and that the key to that platonic sphere is handed down from father to eldest son, generation after generation. That grand illusion is nurtured through education: from infancy on, princes and princesses are never permitted to forget their exalted identities. Their tutors are priests and patriots who dedicate themselves to inculcating the concepts of duty. They are carefully insulated from contact with ordinary people, from everyday life.

In his book *From Caesar to the Mafia*, journalist Luigi Barzini recalls a dinner with King Umberto on the night before Umberto's departure for exile. With his eyes half-shut, Umberto named all the villages along Sicily's northern coast without missing a single one, and describing some of them in detail. Barzini realized that Umberto knew his kingdom "yard by yard" and "always saw places decked out in their best, their faces always newly washed and shining . . . all the bells always rang for him from every bell-tower . . . He loved this non-existent country."

Monarchy depends on chivalry. Could there be a restoration without the likes of Alexandre Dumas's three musketeers willing to risk life and limb for a king or queen? But the king is lost the moment he recoils from the threat of violence; he who is unafraid to risk his life and those of his men inherits the kingdom.

"He is very loyal" is the highest praise from royalty. "He is ungracious" is the ultimate condemnation.

Nonreigning royalty have not been able to find their proper places in republics. Louis Ferdinand Hohenzollern has been mentioned as a possible president of the Federal Republic of Germany, but he has shied away from the honor, uncomfortable with the briefness of the tenure. As president of the Fifth Republic, Charles de Gaulle dangled the possibility of succession in tête-à-têtes with Henri Bourbon-Orléans. Yet perhaps because of his fear of the rough-and-tumble of French elective politics, Henri restricted himself to diplomatic missions abroad, earning himself the epithet the Crown Prince of the Republic. Otto von Habsburg is the only one among exiled royalty who has decided to run for office—for the European Parliament, to represent his domicile in southern Germany. He justifies his decision on the basis of his lifelong commitment to a united Europe. His colleagues without thrones and his loyalists in Austria criticize him for abandoning the monarchic ideal and for associating himself with a political party and with Germany.

The claimants to European thrones this book portrays have little in common. They are trained craftsmen of kingship, but each of them has his own way of coping with this century hostile to the craft. King Umberto keeps an operatic court, charms a long queue of visitors every day and sends telegrams to Parliament offering himself as a solution to Italy's perennial political crisis. Romania's King Michael is a withdrawn, brooding refugee from communism who makes heroic efforts to succeed as a businessman. France's Henri is a wealthy, contented citizen, enjoying an endless feast with leaders of the republic. His rival, Prince Imperial Louis-Napoleon, possibly Europe's wealthiest royalty, has no interest in politics and is not a claimant to the throne, only the head of the House of Bonaparte.

Unlike Rudyard Kipling's gentlemen, the eleven claimants interviewed in this book do not want to be thought of as belonging "To the legion of the lost ones, to the cohort of the damned." They do not like to be considered as a group, compared or even contrasted. Each stresses that he is unique—a sovereign soul, an historic exception. Those who have been kings point out that they once reigned—unlike pretenders who merely claim thrones—and each has his personal version of his dethronement. Among those who inherited thronelessness, some argue that they are not pretenders but heads of a royal or imperial house, or suggest that they are *not* like the Romanoffs (synonymous with hopelessness) or Henri Bourbon-Orléans ("he is a socialist who foolishly put his trust in a republic and in Charles de Gaulle") or Louis Ferdinand Hohenzollern ("a softie who never tried hard enough") or Otto von Habsburg ("he betrayed tradition by running for elective office"). Those from large countries tend to look down upon the others. "After all, what could one do with Bulgaria?" was Grand Duke Wladimir's comment on the failure of the monarchy in that small Balkan country. The one who gives the impression of being above it all and least concerned with his colleagues is the Bourbon pretender Henri. He is much like his ancestor Louis XIV who would rather not be grouped with other kings for fear that they presume "an equality which does not exist." For France, *bien entendu*, is the premier kingdom of Europe, "the first and most excellent kingdom in Christianity" and the one imitated by all the others.

This book deals with claimants to thrones in eleven countries—Albania, Austria-Hungary, Bulgaria, France, Germany, Greece, Italy, Portugal, Romania, Russia, and Yugoslavia—and contains interviews with all the claimants. I did not speak to claimants to thrones in countries that no longer exist as independent states: Bavaria, Hanover, Saxony, and Württemberg in Germany; the Kingdom of the Two Sicilies and the Duchy of Parma in Italy; and Montenegro in Yugoslavia. Nor did I concern myself with Ireland, Scotland, and Poland—countries that do not have royal houses, only descendants of kings with genealogical interests.

The claimants are all big men—the shortest is Portugal's Dom Duarte João, just under six feet; the tallest is King Leka I of the Albanians who measures 6'9". They all speak English, most of them French, and fluency in half-a-dozen languages is the rule rather than the exception. When conversation turns to King Constantine, his royal colleagues always note with derision and surprise that "poor Tino only speaks English and Greek." They all like to travel. They cross borders using an exotic variety of travel documents, ranging from an Italian passport issued to Count Rylski, who is in reality Bulgaria's Czar Simeon II, to the laissez-passer, recognized by the U.N. refugee organization, of Russia's Grand Duke Wladimir, to King Umberto's Italian passport not valid for Italy, to the Royal Albanian passport issued by the court of Leka I.

The problem of where tomorrow's dinner comes from has never occurred to any one of them. Except for King Michael, whose circumstances are modest, they all live in comfort, most of them in luxury. They can afford to live lives of passionless ease; they can even have a make-believe court with real visitors, some of whom are simply curious, others enchanted with the thought of stepping back in time. Among the visitors are royalists who practice unconditional surrender to the cause, and melancholy souls who enjoy partaking of the sadness of kings. What could be more noble than to be dedicated to a lost cause, to be more hopeful of restoration than royalty, to give heart to His Majesty by telling him to ignore the slings and arrows of outrageous fortune or to take arms against a sea of troubles?

Henri, the count of Paris, and King Constantine of Greece are perhaps the wealthiest of the claimants. Or perhaps that distinction belongs to Bulgaria's Czar Simeon, described by his relatives as the craftiest of businessmen and a son worthy of his father Czar Boris, whom Winston Churchill called the Fox of the Balkan.

Except for Prince Alexander of Yugoslavia, who is an insurance executive in Chicago, nonreigning royalty do not have 9-to-5 jobs. They are—or were in youth—enthusiastic airplane pilots ("It's because they like to be up in the clouds," explains Alexander's wife, born Princess Dona Maria da Gloria Orléans-Bragança). They are also sailors, and have a fascination with the sea. Most of them had some kind of military training; they all like hunting.

Five of them are descended from Queen Victoria of England, and, except for Leka, who is Moslem and only second-generation royalty, they are all at least distantly related to one another. Between the Catholic and Protestant dynasties, both opposed to intermarriage, the Orthodox of Russia and the Balkan provide bridges.

Since marriage with nonroyalty is usually frowned upon, European royalty form one family. "It's a soup," Prince Alexander declares, "we all are in one big pot." Prince Louis Ferdinand of Prussia, for instance, is not only the great-great-grandson of Queen Victoria, but married to Grand Duchess Kira—sister of the Romanoff claimant Wladimir and Victoria's great-granddaughter, as well as Louis Ferdinand's cousin on her father's *and* her mother's side. And Wladimir's daughter Maria married Louis Ferdinand's nephew, Prince Wilhelm Franz, who is Queen Victoria's great-great-great-grandson.

The Russian Orthodox Romanoffs, routinely allied to the Lutheran Germans and the Anglican British, are also related to the Roman Catholic Savoys of Italy and all the Balkan dynasties. Romanian Orthodox King Michael—great-great-grandson of Queen Victoria as well as of Czar Alexander II—is married to his third cousin, Princess Anne Bourbon-Parma, a Catholic originally from Italy, who in turn is closely related to the Protestant Danes as well as to the Catholic Habsburgs and Braganças. The missing link in the genealogy of European royalty is Bulgaria's Simeon, who is everybody's cousin.

A minority of nonreigning royalty may enter the country ruled by their forebears. Only Prince Louis Ferdinand was never exiled—but his grandfather, Kaiser Wilhelm, was. Bourbons and Bonapartes were finally allowed to return to France in 1950 through a legislative action that was later emulated in Portugal. Since the late 1960s, the head of the House of Habsburg has been permitted to enter Austria, though he prefers to live near the border, in Germany.

Most claimants have lived through at least one period during which restoration appeared to be a distinct possibility. During World War II, Prince Louis Ferdinand and Archduke Otto seemed to have good chances to recapture the thrones of their ancestors. If it had not been for the American gut distrust of monarchy—unmitigated by President Franklin Roosevelt's one-man lobbying effort—as well as a quaint British inclination to equate foreign dethronements with progress, a Hohenzollern or a Habsburg restoration might have succeeded the Nazi Reich.

In the mid-1940s in Yugoslavia, and in the early 1950s in Albania, a change of regime could have meant a reentry of the monarchy. In the mid-1950s, the Duke of Braganca was slated to succeed Portugal's dictator, Dr. Oliveira de Salazar. And had there been no de Gaulle to rescue French honor from the disgrace of collaboration with Nazi Germany, Henri Bourbon-Orléans might well have emerged as the alternative to Marshal Philippe Pétain of Vichy.

The most recent addition to the ranks of nonreigning royalty is King Constantine, who left Greece in 1967 and finally lost out in a referendum in 1974. At forty, he does not like to be categorized as an ex-king. He firmly believes that he will be called back to restore order in Greece and refuses to speak to the press for fear of reducing his chances of return.

The furthest removed from a reigning predecessor is Henri, the dashing count of Paris, whose great-great-grandfather, Louis-Philippe, was deposed in 1848. Henri reacts with a Gallic shrug when questioned about the possibility of a restoration. But, he declares at the age of seventy-one, he has not given up.

"Do you expect to regain your throne?" No journalist and few visitors can refrain from posing the inevitable question. The variety of response is extraordinary. King Leka proposes revolutionary activism, aimed at landing on the Albanian mainland; Prince Alexander carefully understates his availability; Prince Louis Ferdinand protests that the issue is irrelevant; Archduke Otto focuses instead on European unification.

But what matters is not whether the hopes for restoration grow dimmer or brighter, or whether the claimants—and their wives and followers—really believe that restoration is feasible. What matters is that while each claimant has made his separate peace with the realities of this day and age, those realities are of no overwhelming importance. The claimants do not bother to keep up with the times. Like maiden aunts and provincial cousins at the far end of the wedding table, they are what they are and they are who they are.

They cannot very well become construction workers or retail clerks. Nor do we expect them to—we are surprised by the few who pursue everyday careers. "They have beetles inside their heads," says one chatty princess who has known most of them, "and those beetles do buzz occasionally, and, with some of them, all the time. Those beetles can make a fearfully noisy racket."

In their heart of hearts nonreigning monarchs believe that they will be called back to rule. How could they believe otherwise? They are fed on hopes, and surrounded by people who perpetually say, "Your Majesty, the crown awaits you; it's only a question of time and the right circumstances." Visitors received by royalty leave sighing, "Oh, the problems we have these days we never had in the monarchy!" or "If only the monarchy could be restored!"

This may be the last time that there is a full complement of European claimants who take their roles as heads of imperial and royal houses seriously. Half of today's pretenders are over sixty and less than half of them have heirs able (or willing or qualified) to assume the titles and the pretensions that their fathers are carrying, with so much grace and style and with such a strong sense of duty.

Unlike their uninhibited ancestors—and unlike some of their children who pursue the dolce vita—the claimants portrayed in this book live lives free of scandal. If they have illicit love affairs or shady financial dealings (and suggestions of both exist) the public does not know about them. The family, for all of them, is the last refuge; the oldest, Prince Louis Ferdinand, has six children; Henri Bourbon-Orléans has ten; the youngest, Czar Simeon, is the father of five. Only Dom Duarte João is a bachelor; the rest are intensely concerned with progeny and with posterity.

Most of the claimants are difficult to reach. Some, like Archduke Otto and Czar Simeon, answer inquiries promptly and are open to the press. But the majority do not respond to letters, and even if one obtains their unlisted telephone numbers, one has to work one's way past courtiers and cleaning women, relatives and loyalists. His Majesty or His Highness never seems to be there: he is visiting friends, he is not available this week, this month, this season. He is consulting business associates in Zurich, or touring Communist China as a guest of the government. He is on a safari in Kenya, or attending a wedding in Buenos Aires. Or, simply: His Majesty or His Highness does not receive journalists. Or anyone.

They fear royalty fans and royalty-mongers more than they fear passionate republicans. They create strategies of evasion. "I am so sorry, but I have friends waiting for me," I overheard Archduke Otto say, ever so politely, to a stranger who approached him in the foyer of a restaurant. "Perhaps some other time we could get together."

They live in small and intersecting circles of relatives and aristocrats whose elaborate dinner parties and sports-filled country weekends constitute their social life. They cherish their privacy, which they feel is the one privilege they gained when they lost their thrones.

Royalty visit royalty. Among those in power, the Scandinavians are the most hospitable. Among nonreigning royalty, King Umberto—Uncle Beppo—is the most popular host and guest. His colleagues say he is always cheerful; they stay away from "the gloomy cases" such as King Michael or Grand Duke Wladimir. In the 1960s, Michael accepted an invitation for a cruise on a yacht belonging to his Aunt Frederika, then queen of Greece. Asked why he went, Michael explained, "I like some royalty, but not many and not much."

Old friends are very important; the older the better. Rarely are there new friends; nor is the present worth discussing—except for grandchildren and travel, wines and high taxes, or the rising wave of vulgarity everywhere.

Having interviewed all the claimants to now nonexistent European thrones makes one feel one has accomplished the twelve labors of Hercules. Meeting them—at last!—one is always the petitioner, hat in hand. Even with those who put a visitor at ease— Prince Louis Ferdinand and Archduke Otto are the most skillful at that art—it is hard not to be aware of being in the presence of history.

The institution of kingship may survive in Europe, which has had its regicides and dethronements but which is left with ten stable, successful monarchies (including the tax-haven principalities of Liechtenstein and Monaco) boasting a wide range of monarchs from Britain's and the Netherlands's showcase royalty or the bourgeois Grand Duchy of Luxembourg to the one-of-the-people sovereigns in the welfare states of Scandinavia, from the savior of democracy in post-Fascist Spain to the champion of national unity in binational Belgium.

Unlike the shah of Iran, who was generous with nonreigning royalty with whom he had no family ties, British monarchs have been aloof despite close connections to most of them. "Don't be misled by their placid exterior," a Russian cousin of Queen Elizabeth told me, "the Windsors are mortally afraid of the republican fever spreading to their blessed island. In the 1920s, they asked us Romanoffs not to mention in their presence the Russian revolution of 1917, and they frowned if we used the word Bolshevik."

In 1918, one Russian grand duchess who settled in Britain was shocked to hear that King George V decided against attending the memorial mass for Czar Nicholas II and his family, murdered by the Bolsheviks.

She rushed out of the church and went to Buckingham Palace. Brandishing her umbrella, she demanded to see her cousin, the king. There was no way to stop her short of violence.

She burst in on King George who was taking tea with Queen Mary.

"George," the grand duchess called out, according to one of her descendants who treasures the story, "why are you not with us in church?"

The king tried to defend himself by citing domestic policy implications and the apprehensiveness of the Labour government about precipitating further bloodshed in Russia.

"Nonsense, George," the grand duchess roared. "Nicky was your cousin. You loved him, he was your ally, and he is dead. You come with me right now to pay your respects to his memory."

She pointed the umbrella at the king as if it were a gun.

And, according to the family story, the king of England rose meekly and accompanied his cousin to the church where he joined the mourners for the concluding part of the service.

The Windsors still adhere to the World War I self-definition, provoked by H.G. Wells's attack on Britain's "uninspiring and alien court." "I may be uninspiring," George V retorted, "but I'll be damned if I am an alien."

Before her marriage to a commoner, a Briton, Princess Anne was mentioned as a possible match for Dom Duarte João, pretender to the Portuguese throne. When the two met at the wedding of Prince Alexander of Yugoslavia, Anne made sure that Duarte, who, eager to get married, struck up a conversation with her, would never think of approaching her again. In a word, the princess was rude.

An invitation to a private dinner at Buckingham Palace, usually unmentioned in the court circular published in the daily newspapers, is the maximum that a relative can expect once he reaches Britain after dethronement. In years to follow, an invitation to tea can be arranged, to introduce someone married into the family or to present children coming of age. Only minor members of the British royal family attend weddings, christenings, and funerals of deposed royalty.

The exceptions are Prince Alexander of Yugoslavia and King Constantine of Greece. The Windsors consider London-born Prince Alexander a Britisher—he is Queen Elizabeth's godson and served in the British army—and expect Constantine to return to the throne in Greece.

Nonreigning royalty present special problems of protocol. Since reigning monarchs take precedence, Constantine has had to swallow the indignity of being seated at a place less important than Monaco's Prince Rainier at festivities marking Elizabeth's jubilee.

"Our royals—like other Britons conscious of their foreign origins—are more British than the British," one Englishman, a frequent guest at Buckingham Palace, suggests. "They don't really like associating with foreigners, and, to tell the truth, nonreigning royalty are a very mixed bag. Public opinion wouldn't like the queen or her consort to get mixed up with them. Although one or the other of King Michael's five daughters is always mentioned as a prospective bride for Charles, the prince of Wales, I bet any amount that he will not marry someone from the ranks of ex-royalty. One doesn't have to be superstitious to think of deposed royalty as a bit of bad luck."

An Incident in Tarcento

Let's talk of graves, of worms, and epitaphs;
Make dust our paper, and with rainy eyes
Write sorrow on the bosom of the earth. . . .

For God's sake, let us sit upon the ground,
And tell sad stories of the death of kings:—
How some have been depos'd; some slain in war;
Some haunted by the ghosts they have depos'd;
Some poison'd by their wives; some sleeping kill'd;
All murder'd

King Richard II

For Samuel Schwarcz, the well-ordered world of his youth began to fall apart on a cold night in November 1917, on the Italian front, where he served as a cadet in the army of the Austro-Hungarian Empire. It was the day of a minor saint, and the soldiers of the two Catholic monarchs observed it with a cease-fire. The officers stole out to celebrate in the nearby town of Tarcento, leaving Schwarcz in charge of some 100 enlisted men, peasants from the dusty Great Plains of Hungary who shivered in the fog of the Alpine mountains.

Toward midnight, an automobile materialized out of the drizzle. The chauffeur opened the door for a tall figure with a general's triple red stripes on the sides of perfectly pressed black trousers. He was Swetozar Boroevich, the commander of the monarchy's forces on the Italian front. He shook hands with the astonished Schwarcz, who was then told to assemble the troops.

The general said he didn't mind that the officers were absent. He had wanted to talk to "the real heroes of the war"—the enlisted men. "You are the bravest warriors the world has known," he told the raw recruits who were either under twenty or over fifty years of age. Then he ordered his aide-de-camp to pass around bottles of choice plum brandy, reserved for officers.

Was the front caving in? Or did the monarchy pull out of the war and reach a separate peace, leaving Kaiser Wilhelm to fend for himself, as many had hoped? Or was there another suicide or assassination—did the curse that pursued the old emperor, Franz Josef, now strike his young successor, Karl? The men tried to guess the purpose of the visit as they looked at their commander for the first time.

Boroevich was one of many Croatian officers in the service of the Austrian emperor. Ramrod straight and with a greatcoat thrown casually over his powerful shoulders, he stood in front of the fireplace of the hunting lodge, which served as the officers' quarters and which belonged to the king of Italy at the time of peace. He spoke in pidgin Hungarian, the second language of the polyglot empire. He repeated the well-worn slogans about the trying times, the need for unity, loyalty to the empire, and the little additional time required for final and total victory. He dropped dark hints about troublemakers and demagogues. Then he gulped down a glass of brandy and lowered his voice: there had been a putsch in St. Petersburg, and the new rulers of Russia were godless anarchists bent on murder and worse, led by a madman whose name—and the men from the Hungarian Plains were hearing it for the first time—was Lenin.

Boroevich proposed a toast to the emperor and the fatherland, then left as abruptly as he came. Schwarcz recalls that he stood for minutes, frozen in a salute even after the fog had swallowed up the commander's regulation-gray automobile.

The midnight visit baffled everyone. Enlisted men went back full of wonder to sleep on the straw spread over the floors in the outbuildings of the hunting lodge. The officers who returned in the early hours of the morning hardly believed Schwarcz's report. But everyone knew that there must be serious trouble if a general drinks with a few dozen enlisted men; something extraordinary must be happening in the distant capitals if the soldiers of the Austrian emperor have to grieve over the misfortune of the Russian enemy.

Two generations ago monarchs ruled Europe, and the divine right of kings was the law. The exceptions were the centuries-old confederation of Switzerland and errant France experimenting with its third republican system. The French Revolution of 1789 was the specter that haunted the palaces, and the United States was still a distant land for adventurers and a haven for fugitives. The

Holy Alliance, founded in 1815 after Napoleon's banishment, failed to unite Europe's monarchs to defend the old order, and the defeated revolutions of 1848 won on one point: across the continent, the great transformation began from absolute to constitutional monarchy.

In the nineteenth century—the century before the majority of Christendom's royalty were disinherited—there arose two monarchs who made good the two promises of kingship: glory and tranquillity. The one who offered the glory, Napoleon Bonaparte, was the apotheosis of the parvenu; the one who brought about tranquillity, Franz Josef, led his ancient empire into ruin.

If Franz Josef was the fixed star around which the European firmament seemed to revolve for more than half a century, Napoleon was the comet whose brilliance others tried to evoke long after its brief appearance ended. Napoleon proved that will, rather than class, shapes destiny. In France he rejected the course of restoring the Bourbons, and throughout Europe he defeated an aristocracy justified by nothing more than mere existence.

It is a quirk of history—for history is non-Spenglerian and anti-Marxist—that in that last great century of kingship, not only was monarchy fulfilled in Franz Josef, but the bloodiest egalitarian revolution, in France, ended up by sealing a new pact with monarchy.

Napoleon began his career as the victorious general of the Revolution who conquered Italy and Egypt, and later became France's first consul, then first consul for life. Finally he created an imperial crown, a replica of Charlemagne's, which he took from the pope's hands to place on his head. He established a new aristocracy, a new court, a new knighthood. His admirers even devised a genealogy that identified him as an authentic Bourbon—a descendant of the Man in the Iron Mask, the fictitious brother of Louis XIV, held in an inaccessible fortress all his life for reasons of state. But Napoleon ridiculed the effort. "My family begins on the 18th of Brumaire," he said, referring to the day in the revolutionary calendar when he staged his coup d'état.

Napoleon's military victories were so decisive that there was little resistance to his seven brothers and sisters marrying into the reigning European dynasties and becoming rulers in German, Dutch, Spanish, and Italian lands. His only legitimate son's mother was the daughter of the Habsburg Emperor Franz, the great-grandniece of Marie Antoinette, guillotined along with her husband, Louis XVI, in 1789.

Yet in the folk memory of Europe, Napoleon was the Man of the Revolution—the revolution that swept away feudal privileges and opened careers to all talent regardless of class. He was the liberator manqué, the doomed hero who realized the daydream of the century. He was the prototype for the restless spirits celebrated by Stendhal and Schiller, Lermontov and Beethoven, Verdi and Byron.

Napoleon was obsessed with the past. In imitation of the Romans, triumphal arches and commemorative columns marked the march of his armies. The imperial eagle spread its golden wings; the laurel wreath of antiquity was again a symbol of honor; classical caryatids supported public buildings and jewel boxes. Napoleon saw himself as the new Caesar, the true heir of Charlemagne. He dismissed his army's losses—300,000 Frenchmen a year—as replaceable, a loss the passionate ardors of a single night could restore. In his view, to be French meant to belong to *La Grande Nation*; he declared, "all men of genius are French." He was convinced that the French people preferred glory to liberty, grandeur to peace. His ultimate defeat notwithstanding—"God got bored by him," said Victor Hugo— Napoleon was the century's great success story. His example inspired men throughout Europe: the frustrated commander of a faraway garrison, the thwarted intellectual reduced to futile debates in coffeehouses, the exiled politician forever plotting to seize power, the dreamer in dull provincial towns.

Probably the majority of the French people were glad to see him banished; there had been too many wars, too much instability. Nevertheless they were titillated by his return from the Island of Elba, but then resigned themselves to his final exile on St. Helena. After his death in 1821, after the restoration of the Bourbons, "who forgot nothing and learned nothing," Napoleon became a martyr, and suddenly it was not only the faithful Bonapartist who longed for "the little man in the gray riding coat who crossed the Alps and the Rhine, and carried the tricolor as far as Moscow."

In André Maurois's words, "there remained within Napoleon something of the Corsican subaltern, of the Jacobin and of the cynic; Machiavelli and Plutarch vied for his heart." Napoleon was a complex artist while Franz Josef was made of one piece, an autocrat in the traditional genre, contemptuous of new ideas and determined to reign the way his medieval ancestors had. Napoleon relied on his instincts, and was undone by his impulsiveness; Franz Josef was inhibited, ponderous, and excruciatingly prudent. Believing in the wisdom of endless delay, he avoided confrontations and searched for the golden mean as if it were the Holy Grail.

Franz Josef was installed as emperor at the age of eighteen in the fateful year of 1848, when revolutions were rocking the Habsburg Empire in Vienna, Budapest, Milan, and Prague. People were demanding independence or at least autonomy; an end to absolutism was the common cry. It took the armies of Czar Nicholas I to crush the Hungarian revolt; the Brezhnev Doctrine of the day protected monarchy. But the repression that followed gave way, gradually and cautiously, to reconciliation. By the late 1860s, the Austro-Hungarian monarchy was enjoying a golden afternoon of liberalism.

Franz Josef's long reign—a record sixty-eight years—set a standard for serenity and a focus for nostalgia. *Mitteleuropa* had not known such fat years of peace, such ceremonious insistence on the letter of the law, such self-confident tolerance of diversity, even of dissent.

Franz Josef personified predictability, the most solid bourgeois virtue of an age in which the bourgeoisie, growing and prospering, believed in continued growth and prosperity. In a culture devoted to comfort, Franz Josef was a puritan who slept on a narrow, steel-framed army cot, rose at five every morning and retired at nine, unless a state dinner kept him up slightly later. He ate very little; his one indulgence was a baby biscuit called ladyfingers that he dipped in champagne. Every spring he caught a cold, a temporary indisposition that served only to underline the robustness of his health. His schedule was sacred; his mind, once made up, was unchangeable. He was the Austro-Hungarian monarchy's number one civil servant, dedicated to paperwork and parades, inaugurations and inspections. He was a most dutiful emperor, as reliable as the mechanical knight of a clocktower.

To keep calm is the citizen's first duty, he declared. He believed that the Austro-Hungarian Empire was "the one vital, crucial, indispensable ingredient of European peace." He was convinced that doses of repression, however regrettable, were necessary whenever domestic tranquillity was at stake, and that nationalism spelled a mortal danger. He believed that certain books and individuals ought to be quarantined if they threatened "to confuse the public," and to confuse the public was never too difficult. But repressive measures, applied with the good-natured sloppiness immortalized by Johann Strauss's *Fledermaus*, were easy to evade and in any case temporary, because the authorities always left the door open or at least slightly ajar, for a compromise at a later date. Franz Josef presided over his realm using a collection of stock phrases that praised Austrians and Czechs for their industry, Hungarians and Poles for their passionate attachments, Croatians and Slovenes for their loyalty, and Italians and Jews for their love of family.

His private life was relentlessly unhappy. His marriage—a love match, not an arranged marriage—turned out to be a union of irreconcilably opposite temperaments; his relations with members of his family were always strained. His subjects believed that he was hounded by a curse, pronounced by the widow of a Hungarian aristocrat executed after the defeat of the 1848 revolution. An Italian anarchist murdered his beautiful, artistic wife Elisabeth; their only son Rudolf committed suicide; his brother, Maximilian, installed as emperor of Mexico, was executed by revolutionaries; a South Slav nationalist assassinated his nephew and heir, Franz Ferdinand.

This dyspeptic, humorless clockwork emperor was the most popular Habsburg in the seven centuries of the dynasty, the Good King mourned by his fifty million subjects. Pious Jews believed that the prophet Elijah rewarded him with long life; even rebellious Hungarians learned to bask in the favor of the imperial sun. His subjects copied his muttonchops, his dignified gait, his terse manner of speech. People born the same year as Franz Josef cited that fact as if it had been an act of loyalty. Tens of thousands of children were named after him, including Josip Tito of Yugoslavia, who was born a citizen of the Habsburg monarchy and fought in its army in World War I. It is an odd coincidence that Stalin, in distant Caucasus, was also christened Josef, and that Franco, the third twentieth-century champion of dictatorial longevity, bore a name that is the Spanish equivalent of Franz.

The socialists who emerged on both sides as victors of the Great War promised equality and a break with the past. They saw social and economic justice rather than mystical destiny as the call of the twentieth century. But the dictators who then took over from the socialists were ersatz emperors who offered to recapture the old glory that so many people yearned for. When defeating the Weimar Republic at the polls, Hitler pledged a "Thousand Year Reich." No czar was as absolute a ruler of Russia as Stalin, who substituted the Communist Party for the Holy Orthodox Church, and, in his finest hour, issued the traditional appeal to save Mother Russia from the foreign invader. Austria, stripped of its subject dominions, produced ineffectual strongmen until it was taken over, in a bloodless march, by the Austrian-born Hitler in the name of greater German glory. A bit more fortunate was the other part of the sundered monarchy, Hungary, because its regent, Nicholas Horthy, attempted to emulate Franz Josef, for whom he was once an aide-de-camp.

In Rome, King Victor Emmanuel survived World War I but was reduced to a baroque figurine, the kind Italians are fond of. The real sovereign was Benito Mussolini. In Madrid, the collapse of the monarchy was followed by a succession of dictators, the last of whom, Franco, ruled for more than four decades. His reign was ended—both ruptured and fulfilled—by the coronation of Juan Carlos.

Those who live through the fall of empires do not forget it. Cadet Schwarcz, now a retired bookkeeper in Budapest, remembers a numbness, a sudden incapacity to engage in the confident analysis of the officers' mess.

Schwarcz was nineteen, the eldest son of a landowner, an heir to status and privilege. He did not know, could not even suspect, that the czar's dethronement meant that his carefree youth was over, that the wealth his ancestors had accumulated would soon go up in fires set by soldiers returning from a lost war in a Bolshevik mood, and that the land would be auctioned off later to pay off investment loans contracted in the optimistic years before the war. He could not know that for the rest of his life he would carry the markings of a man born under the ancien régime. He would always be preoccupied with questions of duty, conscience, and honor; he would look down upon opportunists, time-servers, self-promoters. He would charge that there are no more men worthy of being called leaders, and he would be most contemptuous of those who claimed the mantle of The Leader—"impostors"—such as Mussolini, Hitler,

Stalin, and their provincial imitators. The way he kissed a lady's hand during the darkest years of Hungarian Stalinism was a gesture defiantly decadent. Against the mandatory proletarianism of manners, his chivalry was a futile if not ludicrous act of terrorism in memory of a better world. In his way, Schwarcz was to be as déclassé and as passé as members of the imperial families banished from lands they had ruled for centuries.

Schwarcz mourns the passing of the old order. "How could I not," he sighs, "when that old order was my youth? I blame the methodical madness of the Germans who instigated World War I and destroyed themselves by sending Lenin to St. Petersburg. They created the monster that was to end their dream of world domination twenty-five years later.

"We have been dispossessed of tranquillity. We are always on guard because of the *lumpenproletariat*, the kith and kin of that unskilled laborer Stalin and that unemployed housepainter Hitler. The rest of us may have dreams of prosperity, professional success, a happy family. They can only think of power, of revenge, of control that must always be total."

The Archduke of Europe
Otto von Habsburg

It is to be all made of fantasy,
All made of passion, and all made of wishes;
All adoration, duty, and obedience,
All humbleness, all patience, and impatience,
All purity, all trial, all observance

As You Like It

In March 1943 a strange assortment of young recruits with orders
to join the 101st Infantry Battalion found themselves assigned to
the same car in a troop train leaving Philadelphia and heading west.
Some of them were recent refugees from Hitler-occupied Europe,
their English halting or stilted; others barely remembered their
European birthplaces, having come to the United States as children
with their immigrant parents. Among them were blue-collar
workers from New Jersey born in northern Italy and southern
Poland; Hungarian and Croatian coalminers from West Virginia;
former students from the universities of Vienna, Prague, Budapest,
Zagreb, and Cracow; observant Catholics, freethinkers, and a
goodly number of Jews in various phases of unbelief and the only
ones to speak the others' languages. They were passing through the
flatlands of Ohio when one erstwhile habitué of a Budapest
coffeehouse announced the astonishing conclusion of his informal
survey: the men in the car had all been born in the Austro-
Hungarian Empire as of its borders in 1859, just prior to the
Austro-Italian War that Emperor Franz Josef lost to King Victor
Emmanuel II.

Laughter and incredulity greeted the announcement.

But it was still a shock when, upon arrival at six a.m. at Camp
Atterbury, Indiana, in the heartland of the great American Mid-
west, a sergeant of the U.S. Army greeted them with a crisp *"Guten
Morgen, Soldaten."* He explained that they were to join the so-called
Austrian Battalion, organized for the purpose of liberating their
homeland, Austria. Their special responsibility was to demonstrate
to the American public that Austria was not a part of Hitler's
Germany, but an independent country invaded by Hitler, and thus

an American ally like Poland or the Netherlands.

The eminent Hungarian poet George Faludy, now a professor of literature in Toronto, recalls that as he put down his baggage by his bed, a tall youth materialized and introduced himself in German as Felix von Habsburg. Faludy learned that his new buddy's brother, Otto, head of the House of Habsburg and a friend of President Franklin Roosevelt, was now an exile in America and the man responsible for organizing the Austrian Battalion.

The poet thought he was dreaming. He had come to the United States via France, North Africa, and Portugal. He was a Hungarian patriot, a social democrat. He came from a milieu in which the Habsburgs were considered the historic oppressors of the peoples of Central Europe. He had heard much about the unpredictable, crazy United States, but he was not prepared for the experience of being told there that he had to fight for an empire that belonged to antiquity.

At night, Faludy dreamed of being captured by Nazis dressed in medieval armor. They ordered him to write poems in German. He refused and was sentenced to be burned at the stake as a heretic.

He was still in a haze when at dawn he witnessed Archduke Felix getting ready to scrub the floor and vomiting because he was so unaccustomed to such an exercise.

The men marched off to their first drill, which included a class in German. They were to memorize the full title of Charles V, the great Habsburg emperor of the sixteenth century, whose realm included Spain, Austria, and the Low Countries, parts of today's Germany, Italy, and Czechoslovakia, and the newly discovered lands of Cuba, Mexico, and Peru. Charles V's title was 300 words long.

The poet protested. He disliked the German language, and he was not a monarchist. He joined the army of the American democracy to fight Nazism and to help liberate his homeland, Hungary. Austria was of no particular importance to him.

He was ordered to paint the shingles of the officers' club. After he finished, he put through a telephone call to Dorothy Thompson, a journalist he had met a few weeks earlier as a new arrival from overseas. The next day, *The New York Post* carried a story about the strange goings-on at Camp Atterbury, including fistfights between Italian-Americans and Croatian refugees. In Washington and London, the Czech and Yugoslav governments-in-exile sharply condemned the Austrian Battalion for promoting the reactionary Habsburg monarchy. The majority of Austrian émigrés joined in the protest and asked for permission to form *their* Austrian Battalion. President Roosevelt backed his friend Otto, who had just turned thirty, but felt it necessary to deny at a press conference that a Habsburg archduke, the son of Karl, the last emperor of Austria, was in charge of the project. The War Department reluctantly followed Roosevelt's orders, but sent him memoranda arguing against "the presence of a foreign body in the U.S. Army." As usual, State Department opinion was divided.

According to rumors at Camp Atterbury, the idea for the battalion had come from Otto's ambitious, tough-minded mother, Empress Zita—another frequent visitor at the White House and the Roosevelt estate in upstate New York. It was also known that Eleanor Roosevelt, the First Lady, did not share her husband's enthusiasm for the Habsburgs.

In a few weeks, the War Department had had it. There was no end to telegrams containing protest resolutions by governments-in-exile and groups-in-formation, six-page letters in incomprehensible English from international organizations all headquartered in the same blocks of the Upper East Side in New York, numerous visits by delegations of solemn little men with strange accents and dressed in blue serge suits. Officers had to remind themselves that they were, after all, fighting a common enemy. But who needed a battalion of archdukes?

In April, the battalion was still only 199 men strong, including Otto's three younger brothers, also archdukes, Felix, Robert, and Karl Louis. Otto did not seem to be able to make good his pledge of 5,000 recruits. The slow recruitment rate offered a pretext for an investigation, and a general was dispatched to Camp Atterbury to conduct a full and immediate one. He called in the men one by one and asked: "Do you want to stay in the Austrian Battalion or do you want to join another part of the U.S. Army?" Few elected to stay, and in May the unit was disbanded.

Thus ended the one American project to restore a monarchy in Europe, an uncertain, brief prelude to far more costly and complex projects to shore up foreign leaders. It was an amateurish exercise by a rising superpower—and a personal favor by a patrician president of the new world who loved meeting heirs of ancient dynasties.

For Otto, it was yet another disappointment, the story of his life. In vain he looked for faithful subjects and prayed for the unconditional surrender of loyalty. In a world war fought over fierce new fealties to race and class, his old idea of a supranational, tolerant, pluralistic confederation of peoples could not even raise a battalion of men.

Otto visited Indianapolis but never inspected his troops at nearby Camp Atterbury. He did not think of talking to the men, or of trying to exchange thoughts with them directly. He stayed among his books and abstractions, won the support of the editorial board of *The New York Times*, dined with Roosevelt and fascinated statesmen who afterward dismissed him as a man whose kingdom was not of this world.

In his definitive 1979 book, *Austrian Emigration*, ex-émigré Franz Goldner regrets the dissolution of the battalion: "If the Austrian Battalion had already been functioning at the time of Stalingrad, then Roosevelt would have held a trump card in the confrontation with Russia over Central Europe." Goldner puts the blame on squabbling Austrian émigrés as well as on Otto von Habsburg for assuming a leadership position he should never have accepted.

"Otto asked for our pledge of fealty," a Hungarian émigré leader of those days recalls, "and we said, 'we'll give it once a plebiscite decides in your favor. But not before.' 'Then I won't work with you,' was Otto's reply. We knew that it was his mother, Zita, speaking."

"I tried to be helpful to both Austrians and Hungarians," Otto told me in 1979. "I did what I could to save both countries first from being labeled Nazi and then from being taken over by the Communists.

"I was fronting for President Roosevelt. He told me that if we wanted an independent Austria in a postwar settlement and if we wanted recognition as a government-in-exile, we ought to have our own fighting force. He suggested that I go ahead and organize an Austrian battalion. But we were not supposed to say that the idea had come from him. I was not very enthusiastic, but I went along.

"Churchill and Roosevelt were for it," Otto explains with a smile that suggests that this part of his past is well behind him, "primarily because they were gamblers. They loved to play, and they liked to keep in the air a lot of ideas, and they liked to have a lot of players engaged in action and ready to do their bidding. Ah, the funny projects they launched and encouraged others to launch! At one time they thought that Lord Louis Mountbatten, Prince Philip's uncle, should become the emperor of postwar Germany. Or Ernst, prince of Hanover. Or a Hohenzollern prince, Louis Ferdinand. They also toyed with the notion of splitting Germany into a Protestant north and a Catholic south, the latter to be joined by Austria. Churchill was particularly fond of a Bavarian-Austrian-Hungarian confederation. Ah, how those two loved playing world politics!"

Otto chuckles. Time has passed, and the grand old men of his youth have died. It is not easy to see behind his tolerant, avuncular mien the anxious young émigré pleading the cause of his not one but two countries—negotiating with the American and British cabinets, with generals fighting a war and politicians concerned with their constituencies, lecturing audiences in small-town America, and arguing with State Department experts who would have trouble passing a geography examination in any Central European high school.

At sixty-seven, Otto is wiry, more mellow and mild-mannered than ever, a bit of a puritan. He does not touch whiskey, has no favorite dish or hobby, but can be induced to sip a glass of white wine or to squeeze into his schedule a day's hunt once in a while—as a youth, he was an excellent marksman—or to drink a cup of coffee without the usual whipped cream, with any of his thousands of visitors. He is a spry professor, rather than a sportsman, who has kept himself in good shape; his tall frame has the awkwardness of a man who has spent the best part of his life in the library. What invariably impresses people who meet him is his friendliness; he is open and direct, and astonishingly free of arrogance and pretension—he is aware that his friendliness wins over people who expect a Habsburg to be distant and haughty. But he is also unmistakably the classical elitist, charged with a mission to teach. His is a world rounded with duty and enclosed by law.

"I tried to avoid talking with Roosevelt and Churchill about the future form of government for Austria or Hungary," Otto declares, suddenly turning very serious. "I do not believe that it is right to discuss constitutional issues with your allies while your country is under occupation. You imply a surrender of sovereignty if you do.

"Roosevelt was a poker player, and the great problem with him was that he was too successful. People learn through adversity, not through success. Roosevelt had had polio, but apart from that, everything he touched turned to gold. So he believed that he would always be successful. Always. What an illusion for a politician! It's because of that illusion that the West lost Eastern Europe to the Russians. Roosevelt was sure that he could outsmart Stalin."

Charles Mayer, a veteran of the Austrian Battalion and a Vienna-born business executive whose family has served the Habsburgs for three centuries, is now Otto's closest friend in Washington.

"Were Otto and FDR friends?" I ask.

"Otto is a charming man. His learning and wit appealed to FDR. Besides, FDR liked being a friend of royalty—a common weakness among American presidents."

"Did FDR encourage Otto to believe that there could be a Habsburg restoration after the war?"

"FDR was too smart for that. It's one thing to have dinner with a pretender to the throne, but it's quite another to go to bat for him. There was no chance of Habsburg—or Hohenzollern—restoration during or after World War II. None whatsoever. But there was no deception. Otto is an optimist, and he is just as capable of deluding himself as someone far less knowledgeable. It's in the character of an exile to live with illusions."

Mayer tells the story of a U.S. congressman who once congratulated Otto after an appearance before the House Foreign Affairs Committee. "Otto," the congressman gushed, "you ought to be running Austria."

Mayer's smile is a man-of-the-world smile. "After Otto, very pleased, told me what the congressman had said, I asked him, 'So what is he prepared to do for you?'"

Otto acknowledges "having enjoyed excellent personal relations" with Roosevelt and Churchill, but his face says, "So what?"

He responds with a weary sigh to my question about his hopes at the time for restoration. "Restoration of the monarchy had no real chance after the *Anschluss*. Before 1938, yes—then restoration seemed a very real possibility. But not after. And not as a result of any agreement with Roosevelt or Churchill." He cites as his objectives during World War II securing Austrian independence and engineering Hungary's switchover to the Allies.

Whatever Otto now says, Roosevelt and Churchill did at that time hold extensive discussions with him on the possibility of reconstituting the Austro-Hungarian monarchy. The two great allies of World War II both believed that the Habsburg Empire ought not to have been disbanded after World War I, that subsequently no other force could and did balance German ambitions in Europe, and that the best solution would be a Danubian confederation of Austria, Hungary, Czechoslovakia, Yugoslavia, and perhaps Romania. The ideal man to head that unit would have been their young friend Otto, charming and earnest, historic in name and democratic in temper.

The Anglo-American failure to implement such a project was due to Russian ambitions that grew in proportion to Roosevelt's declining health and to the success of the Red Army. But there was also an Anglo-American half-heartedness due to Otto's inability to translate into a political movement his sparkling dinner table conversation at Allied summit meetings or the ideas in his fine articles such as the one on Danubian reconstruction in *Foreign Affairs*.

In his 1966 book, *Die Balkanisierung Österreichs*, the respected Austrian writer Alexander Vodopivec sums it up: "The roots of all subsequent evil lay in the fact that Otto von Habsburg never personally experienced conditions in Austria. For him, they are a mosaic composed of many small pieces, each of which he knows, each of which is correct in itself, but from which he had put together an incorrect total picture."

"When he descends to our level," one former associate of his says, "he is seductively open and friendly. But he can also cut you off. Once you joined him—or he thinks that you joined him, and he can think that with surprising facility because he is a wishful thinker if there ever was one— you may not contradict him with impunity. If you do, he cuts you dead. He is overwhelmingly charming with those he expects to influence and who do not agree with him on this or that point, but when it comes to his followers, he expects complete, unquestioning loyalty. Remember: he is a monarch."

Otto's historic achievement came in 1944, when he convinced Roosevelt and Churchill at their Quebec summit meeting to divide Austria into four—rather than two—occupation zones, which decreased the Russian share from one-half to one-fourth, and which, some experts believe, enabled Austria to emerge from occupation as a democracy, neutralist but Western-style, not a people's democracy *à la* Moscow.

From 1943 to 1944, Otto was a middleman in secret peace

negotiations between Hungary and the Allies. The Hungarians asked for the landing of an Anglo-American force, and Otto—and the Americans—urged them to turn against the Nazis as soon as possible. The liaison officer was Otto's brother, Karl Louis, who operated out of neutral Lisbon. The Hungarian government was glad to have the services of a man as close to Roosevelt as Otto. But Hungarians knowledgeable about the negotiations note that Otto spent a bit too much time and effort getting himself recognized not only as Hungary's official emissary but as head of state, in case the Germans replaced Regent Nicholas Horthy, which in the end they did. Had Horthy been less clumsy and hesitant in quitting his German allies, and had Roosevelt lived up to his word about keeping Hungary in the Western camp, in the spring of 1945 Otto von Habsburg could have returned to Budapest from Washington rather than a phalanx of Stalinist émigrés from Moscow.

"What is behind us is unchangeable, and therefore cannot be resolved," Emilio Vasari quotes Otto in his biography. "We can defeat the past only if we turn away from it and look to the future. The past divides us, but the future integrates us."

For gourmets of historical ironies, the Habsburg saga in this century offers a feast.

In 1921, Otto's father Karl, the last emperor of Austria and king of Hungary, was twice sent back into exile by Hungary's head of state, Admiral Horthy—the man who had once served as Franz Josef's aide-de-camp and who had himself assured Karl of his "unswerving, eternal fealty." On Karl's part, Otto explains, "there was a completely understandable misjudgment of Horthy's character." Horthy had been sending messages to Karl, then in exile in Switzerland, that he, Regent Horthy, was only in charge temporarily and was waiting for a "suitable moment" to hand back the kingdom—constitutionally, Hungary remained a kingdom until 1946—to its legitimate ruler, Karl.

The first attempt, in the spring, began with a train ride from Strasbourg, France, to Szombathely, Hungary. An automobile then took Karl to Budapest where Karl warmly embraced the thoroughly embarrassed Horthy. Horthy cited the possibility of civil war and the opposition of the old empire's successor states—Czechoslovakia, Yugoslavia, and Romania—and asked Karl for more time to prepare the climate for a restoration. Karl's return to Switzerland says more about his innate optimism than about Horthy's diplomatic cunning.

I ask Otto about Horthy's vaunted monarchist sentiments and his devotion to Franz Josef, called "the ideal ruler" in Horthy's memoirs.

"It is easy to be loyal to a dead man," Otto answers, his voice pedagogically low and his face a portrait of dynastic wisdom.

The second attempt took place in the fall, seven months later. Karl, this time accompanied by his wife Zita, flew to an airstrip in western Hungary and then took a train to the capital with a monarchist general's 3,000 soldiers sworn "to fight to the death." Members of the cabinet and Catholic bishops joined them en route. At several stops, demonstrations greeted the king, garrisons pledged their loyalty, and Catholic clergy blessed the enterprise. But near Budapest, Horthy's men opened fire on the train. The astonished Karl disregarded the advice of his supporters, forbade resistance, and declared that he would allow no bloodshed. Horthy sent messages warning that Hungary's neighbors were ready to attack unless the king left immediately. Karl called off the venture after a few days of desultory negotiations, during which he hoped in vain for French support (promised by Prime Minister Aristide Briand, but only in case of success, for France would not endorse failure). Karl, in tears, boarded a British steamer that eventually took him to the Portuguese island of Madeira in the distant Atlantic.

"My father knew full well that it was his last chance," Otto observes. "But he had no choice but to try. He felt it was his duty to return to his people. Whether or not he believed that he would be successful is another matter. He lost because Czechoslovakia, Yugoslavia, and Britain were against him, and Horthy's advisors, set against the monarchy, forced his hand."

Otto's biographer Vasari records that when the Swiss police investigator asked Otto, then nine, if he knew about his father's illegal departure from Switzerland, the eldest son and heir responded: "Yes, Papa has left. For a ruler, duty is more important than personal happiness."

The following year Karl died of pneumonia, and thirty-year-old Zita was left a widow with eight children and no funds other than contributions from friends. Legend has it that it was in those days of tight budgeting that Zita, a strict authoritarian even by the standards of that strict age, established the special rights—and obligations—of her eldest son and had the other children acknowledge his privileges with regard to clothing, gifts, and even food. Upon reaching maturity at eighteen Otto declared, "I am the rightful ruler." Zita curtsied before him, as did his sisters. His brothers bowed.

Zita first accepted an invitation from Spain's Alfonso XIII to live in a castle near Madrid, built by Charles V, the great Habsburg emperor who later became Otto's historical model. But even before Alfonso lost his throne, Zita had moved her family to a small, quiet Basque fishing village, Lequeitio, where private tutors—volunteers from the old Austro-Hungarian army and Benedictine fathers— taught the children. Zita, born a princess of Bourbon-Parma and never popular in Austria or among Habsburgs because of her strictness, believed in education. She was determined to prepare Otto for the throne in a way that no Habsburg emperor had ever been prepared, and his brothers and sisters had to help. Each child pledged to contribute a tenth of his or her future income to keep the head of the House of Habsburg financially independent, and thus able to devote his full attention to dynastic duties and the recovery of the throne.

After Spain, the family moved to Belgium where Otto enrolled at Louvain, the 500-year-old Catholic university near the birthplace of Charles V.

For close to seven centuries, the Habsburgs had a reputation for being dull-witted and limited in their interests. But in Otto, the last Habsburg crown prince, the dynasty finally had an intellectual. As a child, he studied ten hours a day and passed not one but two grueling matriculation examinations, one ending the Austrian curriculum, the other the Hungarian. Zita forced on him a most stringent regimen, and he was obedient. He learned to enjoy excelling in his studies. He became the first Habsburg with a Ph.D., which he earned at Louvain in political science, and with *La Plus Grande Distinction*—granted once every two or three years. He has since authored close to twenty books on history, politics, and social problems. He writes in six languages and can converse in a few more, such as Croatian, Walloon, and Basque. His interests range from the history of farm ownership legislation in Austria (his Ph.D. thesis) to Hungarian lyric poetry (a favorite recreation), from Catholic theology (for spiritual nourishment) to Far Eastern economic development (a frequent subject of his articles).

As a student at twenty, Otto showed unusual foresight in declining repeated invitations to meet with an ambitious politician, slated to become the next chancellor of Germany, Adolf Hitler—a declared enemy of the Habsburg policy of ethnic pluralism and religious tolerance. Otto, doing his research for a Ph.D. thesis in Berlin, felt that he had nothing to discuss with a man who found Franz Josef's Vienna "a disgusting racial mix" that included Jews and Slavs, and who had called the Habsburgs the enemy of the German race. Hohenzollern princes—sons of the deposed Kaiser Wilhelm—and others seeing in Hitler the future führer told Otto that Hitler was willing to work with him and pleaded with Otto to go see him. Otto was inflexible. He said he could not deal with a man who believed in racial supremacy and racial hatred.

"In the 1930s, Hitler was the wave of the future," Otto says, his arms suddenly in the air in a parody of the führer's style. "Hitler was the reality that people, even well-meaning people, advised me to adjust to. I am old enough, you see, to have known so many realities."

In the 1930s his return to the throne of his ancestors seemed likely, and even, on several occasions, imminent. But the heads of state and prime ministers he dealt with were monarchists only in sentiment; in practice, they prevented him from setting foot in Austria or Hungary.

The closest Otto came to restoration was on the night of July 24, 1934, when Chancellor Engelbert Dollfuss told Otto's emissary that although once an opponent of the Habsburgs, he had come to the conclusion that only the historic appeal of a Habsburg could stop the psychological attraction of Hitler. "Against Hitler, only a Habsburg!" Dollfuss exclaimed. Dollfuss, a rightist strongman, was convinced that countries such as Czechoslovakia and Yugoslavia feared Hitler so much that they would eventually acquiesce in a Habsburg restoration if it were to take place decisively and if it brought stability to Austria.

The next day, Hitler's hired guns took over the chancellor's building and assassinated Dollfuss. His successor, Kurt von Schuschnigg, was an avowed monarchist. Before he became chancellor he had pledged fealty to Otto. But once in power, his answer to Otto's query was "not timely." In secret meetings with Otto and in handwritten letters delivered by trusted couriers, Schuschnigg sent the same message for four years: the domestic as well as international climate was hostile to a Habsburg restoration, and Otto must wait and wait patiently.

Four weeks before the *Anschluss*, Otto appealed to the chancellor, reminding him of his officer's oath under the empire and citing his "unswerving loyalty to the legitimate ruler." Make no further concessions to Germany, Otto demanded, and, should pressures become intolerable, hand over the reins to him. Schuschnigg, a model of Austrian caution, declined the impulsive offer. Otto had been counseling Schuschnigg to enlist the support of the Western democracies, to build up the army, and to fight the Germans if they tried to march into Austria. Schuschnigg made it clear—all too clear—that he opposed resistance to the Nazis. He tried to be a diplomat and a man of peace; he became the chancellor who submitted to the *Anschluss*.

Listening to the monarchist account of the history of the 1920s and '30s, one's impression is that in Austria as well as in Hungary the majority of the population, or at least most of the leading politicians, were monarchists in thought but not in action.

In Austria, a succession of presidents, prime ministers, and cabinet members called Otto "Your Imperial Majesty." They were all born as subjects of the unforgettable Franz Josef, and whether soldiers or civilians in 1916, they had sworn allegiance to his grand-nephew Karl. Monarchy was the one legitimate system and their only true love, and they believed there would be a restoration once the paltry men of the hour and their vulgar, mob-pandering realpolitik were defeated.

But they were given pause throughout the 1930s by "the one million soldiers of the Little Entente" who threatened to undo a Habsburg restoration in Vienna or Budapest. Yugoslavia, whose Catholic Croatians and Slovenes looked to Vienna rather than to Serbian Orthodox Belgrade, pledged to attack Austria immediately if Otto returned there. "Better a Hitler in Berlin than a Habsburg in Vienna" was the private slogan adopted by Eduard Benes, foreign minister and later president of the Czechoslovak Republic.

While even socialists, opposed to the monarchy, wryly called Austria "a republic without republicans," Hungary remained a kingdom in name, and its head of state, Horthy, had the title "Regent." But Horthy had dynastic ambitions of his own. After rebuffing Karl, he maintained his distance from Otto, and denied Otto's request to study one semester at a Hungarian university.

Horthy even advised Chancellor von Schuschnigg that Austria ought to avoid a restoration and link up with Germany instead.

Ironically, Otto's most powerful early supporter was Benito Mussolini, who in the early and middle 1930s thought that a strong Habsburg empire could balance German ambitions. The controlled Italian press floated rumors of Otto's impending marriage to a daughter of Victor Emmanuel III. Mussolini was attracted by the possibility of installing either an emperor of Austria or king of Hungary who would have an Italian princess for a wife, and another for his mother.

From the 1920s on, Otto's Austrian supporters were consistent, outspoken opponents of pan-German nationalism and of any union with Germany. (Socialists and Communists on the other hand often spoke of the progress that a united Great German state would represent.) Monarchists were among the first to be taken to Nazi concentration camps.

When Hitler invaded Belgium, Otto fled with his family to France. The Nazis put a price on his head. When France lost the war, Otto first placed himself under the protection of the Vichy government, then was advised to cross the border to Spain, and, finally, to flee to the United States.

In 1945, Otto and his brothers returned to Austria and took up residence in the French occupation zone. The Russians vetoed the application to form a monarchist party, signed by former prisoners in Hitler's concentration camps. After six months Russian protests, echoed by social democrats and Communists, forced the Habsburg brothers to leave Austria.

This was Otto's third emigration. The first flight was his father's; he was not yet seven. The second, from Hitler, was, he thought, a prelude to victory. But this third exit felt like being struck in the face without warning or provocation.

His Belgian diplomatic passport, a souvenir of his prewar stay in Belgium, was canceled because of the crisis over King Leopold, who had stayed in his country during German occupation. Otto received a new passport from the Principality of Monaco, embarked on a lecture tour in the United States, and began his writing career. He also spent time with refugees. On a visit to a hospital in Germany he overheard a patient trying to explain his aches to a nurse in broken German. He recognized the Hungarian accent and volunteered as an interpreter. The nurse turned out to be Princess Regina von

Sachsen-Meiningen, a penniless German refugee whose father had starved to death in a Russian concentration camp.

Within a few months, Otto, thirty-eight, and Regina, twenty-five, were married. The wedding was held in Nancy, France, once part of the Habsburg patrimony of Lotharingia, in a church that had belonged to Otto's ancestors. The couple honeymooned in the Basque village of Otto's childhood and then settled in Pöcking, a village twenty miles from Munich.

After the Austrian peace treaty of 1955, Otto tried to return to Austria. In 1957, he was issued an Austrian passport, but with an unusual proviso: not valid for Austria. The authorities informed him that he could return if he signed the abdication statement, originally drafted in 1920, renouncing all claims as a Habsburg.

Otto decided that he, too, would sign. Zita told biographer Vasari, "In no way did I influence my son. He only asked that I pray for him. I knew that he would weigh carefully what he might do." Zita would not criticize her son; nor would she approve the compromise with a law that she considered unfair and illegal. Never having worn anything but black since her husband's death in 1922, Zita lives a Spartan life in a convent in Ziziers, a wine-growing village in Switzerland. She is the only living Habsburg—there are about 100 of them in various parts of the world—who has not signed her peace with the Republic of Austria.

Otto's sister Adelaide, who once taught at Fordham University in New York and was also a Ph.D., was supportive. "If we want to do something for Austria, which is what our family tradition requires, we have to adjust to today's conditions. In order for us to return, abdication of our rights was the only possibility."

In 1958, the socialists viewed with sympathy the idea of Otto's return. They hoped that he would form a monarchist party and thus divide the camp of the majority conservative force, the People's Party. They said that as soon as Otto signed the abdication statement, he might reenter Austria. But after Otto assured the apprehensive conservatives that he planned no new party, the socialists turned against him.

German Chancellor Konrad Adenauer brought Austrian Chancellor Julius Raab together with Otto von Habsburg in 1960. Otto expressed his readiness to sign the abdication statement and assured Raab that he had no intention of suing the republic for the private Habsburg wealth that Franz Josef had separated from state property. In 1961, Otto's first son, Karl, was born. Five months later, Otto signed the abdication statement. But the Austrian cabinet split in its response: the People's Party voted in favor of permitting his return but the social democrats objected. Since coalition practice demanded a clear consensus, the issue was shelved.

Otto received no answer. When he turned to the high court, it ruled, in 1963, that the government was in error, and authorized Otto's return. Conservatives acclaimed the victory of the rule of law and praised the independence displayed by the judiciary. *Rechtsstaat* is a key concept in Central Europe.

But the socialists charged "a lawyers' putsch." Having lost the election—although still in the coalition—they sought to make political capital out of anti-Habsburg sentiment. They went as far as opening negotiations with Austria's third party, the small rightist Freedom Party, which they had previously called neo-Nazi. The anti-Habsburg plank was to be a basis for a united front.

The debate over Otto von Habsburg and the law led to stormy parliamentary sessions and lively articles in the press. Dull Austria, a stagnant backwater of European politics, had a cause to arouse passions. But the decision, if one can call it that, was borrowed from Kafka's *Castle* rather than Hasek's *Good Soldier Schweik*. The Lower House of Parliament ruled: "Dr. Habsburg's return is not desired." The Upper House supported the high court's judgment. In practice, Otto was barred. The minister of the interior, who happened to be a socialist, ordered the border police under his jurisdiction not to let Otto von Habsburg into the country unless his passport said "valid for Austria." The minister of foreign affairs, who also happened to be a socialist, instructed Austrian embassies not to alter the phrase in Dr. Habsburg's passport that said "not valid for Austria."

The socialists argued that Otto's abdication statement was not credible—the German term *nicht glaubwürdig* carries the nasty connotation of untruthfulness. They cited a 1958 interview with the picture magazine *Paris-Match* in which Otto explained that once he returned to Austria and was a citizen like anyone else, he could not be stopped from speaking out in favor of his political ideas, i.e., monarchism. Otto's conclusion was, "And what law forbids my fellow citizens from electing me their emperor?"

In 1964, the new Chancellor Josef Klaus, a lawyer, bracketed himself with Otto von Habsburg: "We are both fanatics of the law."

Otto promised Klaus that he would not exercise his right to return, as defined by the high court, but would wait for Klaus to hammer out an agreement with the socialists. Socialist propaganda intensified; much was made of the tens of millions of dollars Otto allegedly claimed, and the unrest at home and abroad in the event of his return.

In the 1966 elections, the socialists lost additional seats; monarchists claimed it was because of the vendetta against Otto. Two months later, Otto received his new Austrian passport—this time without restrictions. But Otto waited several months before entering Austria, and talked his supporters out of torchlight rallies and welcoming celebrations. He drove across the border—his Pöcking home is not much more than an hour away on the superhighway—unheralded and unobserved.

He delivered lectures, first in the provinces, then in Vienna. He drew crowds and received strong applause, but aroused no overwhelming passions. There were a few incidents. In one small town, leftwingers threw red paint on him and his Volkswagen. He smiled and went through the lecture as scheduled. The socialists charged that he expected people to call him Your Majesty. "I can't very well say that I am not an archduke," he countered. "I cannot tell people not to call me what they want to call me." But he said he preferred to be called Dr. Habsburg. In one village, a middle-aged man walked up to him, bowed as low as his father might have bowed to Otto's father, and said, "Your Majesty, I humbly report I am a Communist." Austrian newspapers found Otto an American-style politician—comfortable in crowds and able to speak with the common man.

In 1972, Otto publicly shook hands with Chancellor Bruno Kreisky, the socialist he had once called his primary opponent. "I have no resentment," Otto claimed later in an interview. The two ex-émigrés—Kreisky was in Sweden during World War II—have met frequently since 1972, but Otto's statement has a hollow ring. No exile, royal or otherwise, can spend ten years fighting for his return to his homeland without some bitterness toward those who blocked him. But Otto, Catholic and Habsburg, proclaims forgiveness.

Otto's presence in Austria has not made any appreciable difference to a country where grandeur is conspicuously absent and where the ambitious are plotting careers in international civil service. Their model is Kurt Waldheim, a dull apparatchik of the Western world who rose to become the secretary general of the United Nations by saying little, offending no one, and being always compassionately neutral. "Ours is a small country," one hears again and again, or, "We are content with just being alive."

"Just being alive" is disingenuous. Austrians live very well. Their homes boast Oriental carpets and color tv sets. Austrians are still thankful that the Russian occupation forces left more than twenty years ago, and the motto "bend not break" is repeated so often that it sounds like a prayer.

Otto von Habsburg may be the best known Austrian in Europe and a most capable man, but many Austrians objected to his return simply because it might perhaps upset things, and Austrians love their comfort. They also have a horror of doing anything rash; cautiousness is a way of life.

There is a fascination with Otto. Austrians applaud his lectures and read his articles and books. They cannot get over the fact that a Habsburg can be so knowledgeable, so thoughtful, so industrious, that Otto is "the finest Habsburg there ever was," that indeed Otto is a Habsburg at all.

But they do not want him as a ruler. In an electoral test—which will never occur because Otto would not want to lose and Austrians loathe the unpleasantness of such a political campaign—perhaps 20 percent might vote for him. Perhaps 40 percent would vote for Franz Josef if he were still alive.

The Austrian attachment to monarchy is not a theme for a rousing speech in a rally at the local movie theater or for an important get-together of a select group of men in a private room of a quiet restaurant; it is a subject for a chat with an old friend while ensconced in one's favorite armchair—the one inherited from a beloved great-aunt—or a memory evoked between sips of the new wine tested under the grape arbor of one's usual wineshop. Monarchism is impractical, and impractical is as damning an adjective in Austria as un-German is in Germany. And being impractical is as profoundly un-Austrian as lack of caution.

The empire survives in the so-called Wiener schnitzel (originally from the Italian provinces), the goulash (cooked with less potent paprika than in its native Hungary), and the strong black coffee (first imported by Turks stranded in Vienna during one of the wars between emperor and sultan). There are imperial echoes in

Austrian names that retain the consonantal crowding of the Slavic languages or the ultimate "y" of Hungarian nobility. But the power and the splendor of seven Habsburg centuries are gone.

Otto is a man of the past who sees himself as a man of the future. His ambition, he says, is to be remembered a generation from now as a builder of a united Europe. In 1961, he explained that he had signed the abdication statement because he did not want to spend his life in the pursuit of an abstraction. In 1973 he took over the presidency of the Pan-European Union, a citizens' lobby—or is it an order of chivalry?—established in 1912 by Count Richard Coudenhove-Kalergi. In dedicating himself to the cause of a united Europe, Otto has fallen into the service of another abstraction.

In the early 1960s, Otto said he wished to return to Austria because "life abroad is not life." He also stated that he had always intended to serve Austria. But in the early 1970s, when the repentant socialists offered him the post of ambassador in London, he not only declined the honor but chose to remain in exile, in Germany, and took up German citizenship. Austria is just not that important, some of his critics say, because it is too small to serve as a launching pad for his ambitions. Others suggest that he turned to German politics and European affairs because his return to Austria failed to make an impact there.

Otto is the only European royalty who has run for an elective office (European Parliament) and of all nonreigning royalty, he is the least squeamish about getting involved in the nitty-gritty of twentieth-century politics. He addresses village rallies and civic groups no matter how small, and writes a weekly syndicated newspaper column. He is readily available to the press. He dines and corresponds with hundreds of politicians around the world, and has an astonishing memory for faces and names. Yet he has a churchy otherworldliness about him. He is a pilgrim refusing to be discouraged by mocking laughter and triumphant unbelief. He imparts a whiff of incense.

In April 1979, I attended a political rally of his in Munich. The beer hall—a cross between a railway station and a theater—was festooned with the blue-and-white flags of the Free State of Bavaria, with the emblem of the Pan-European Union—a red cross in a gold circle surrounded by yellow five-pointed stars—and with the lion of Munich's pride: the trademark of Löwenbräu beer. Along the long rectangular tables, covered with blue-and-white tablecloths with mugs of beer printed on them, some 400 people drank mugs of beer. When the food arrived, on noiselessly rolling steel carts, everyone wished good appetite. Some ate a hearty dinner; others ate hot dogs with grated horseradish. Mugs of beer kept arriving as the speakers discussed the forthcoming elections.

For the first time in history, people in nine West European states vote directly for candidates for European Parliament. The jurisdiction of that body is as yet hazy, but it has the potential of becoming the Continental Congress for a United States of Western Europe. Dr. Habsburg, who knows many of the future parliamentarians and speaks almost all their languages, may well emerge as a leader.

The audience was sympathetic, mostly middle-aged and older, from rumpled lower-middle class to well-pressed upper-middle. No beards, and only a few people were under thirty. There was no passion in the applause; no electricity in the speaker. Otto spoke without notes, with plenty of "permit me to explain" and "I wish to emphasize once again." His hands were in the air all the time, touching, clasping. His gestures were always symmetrical.

His appeal for a united Europe—a free community of free nations, a federation without frontiers and other restrictions, and eventually extending from the Atlantic to the Urals—seemed eminently sensible. He dwelled on the Christian tradition of spirituality. He urged higher standards of morality in public and private life. He got his strongest applause for his stands against abortion and pornography. In pursuing the goal of a united Europe he prescribed practicality, not romanticism; federalism, not centralism; a Europe growing from below instead of one imposed from above.

Dr. Habsburg was in the number three slot of the Christian Social Union, Bavaria's conservative regional party, an ally of the opposition Christian Democrats. But he was not a member of CSU, and it took Party Boss Franz Josef Strauss to arrange such a slot—a safe one because CSU was expected to carry eight to ten candidates.

There was opposition to the Habsburg candidacy. Within CSU, Dr. Habsburg was considered an outsider. The party's youth wing, demanding more representation for itself, voted against him, as did others who cited the fact that Dr. Habsburg is not a Bavarian, not even, strictly speaking, a German. His citizenship was less than a year old, arranged by the prime minister of Bavaria (who addressed him as "Your Majesty" during the ceremony), and in a haste that smacked of personal favoritism.

Otto's condemnation of pop music added more controversy to his candidacy. He had said that Bob Dylan and other singers like him "are highly Communist-influenced, whether they know it or not, and in this way act as agents of the Soviet Union." He explained that the texts of popular songs are "very destructive of moral values and liberal society. Many of them are highly pornographic. They are trying to undermine our own free society."

In an interview with *The New York Times*, Otto reflected a more politic stance: "I'm really for diversity. That's the old Central European way." And he conceded that he would not be able to do much about pop music in the European Parliament.

Among the Social Democrats, West Germany's ruling party, the Habsburg candidacy aroused furious opposition. Chancellor Helmut Schmidt declared in Parliament: "Everybody has got some tic, so why shouldn't he call himself His Imperial Majesty?" Schmidt's colleagues cited a statement, made by Dr. Habsburg in a symposium on nuclear blackmail, which recommended that a strongman take over for nine months and suspend laws if such blackmail does take place. In today's West German atmosphere, charged with the fear of terrorism and of the state reverting to Nazi practices, it seems natural that the rest of the Habsburg article, which stipulated that such a strongman be accountable to an independent judiciary elected by Parliament, was not mentioned.

Otto von Habsburg is a conservative. He defends some aspects of South Africa's policies. He supported white rule in Rhodesia. He praised Richard Nixon's administration for producing two years during which the United States, rather than the Soviet Union, took the initiative in international affairs. He has identified himself with the firmly conservative stance of Franz Josef Strauss—known as the king of Bavaria—and he was an admirer of Spain's Francisco Franco. And with a monarch's forgiveness, he has accepted pledges of fealty from several ex-Nazis and ex-Communists. One little-known member of the German Parliament has made a name for himself by attacking Otto von Habsburg as a Fascist, an émigré archduke scheming to turn the progressive Europe of the future into the Holy Roman Empire of the reactionary past.

"You can't imagine how they hate him," a slim, well-educated woman in her early 40s told me at the rally. There was a hint of tears in her blue eyes. In front of her was an aspic salad and a glass of Beaujolais. "They say the most terrible things about him. They try to hurt him. It is cruel and vicious. But he never responds in kind, or even in anger. He is so pure, so chivalrous. He is too good for our times."

"The more they attack me," Dr. Habsburg told me after the lecture, "the more I like it. I am delighted with the rough-and-tumble of politics. This is the real life."

A smile settled on his face. It was a dutiful smile, with a measure each of Austrian affability and American public relations, of Habsburg self-discipline and Catholic self-hypnosis. His is the jovial, round-featured face of a Central European; he could pass off as a native in any part of the old monarchy. It is his eldest son, Karl, eighteen, who is the typical Habsburg: pale, blond, with thick lips—handsome but with a suggestion of decadence. In meeting with people after the speeches, the two Habsburgs, father and son, bowed more deeply than anyone else.

A dozen men and women in polyester suits and dresses much too tight for their ample midriffs assured His Imperial Majesty or *Herr Doktor* of their votes and those of their friends. They were ethnic Germans whose mass expulsion from Czechoslovakia's Sudetenland after World War II Otto protested—a most unpopular act of political chivalry. When in 1942, Benes' government-in-exile floated the trial balloon of the expulsion plan, Otto argued that deportation because of national origins would be an imitation of the lawlessness of the Nazis.

Two Hungarians in their seventies bowed to His Majesty, and wished him success and good health. "So very, very good of you to have come," Otto answered in Hungarian. "I am always very, very happy to be among fellow Hungarians."

There are Hungarians who remember Otto as an angelic four-year-old—the only one dressed in white at Franz Josef's austere, wartime funeral under gray November skies, and then, a few weeks later, in Budapest, at his father's coronation dressed in a fantasy of silk and ermine, white and gold, designed by the great romantic painter of the time, Gyula Benczur. They also remember Karl's horse stumbling—an ill omen—and the mystical crown of St. Stephen slipping back and forth on Karl's small head. When Karl made his horse rear up and swung his sword in the four directions—symbolic of his readiness to defend the realm—the crown very nearly fell off.

But that was two generations, two world wars, and two revolutions ago. "I am the oldest Hungarian émigré," Otto is in the habit of saying. He last saw Hungary in 1918, at the age of six. Hungarians who meet him are almost always impressed that he speaks such good Hungarian, and that he is so humble. No Habsburg was ever as fluent in Hungarian as Otto. And no Habsburg was able to say, "we Hungarians" and be convincing.

Hungarians remember the Habsburgs as the foreign oppressors who liberated Hungary from the Turks in the seventeenth century, just as the Russians liberated the country from the Germans in 1945. Even Franz Josef was at first the murderous tyrant whose armies, with the help of Czar Nicholas I, crushed the revolution of 1848. It was only after 1867 that Franz Josef's image changed to that of a kind-hearted old soldier who made Hungary an equal partner of Austria in the empire. He taught Hungarians the virtue of compromise between the computation of self-interest and the passion of nationalism.

"Is Otto an Austrian or a German or a Hungarian?" the question is often asked. "I hear that Otto speaks Czech and Croatian. Marvelous. But is he a Czech and a Croatian as well? Who is he going to represent in the European Parliament?" For Otto, there is no contradiction, no inconsistency. "I am a European," he says.

In June 1979, he was elected a member of the European Parliament, and he may begin a new political life there. But what is a European? "Otto is at home nowhere," says one Hungarian émigré who knows him. But he is not a rootless cosmopolitan. He believes in a supranational past that he envisages as a model for a supranational future.

Of Dr. Habsburg's sixteen books, the closest to his heart is his biography of his ancestor, Charles V, the last Universal Emperor of the West. Otto notes that Charles V was rejected by the nationalist nineteenth century that "could have nothing in common with a sovereign who, while wearing the German crown, maintained, as King of the Romans, continuous relations with Italy; a man, too, who spoke and wrote fluently in French, Dutch, Spanish, and German, and whose political horizon extended from the Americas to the Far East."

Otto paints Charles V's birthplace, the dukedom of Burgundy, as the Holy Land of Europeanism: French and German were spoken interchangeably; ideas and products from the Mediterranean basin mingled with those of the North Sea coast; nobility and a merchant class coexisted peacefully; and the art of the troubadours, born here, spread in every direction. Chivalry flourished in Burgundy, the headquarters for the Knights of the Golden Fleece. Their master, the duke of Burgundy, gave up a measure of national sovereignty in the name of a supranational ideal: he agreed not to declare war unless endorsed by the Order, whose knights hailed from various parts of Europe.

Otto's attitude toward Charles V is one of filial piety; he kneels in front of the emperor's portrait. Charles V's amorous adventures were fewer than those of his colleagues, Otto assures us, and recalls that "opinion of the time was very tolerant of sins of the flesh." He does not mention Charles V's notorious gluttony—oysters, choice fish, pies, and pâtés were carried on muleback from various European countries to the imperial retreat in central Spain.

Otto can hardly bring himself to mention the Inquisition and other massacres that occurred during Charles V's reign. (In the Netherlands, Charles V recommended that "all those who remained obstinate in their errors be burned alive and those who were admitted to penitence be beheaded.") Of horrors, Otto speaks only if critics have exaggerated them. He not so much excuses the slaughter of the conquistadors under Charles V's banner as he countercharges that the atrocities do not tell the true story of the Spanish conquest; historians ought to focus on the condemnation that Charles V hurled at the un-Christian excesses.

Otto holds himself back from harsh words and damning judgments. His is the good Catholic's gentle reproof; he hopes that opponents will come to see the error of their ways.

Charles V failed in his plan to unite Christendom against Ottoman Islam and could not prevent the great schism that occurred during his reign between Rome and Martin Luther. Otto did not succeed in his efforts to form coalitions against nazism and communism. Otto has pursued goals that Charles V would have pursued; Otto's Charles V is Otto, had Otto lived in the sixteenth century. Biographer and subject merge; it is a most Christian union by emulation.

The prizes Otto sought have eluded him; the high ideals he

emblazoned on his standard have been ridiculed. The masses have not understood him; nor has he understood them. He lacks the knack of knowing what the common man wants to hear; he has not mastered the craft of charisma. But unlike Charles V who retired from politics a few years before he died, this vanquished knight has plenty of fight left in him.

In his books and articles, lectures and interviews, Otto defines the Habsburg concept "as the integration of different nations into one unit, and the gathering together of as many peoples as possible." He is fond of quoting his nineteenth-century ancestor, Emperor Franz: "I know I have ruled well when all my peoples are equally dissatisfied."

One fault biographer Emilio Vasari finds with Otto is that he cannot blow up, cannot bang his fist on the table. "We Habsburgs have always tried to harmonize different peoples and differing interests," Otto's sister Adelaide, who was his secretary for years, explains. "From childhood on, we taught every future ruler to bridge over contradictions and difficulties rather than to pursue aggressive policies; to hold on and to keep together, and to follow the course of compromise rather than that of conflict; to say yes rather than no . . . Compromise is in the blood of many of us, and it is hard to fight. . . . But it seems to me that compromise is good politics in the long run."

"The Habsburg idea is the opposite of Bourbon centralism," Otto says, "and my interest in a united Europe is the absolute continuation of the Habsburg idea of internationalism." He contends that the majority of Austrians understand his position.

"In history, you cannot repeat exactly," Otto says, stressing the word 'exactly.' "You cannot ever successfully reestablish the form, you can only bring back the spirit." As his father Karl handed over the reins in Vienna but never surrendered his rights in Budapest, Otto abdicated in Austria but not in Hungary. Of that throne he says, "To whom should I hand over my abdication? To János Kádár? To the Communist Party? There is no reason for me to abdicate.

"Monarchy may come back in the future," Otto muses, "but it will be with different trappings and appurtenances, and with different protagonists. We cannot even visualize what form a monarchy of the future may take. Let's remember that a hereditary dynasty is not absolutely essential to monarchy, and that monarchy originally came from the judiciary."

Otto acknowledges that "on paper," Karl, his eldest son, is his heir. "But what does that mean in practice?" he shrugs. "If you talk about special rights, there aren't any. If you talk about special obligations, there are some. You have to be at the disposal of your fellow countrymen. You simply can't get rid of history, even if you wanted to. But you can accept history as a challenge.

"I hope that Karl will follow my line of thinking. He shows interest in politics, and he has done well when I sent him out to substitute for me. He knows a little Hungarian; I wish he knew more. But he has so much studying to do, and he doesn't have the opportunity to speak Hungarian that I have had all my life."

Otto and his wife Regina—a tall, blonde aristocrat the press describes as a perfect mother and wife—have seven children. Like Otto's own brothers and sisters, they have all learned, or are going into, professions. The two boys, eighteen and fourteen, are interested in law. Of the five girls, two are married (one to a count, the other to a commoner) and have degrees from German universities. The others are pursuing careers: one is a commercial photographer in Germany, another is in law school in Austria, and the last is the manager of a giant French cosmetic firm in Japan.

Otto believes that the institution of monarchy began to decline when kings no longer fought on the battlefield but set themselves apart and walled themselves in their palaces. "In competing for the European Parliament, I am returning to the battlefield, to reality," he says. "I am not running away from my responsibilities and from the past, as some well-meaning people think; no, to the contrary, I am returning to history, and I am fulfilling the Habsburg tradition."

Rebel Prince
Louis Ferdinand
Hohenzollern

Happy is your grace,
That can translate the stubbornness of fortune
Into so quiet and so sweet a style

As You Like It

We drink to America, my host's "second fatherland," and to *shalom* between Arab and Israeli. We drink to *shalom* of the soul, and then for a better world that is sure to come. Our crystal goblets, cut in the eighteenth century, bear the black eagle of the Prussian coat of arms; an old damask cloth with swirling roses and a lace border covers a table that can accommodate twenty. The golden, delicate wine comes from the Mosel region of Germany; it is what the French reverently call *un grand vin* and partake of only on great occasions. The toasts are by His Imperial Highness, Prince Louis Ferdinand of Prussia, the claimant to the German throne. He is in a high good mood.

He has just returned from a visit to Israel, and he is one of those cultured Germans revivified every time they go abroad. A few months earlier, he toured Latin America and was impressed by its vitality. The Holy Land strengthened his piety. "I wish I had gone to Jerusalem when I was young," he says. "I was overwhelmed by the presence of God in that city."

Louis Ferdinand has another reason to be jubilant. He is looking forward to seeing his clan, gathering the next day to celebrate his seventy-first birthday. Three of his six children, two daughters-in-law and two small grandsons have already arrived at his house in Borgfeld, a little town on the outskirts of the old Hanseatic city of Bremen. Tearfully, he remembers two members of the family who will be absent: his wife Kira, who died in 1967, and their third son, "a wonderful boy", killed in an accident in 1977.

Louis Ferdinand is a patriarch. His children address him as respectfully as musicians address their conductor. They are polite men and women in their thirties—slender, handsome, and well-groomed. Unlike their father, who has studied and worked all his life, they have accomplished little besides attending universities for a few years, or trying out jobs in banks and airline companies for a year or two. Father, who manages the extensive complex of family wealth, arranges their jobs but disapproves of some of their marriages and has felt uncomfortable about their divorces. He worries a great deal about their drifting and shifting and spends long hours in heart-to-heart talks with the boys about "women who are not worthy." But subsidy—houses, cars, money—is never used as leverage.

"Louis Ferdinand is a kind and good man," says my taxi driver, who, in his tweed jacket and plaid wool tie looks like an English country squire out for a spin. Too modern to believe in monarchy, he nevertheless approves of Louis Ferdinand. "He is not what you might call a public figure, but everybody in Bremen knows him. He has many friends in many circles. He is a Prussian, of course. But don't worry, he'll give you a good time."

He gets out of the car to shake hands with the prince, bows, and asks if all is well with the family. "Yes, everyone is healthy, God be praised," Louis Ferdinand replies, and thanks the driver as if bringing me to his house were a personal favor to him.

The head of the House of Hohenzollern exults in being a host. His large frame shakes with pleasure as he receives me. He has soulful brown eyes, and the long, pointed nose of his ancestor, Friedrich the Great, Voltaire's mentor. He lacks the stiffness one expects of a Prussian prince. His critics say that he lacks dignity, smiles too often, and tries to be everybody's friend. He has been known as Lulu, the "democratic" or the "American" Hohenzollern. He wears a baggy, blue-gray suit of undistinguished cut, a white shirt, and a dark blue tie. He has a comfortable paunch and thinning gray hair; his complexion is ruddy. He has a radio announcer's baritone; his English is idiomatic, American-accented. A storyteller, he loves to talk. He is at his best at the dinner table, where he holds court, eating and drinking slowly, savoring every bite and sip, and expounding on the pleasures of life. As he dunks thick slices of dark brown bread in the rich gravy of his sauerbraten, he is the image of the soft, jovial German who considers a hearty dinner the reward for a hard day's work.

"I am a God-fearing man," he says, sounding like an old-fashioned German reassuring a stranger. He explains that his pilgrimage to Jerusalem was in response to an invitation to celebrate the eightieth anniversary of the founding of the Redeemer's Church, built with funds provided by his grandfather, Kaiser Wilhelm II, the last emperor of Germany and king of Prussia who abdicated in 1918. Wilhelm had prayed in that church on his visit to the Holy Land in 1899. Louis Ferdinand was moved to tears at the anniversary ceremony when the Lutheran pastor quoted the words of Kaiser Wilhelm's spontaneous prayer "for all humanity and peace."

"Kaiser Wilhelm did not deserve the bad name given to him," Louis Ferdinand says softly, and I know that I am in for an emotional plea. He has a crusade ahead of him to exonerate his grandfather. "The Kaiser did not cause World War I, as English historians and many Germans believe," he begins. "He was not a monster. To the contrary, he was a thoughtful, gentle man, a loving grandfather. As the ex-emperor living in exile in Holland, he gave money to his grandchildren to study and to travel, and he never interfered with our plans. I, for one, wanted to go to America, and he encouraged me. 'I wish I had had a chance to visit America,' he once said to me, 'history might have turned out differently.' I agree with him completely. It's a great tragedy that he didn't see America. He and the Americans would have liked each other, and there might have been no World War I.

"Thanks to the Kaiser, I could go and work for Henry Ford. I had many, many American friends. Those were lovely days. I met Franklin Roosevelt who was like a father to me. He was a true aristocrat, in the finest sense of the word. I shall never forget him as long as I live."

The prince proposes a toast to the United States, his "second fatherland," and downs his wine. A smile settles on his face. His times in America in the 1930s are among his favorite memories; he was a young European aristocrat at large in a young country. He was honored or unrecognized, depending on his whim. He toyed with the notion of starting a new life on a new continent.

"America was the most important influence on my life. I saw there a free people working diligently for a better life. They could not be coerced or fooled. At the Ford plant, people wore Hoover buttons because our boss, Henry Ford, hated Roosevelt. But Roosevelt drove a Ford car because he knew that it was a good car.

"The Ford workers told me they wore the Hoover button but voted for FDR. And, in retrospect, they were wise. With Roosevelt's help, they joined the middle class—a move not welcomed by agitators of the Left. The middle class is too comfortable to make a revolution. Since the war, in Germany the proletariat has risen socially, too; it has become bourgeois—in fact, more bourgeois in its ambitions than the bourgeoisie itself."

Louis Ferdinand is exceedingly careful not to identify himself with a political ideology or party. Some people suspect that beneath his apparent neutrality he has definite views, close to the conservative Christian Democrats—if not to their Bavarian allies further to the Right, the Christian Social Union of Franz Josef Strauss. Louis Ferdinand protests such a description, citing his friendship with labor union officials.

"I don't dislike socialists. I like *people*, and I have never cared what part of the class structure they come from or what their politics might be. We sit and talk, drink a glass of wine, have a meal together. I have good friends among the Social Democrats, and I have always liked Willy Brandt a great deal; he came to the wedding of one of my daughters. I have friends among Christian Democrats too, of course."

The subject of German monarchists brings a guffaw, then another. Finally, he says, "A dear old friend of mine, a Spaniard, used to tell me that some of the worst enemies of monarchism are the monarchists themselves. He was right. People who call themselves monarchists often look out for their own interests or have their own formulas to promote. They want to use royalty. I wouldn't let myself be used. I don't want to be anyone's follower. I don't like political parties and labels and dogmas. I am an individualist."

Louis Ferdinand's life is a *Bildungsroman*: a novel portraying the development of a character, a favorite German genre. His is a story of an earnest, sensitive youth in pursuit of higher values guided by paternal men of good will and accomplishment. He rebels against the rigidities and pomposities of his family tradition; he is determined to succeed at the university, in the machine shop, and as a pilot, a businessman, and a musician. But in the supreme test he hesitates and misses. He is not enough of a rebel; he lacks the recklessness of kings.

Louis Ferdinand was born the second son of "Little Willy"—Kaiser Wilhelm's eldest son, the astonishingly handsome, blond, and blue-eyed Crown Prince Friedrich Wilhelm, known as a fast driver of sports cars and an inveterate skirt-chaser—with a preference for women of the lower classes. At times, Friedrich

Wilhelm played the role of an English country gentleman, complete with clothes and accent. But he was also a Nazi, as were two of his five brothers, and was arrested and then briefly interned by the French occupation forces. German monarchists greeted with relief the news of his death in 1951, in the arms of his last mistress, a former chambermaid in his Potsdam palace of Cecilienhof.

Louis Ferdinand's mother, born Princess Cecilie of Mecklenburg-Schwerin, was a brooding, dark-eyed beauty and a long-suffering wife who bore six children to a husband who was more a visitor than a resident in her house. She patronized the arts, particularly music. She and her husband named Louis Ferdinand after a collateral ancestor who died in 1806 fighting Napoleon—a celebrated hero ignored by his jealous uncle, King Wilhelm Friedrich III, and a black sheep of the family because of his excessively generous, democratic nature. He was an accomplished pianist and a noted composer.

"The name Louis Ferdinand somehow has implied a program of life for me," Louis Ferdinand wrote in his autobiography, *The Rebel Prince*. "It has meant full approval and enjoyment of everything beautiful and good that life has to offer. It has also meant a disregard for conventions and uncompromising opposition to any kind of tyranny." Louis Ferdinand then expressed his gratitude to his parents for giving him that name, though he added, "I shall never dare to compare myself to my great ancestor."

Louis Ferdinand resented his older brother Wilhelm, the heir apparent. Between them a classic conflict developed: Wilhelm excelled in sports and showed great interest in soldiering (the Hohenzollern specialty for 500 years); Louis Ferdinand, on the other hand, turned to a study of the arts and humanities, and expressed contempt for the military, which Germans called "the School of the Nation." As a teenager, he enjoyed shocking his family by declaring his admiration for the Weimar Republic that succeeded the empire.

Louis Ferdinand found life in Potsdam, the seat of Prussian kings, much like residing in a mausoleum. He was "completely choked," he wrote in his autobiography, because "everything was calculated to remind us of our glorious past." The atmosphere was "sinister" because of the view that life, particularly a Prussian prince's life, "was nothing but a duty to be performed under any and all circumstances." Home was a mixture between a convent and a casern," lacking "that simple cheerfulness which makes even the most difficult conditions in life endurable."

He longed to be someone else and somewhere else. As a small child during World War I, he embarrassed his family by expressing his preference for the Russian enemy and by asking to visit his maternal grandmother, a Russian grand duchess. In high school he developed what his parents called "Hispanomania": he studied Spanish and wrote to his godfather, King Alfonso XIII, who eventually invited him to Spain.

At eighteen, Louis Ferdinand prevailed upon his reluctant family to let him go abroad for the first time. The south—since Goethe, the traditional German route for travel and self-discovery—enchanted him with its colors and conviviality. Others found Spain stifling, somber, and seething with the tensions that were to lead a few years later to civil war. But for Louis Ferdinand Spain was a liberation; he could at times go about unescorted, speak with ordinary people, even flaunt protocol with impunity. For instance, he took a liking to an old Catholic cardinal and kissed his hand—a gesture that raised eyebrows in Lutheran Germany. King Alfonso, a man who conversed with peasants, became the first of Louis Ferdinand's mentors.

Enrollment at the University of Berlin, the next step in Louis Ferdinand's life, represented a departure from the Hohenzollern tradition of attending a military academy. But under the republic, princes of former ruling families were not welcome in the small army Germany was permitted after World War I.

At their father's insistence, Wilhelm and Louis Ferdinand joined one of the student fraternities favored by Prussian aristocrats. It was to be a substitute for military training. Fraternity candidates were systematically humiliated, forced to take part in lengthy drinking bouts as often as three times a week, and obliged to fight duels. The exercises—sometimes requiring blind obedience, sometimes courage—were supposed to build character.

Wilhelm took it all in stride, but Louis Ferdinand thought the system was backward, brutal, and preposterous. He felt "the urge of studying for the sake of studying." He was determined to earn a degree on the basis of personal effort, not family connections. He chose political science as his subject, and the theory of immigration as his Ph.D. topic. Kaiser Wilhelm approved a trip to Argentina for field work, and was delighted when Louis Ferdinand, at twenty-two, became the first member of the Hohenzollern family to receive a Ph.D. from a university his ancestors had founded 200 years earlier. It was a cum laude; Louis Ferdinand learned that magna cum laude was first proposed but the university feared being accused of giving preferential treatment to a Hohenzollern prince.

Although he was a hard-working student, Louis Ferdinand found time to play the violin, go to concerts and theater, and befriend musicians and artists, many of them Jews. He also fell in love—his first love, and at first sight—with Lily Damita, a Portuguese-born actress. Seemingly by chance, the encounter was overseen by an old friend of Louis Ferdinand's, a diplomat and a man of the world. A poorly dressed Berlin student, Louis Ferdinand could only talk about his courses.

Lily Damita left for Hollywood, and Louis Ferdinand soon followed her. There he struck up two friendships that decisively influenced his life. Henry Ford gave him employment, first in Detroit, then in Los Angeles (Louis Ferdinand wanted to be close to Lily), later in Buenos Aires (where Ford sent him to keep him away from Lily), and finally, after World War II, in Germany. The descendant of warrior kings became a skilled automobile mechanic, a successful corporation executive, and a lifelong admirer of assembly-line production.

Franklin Roosevelt, governor of New York when Louis Ferdinand first met him, gave his royal visitor a lecture on the American constitution. It is hard to tell which man was more enchanted with the other. A "grand seigneur" was Louis Ferdinand's first and lasting impression. A charming young man who ought to have a political future in Germany, thought FDR. Later, in 1938, when Louis Ferdinand visited Roosevelt in the White House, they were in agreement on the dangers of nazism. The president asked Louis Ferdinand to convey to Hitler a confidential proposal for a summit meeting in the Azores. The führer, however, did not entrust his reply to the Hohenzollern prince.

In Chicago and Hollywood, in midwestern hotels and on California beaches, Louis Ferdinand pursued his elusive amour, Lily. At first his family did not object, believing the affair to be a necessary learning experience. Louis Ferdinand, though, promised not only eternal love but marriage, and he planned an elopement to Tijuana. When details of his intentions appeared in the press, it dawned on the prince that Lily was using him for publicity.

"I wonder if Lily Damita ever loved me," Louis Ferdinand muses in his autobiography. "I have never found out. But at least she did not destroy my illusion." It was a platonic friendship, he insists. "I suppose that was the main reason why it took me such a long time to get over it."

Louis Ferdinand was an earnest young man. At a party in Hollywood he toasted the film industry with a reminder about their "tremendous responsibility toward the entire human race." As a worker on the Ford assembly line, he described himself as belonging to "the largest army of the world." He clocked-in punctually, and noted with pride that the tin badge on his overalls was in the same position as the Order of the Black Eagle on his frock coat.

At one point he considered the possibility of remaining in the United States, but after his older brother married "below his station"—thus disqualifying himself as a claimant to the throne—a cable came from Kaiser Wilhelm with instructions to return home immediately. Louis Ferdinand could not let his grandfather down. The Lulu of Hollywood and the Mr. Ferdinand of Detroit suddenly became an important Hohenzollern prince. Lily Damita, a little later, became Mrs. Erroll Flynn.

Upon Louis Ferdinand's return to Germany, President Paul von Hindenburg, Kaiser Wilhelm's old chief of staff, invited him for a meeting and confided, "I am a monarchist and shall always be loyal to your house. At the same time, I must do my duty towards the German people who have twice shown me their confidence." In his political last will and testament, suppressed by his successor Hitler, Hindenburg recommended the restoration of the Hohenzollern dynasty.

The Nazis courted Louis Ferdinand, hoping to recruit the impressionable prince. The führer gave him a forty-minute private audience, explaining that while as a poor man he had hated everybody who drove luxurious automobiles, he subsequently came to the conclusion that "instead of being a class-dividing element" the motor car "can be an instrument for uniting class differences just as it has done in America, thanks to Mr. Ford's genius." Hitler's intensity shook Louis Ferdinand. His first impression was that the man had charisma; but very soon he decided that Hitler was "a frenzied corporal" and, later, "a satanical tyrant."

In 1938, Louis Ferdinand married Grand Duchess Kira, daughter of the emigrés' czar, Cyril, claimant to the Russian throne. She was tall, aristocratic, and had the sharp good looks of the Romanoffs, as well as the Hohenzollerns and the Windsors. Both Kira and Louis Ferdinand were descendants of Britain's Queen Victoria; Louis Ferdinand's mother was a cousin to Kira's father and a second cousin to her mother.

Louis Ferdinand liked Kira's sense of humor and her decisiveness. There was no courtship; he asked Kira to marry him after their second meeting, following a family Christmas party and a long friendly poker game in which Louis Ferdinand did not seem to mind his extended losing streak. Kira liked her cousin's good-natured smile and lack of stiffness; she said yes without hesitation. Ever impetuous, Louis Ferdinand phoned his friends in the middle of the night to inform them of his engagement.

The couple honeymooned in the United States and planned to spend one year traveling around the world. But after six months they returned home: Kira was pregnant. She continued to bear children during World War II and after—seven in all.

Louis Ferdinand's disapproval of the war and his hostility to the Nazis were no secrets. He had joined Lufthansa in 1935, and was drafted by the German air force four years later. In 1940, his brother Wilhelm was mortally wounded in France, and the private funeral in Potsdam turned into a monarchist demonstration with an anti-Nazi message. Some 50,000 people attended, and Hitler was so furious that he issued a confidential order to discharge gradually all Hohenzollern princes on active duty—thirteen in all.

One year later, Kaiser Wilhelm died in German-occupied Holland. He had cabled his congratulations to Hitler on the victory over France, and the cable received much publicity. But in his last will and testament the Kaiser commanded that there be no swastika flags flown at his funeral, no delegation from Germany, no wreaths. He was to be interred in his garden, next to his favorite rhododendron bush—not in Germany. It was a decision universally understood as a slap at Hitler's face, an affair of class contempt. German armies may have been marching triumphantly through Europe in the name of a Thousand Year Reich, but the one legitimate heir to the German crown would not permit the "vulgar upstart" Hitler to preside over a grand state funeral. The ex-corporal and his followers could not consummate their union with German history; in his last act, the Supreme War Lord of Imperial Germany had his revenge.

Hitler retaliated by instructing the press to play down the story of the Kaiser's death. He also ordered the commander of the German forces in Holland to disregard the dead man's wish by placing a wreath on the bier with the inscription "Der Führer." Hitler distrusted and feared the Hohenzollerns, even those who had joined the Nazi Party. Perhaps he was conscious of his own social inferiority, uncomfortable with those in an historical role to which he could only pretend. Ironically, he was the only German politician who thought a Hohenzollern restoration a realistic possibility.

Louis Ferdinand was advised to ask for a discharge; in December 1941, at the age of thirty-four, Lieutenant Louis Ferdinand Hohenzollern became a civilian again. He retired with his wife and two children to his family estate at Cadinen in East Prussia, "a small paradise on earth," with a unique combination of "woods, hills, fields, the inland sea and the Baltic." Grand Duchess Kira felt at home so close to Russia; Prince Louis Ferdinand became increasingly attached to this ancestral province of his dynasty.

The Gestapo watched him closely. He wrote in his autobiography, however, that the Nazis considered him indifferent to politics. "A fellow who played the organ during the Sunday service of his church was something of a crackpot in the eyes of these hardboiled roughnecks. This opinion of us and our retired way of living to a large extent saved our skins."

From the late 1930s on, Louis Ferdinand had been in close contact with anti-Hitler Germans, both army officers and civilians. In 1942, he approached a former chief of staff with the suggestion that as the heir apparent he could issue an order calling upon the army to move against Hitler. The general countered that only the army itself could decide to get rid of Hitler, and that it would never do so due to its lack of "civil courage." He advised the prince to return to his hiding place in the country and keep alive.

Somewhat discouraged, Louis Ferdinand nevertheless continued to meet with men opposed to Nazism, including, in 1942, their leader, Karl Goerdeler. One plan, advanced by a conservative Prussian aristocrat, had Louis Ferdinand taking command of the army. In 1943, a group of anti-Nazis invited Louis Ferdinand to Berlin and urged him to issue a proclamation for the overthrow of Hitler. The consensus was that the generals, many of them by that time opposed to Hitler and his war, would obey such an order coming from a Hohenzollern.

In his autobiography, Louis Ferdinand explained that he would have been ready to take such a step but that he could not move without consulting his father—the head of the family and legitimate heir to the throne. He went to see Crown Prince Friedrich Wilhelm who intimated that he too had been approached but that he had remained aloof from all subversive movements, and he advised Louis Ferdinand to do the same because success did not seem realistic. By turning to his father, Louis Ferdinand virtually assured his own negative response.

Louis Ferdinand claimed that Hitler had "humiliated" and "terrorized" his father while his father had "maintained a chivalrous attitude towards the former corporal." This is too kind to his father's memory, though. Friedrich Wilhelm was an early Nazi enthusiast who was disappointed when Hitler refused his request to command an army. In the 1932 elections, Friedrich Wilhelm supported Hitler against Hindenburg. Other family members followed suit. His brother, Prince Augustus Wilhelm, coined a slogan: "Where a Hitler leads, a Hohenzollern can follow." Four Hohenzollern princes joined the Nazi Party and allowed themselves to be part of the Nazis' propaganda. They were led to believe—or they wanted to believe—that Hitler himself favored a restoration of the monarchy. Or, just as likely, Hitler's ideology appealed to them for, along with other conservatives, they detested the liberal Weimar Republic. It was not until a German military defeat became a distinct possibility—and a Hohenzollern restoration seemed a possible alternative to Hitler—that the pro-Nazi Hohenzollerns began cautiously to distance themselves from the Nazi cause.

In his excellent book on the Hohenzollerns, *The Soldier Kings*, Walter Henry Nelson cites a moving declaration that anti-Nazi monarchists prepared for Crown Prince Friedrich Wilhelm in the winter of 1942-43. The proclamation catalogued Nazi crimes and declared that "the blood of German soldiers and the happiness of German families can no longer be spilled and destroyed, so as to enable inhuman criminals to conduct such cowardly crimes." Nelson believes that the document would have rallied not only the *Wehrmacht* behind the conspirators but might have won over the German people. Crown Prince Friedrich Wilhelm, however, was angered by the "presumptuousness" of the monarchists and gave them a cold shoulder.

Louis Ferdinand's contacts with the conspirators endangered his life, but an anti-Hitler appeal from him would have guaranteed his execution. Had he been successful in an appeal to the army, he might have recovered not only Hohenzollern honor but the throne as well. But Louis Ferdinand wanted to live, to return to his family, to survive the horror of the war. Perhaps he did not have enough ambition; perhaps not enough self-confidence. In the crucial test he stepped back. Friedrich the Great, even Kaiser Wilhelm, would not have hesitated. Louis Ferdinand let history pass him by. But he has lived to tell the tale.

Following the unsuccessful attempt at Hitler's life on July 20, 1944, the Gestapo investigated Louis Ferdinand. Two high-ranking Gestapo officers visited him at Cadinen; he placed them in chairs facing a large oil painting of Kaiser Wilhelm in a Prussian field marshal's uniform, and put a bottle of good wine on the table. The strategic combination—or was it Louis Ferdinand's luck that the Gestapo did not have enough on him?—worked. After a seven-hour interrogation, he was cleared of all connections with the conspirators.

Less than six months later, advancing Russian armies forced him to flee with his family to the West. The next child born to Princess Kira, in 1946, had an American army captain for a godfather. *The Bavarian*, the official organ of the U.S. occupation forces, ran a story headlined: "Teach Germans Meaning of Four Freedoms, Prince Urges." The subhead read: "Louis Ferdinand Expresses Views on Policies Necessary to Prevent Psychological Chaos in Germany."

Louis Ferdinand concedes that in the summer of 1944 he was closer to the throne than at any other time in his life. But restoration is not a subject he likes to discuss. "The Hohenzollern monarchy was not what mattered in those days," he says with a touch of annoyance. "There were many different people involved in the July coup attempt: Christian Democrats and socialists, conservatives of all kinds, and even Communists. All kinds of groups. I met them, I spoke with them. Only a small group was truly interested in reestablishing the monarchy; others regarded a call for the monarchy as good tactics. There was a feeling that the army might listen to a Hohenzollern or to someone like former chief-of-staff Beck who wanted to set up a regency. Then there was a suggestion that my friendship with President Roosevelt could be helpful in convincing the Americans that they should negotiate a separate peace with Germany. Perhaps the Allied demand for an unconditional German surrender was a mistake. I don't know."

"Louis Ferdinand was not one of the up-and-coming postwar German politicians we watched carefully," recalls one American diplomat stationed in Germany at the time. "But we did pay some attention to him in the early 1950s, primarily because he himself was very busy making contacts with scores of German politicians across the political spectrum. Still, our impression was that he had more ambitions in the economic than in the political sphere. In him, the Ford Motor Company had a hard-working salesman in the Federal Republic."

Louis Ferdinand now says that there was no realistic chance for restoration after the war. But a Romanoff cousin still treasures the memory of one enchanted evening in Berlin's old Titania theater in 1955, when a packed audience applauded Louis Ferdinand's musical compositions with an enthusiasm expressive of much more than mere appreciation of the music. Louis Ferdinand took a bow on stage and then, in response to demands, in the former imperial box. The applause grew stronger and stronger, as did shouts of "Long live the emperor!" The celebration went on, and the beaming Louis Ferdinand continued waving to the crowd, with expert gestures and tirelessly, as if he had been waiting for that moment all his life.

"Failing to become a monarch is all right with me," Louis Ferdinand now shrugs. "Believe me, I have no regrets and I accept my fate with great gratitude. I have lived a very happy life; I have enjoyed the beauty of life. I had a very successful marriage, and we have raised a lovely family. I have lived through tragedies, too, of course."

His voice fades out, his dark eyes glaze with sadness. Did I know about his wife's sudden death, only a few years ago, or about his third son, killed in a freak accident by a tank while on a military maneuver? For a moment there is silence. He looks at the floor; his hands move hesitantly in the air, as if trying to catch an invisible object. "But all in all," he says finally, "I must not be ungrateful. So many people were killed in the war, and I could have been, but for the grace of God, among my friends who were liquidated after the July coup. I am still alive. My soul is at peace." He raises his glass. "This is for *shalom* of the soul," he says softly. "I am grateful. I am comfortable financially. I have traveled all over the world, including the Communist bloc. Albania is the only European country I have not visited. I am a private citizen with all the rights and duties, and I live in a free, democratic society, thank God.

"I don't really care about the monarchy," he suddenly bursts out, sounding like a man tired of nonsense. "What matters is that people live in a state where they are free and the law is observed. The form of government is unimportant; the content of life matters.

"In Germany, the reunification of the country is our most important objective. Everything else is secondary. But reunification is a decision of Heaven, and we, mere men, need not waste our time speculating on that. Restoration of the monarchy? Well, anything is possible. In politics, we should not use the word never. We have to believe in a higher intelligence which defies convention and logic. We have to believe. I tell you, even socialists believe."

There are people who have known Louis Ferdinand for years and who declare that he is not a leader, and that he knows it, and that, given the choice, he would rather not be bothered with dynastic duties and compulsory hopes. Perhaps. But given his family and his upbringing, Louis Ferdinand cannot simply remove himself from the political arena.

He concedes that every so often he thinks of running for office, but always decides against it. "To run for office," he sighs, "you have to be a member of a political party, and I have never had an inclination to join a party. A monarch must be above parties, he must be open to all opinions, all kinds of people. I am not a monarch of course, but I agree with that principle of constitutional monarchy." As for the presidency, he says that "it has been suggested. Friends of mine have thought it might be a good idea. I never liked it though. Suppose I get elected; it could happen. But what happens after the term runs out? What will I do then? Why should I try to be the head of state for four or six or eight years? It's not for me."

The presidency is not an unrealistic option. In 1968, *Bild-Zeitung*, the largest circulation newspaper in West Germany, asked its readers for their preference for the next president of the Federal Republic. Gustav Heinemann, the professor that Parliament later elected, came in second, with 14.3 percent of the vote. First choice was Louis Ferdinand, who drew an amazing 55.6 percent—despite the fact that he was not even running. Similar polls suggest that between 30 and 40 percent of the population would like to have a monarchy, and that such a preference cuts across party lines.

Half an hour after his moody disavowal of interest in the monarchy, Louis Ferdinand talks about a void, a sense of loss in the contemporary German soul, an aching for order and structure that a republic somehow cannot remedy. He repeats what monarchists in one European country after another are fond of saying: "My homeland is a natural monarchy. Hitler catered to that need," Louis Ferdinand adds, "and many Germans supported Hitler because he offered to fill the void left by the dissolution of the monarchy."

As for what he misses in contemporary Germany, Louis Ferdinand mentions Jewish humor. He remembers a play by Ferenc Molnar, a Hungarian Jew, that he saw in Berlin in the 1920s. It was about a carnival man who operated a carousel, a brutal man with a tender heart (the play was the basis for the musical comedy *Carousel*). "Half of the time I laughed," Louis Ferdinand says, "the other half I cried. Jewish humor is more than important—it's indispensable. No one writes in that vein in Germany today; there is too much posturing, no gentle self-mockery."

Louis Ferdinand lives in luxury. Although most Hohenzollern family properties were in the East, and therefore confiscated by the governments of the Soviet Union, Poland, and East Germany, Louis Ferdinand had some holdings in the West. In addition, American friends aided him in the difficult postwar period. Until his retirement some ten years ago, he worked as the representative of the Ford Motor Company in the Federal Republic, and his friends and critics say that he has always invested his money wisely. He is on the board of directors of several companies. He is also a millionaire in his own right.

To replace his father's palace, Cecilienhof in Potsdam—which has served as the Soviet military headquarters in East Germany—Louis Ferdinand built a modern bungalow in a Berlin suburb. It is called "Mon Bijou," and just happens to be located on *Königsallée*, the King's Boulevard. Several times a year Louis Ferdinand organizes a concert there; his guests include musicians, music-lovers, and politicians. He is friendly with a few journalists, and his opinions are published once or twice a year in leading German newspapers.

His house in Borgfeld is roomy and unpretentious. There are fine old oil paintings of the German countryside, etchings of German towns and tradesmen, portraits of ancestors, and photographs and a bronze bust of Kaiser Wilhelm. The library houses hundreds of old leather-bound books and a big oak desk strewn with correspondence and newspapers. In the middle of the disorder is a thick guestbook I am encouraged to sign. In the low-ceilinged living room, the enormous fireplace is decorated with delft tiles more than a century old. The furniture, built for comfort, would look right in a middle-class American home. The chintz-covered sofas and armchairs are arranged to encourage conversation; the well-worn Oriental carpets are in soothing shades of amber and maroon.

The house is in a quiet middle- and upper-middle-class neighborhood. The area was still farmland in the 1950s when Louis Ferdinand bought the property, and initially his immediate neighbors were farmers. Today, the neighborhood boasts ultra-modern villas.

These are the good days in Germany. More than three decades of peace have left their blessings. In Bremen's rathskeller, a plate of Wiener schnitzel with boiled potatoes costs ten dollars, and the place is jammed with middle- and lower-middle-class people. Stores with brown velvet wallpaper offer silver and china at prices considerably higher than stores in Palm Beach or on New York's Fifth Avenue. There are more Mercedes Benzes than Volkswagens. The center of Bremen escaped bombardment during World War II. No bullet holes disfigure the magnificent medieval City Hall; the enormous fifteenth-century statue of the heroic knight Roland is intact, towering over the main square.

Peace and prosperity are so all-encompassing, so natural— *selbstverständlich*, or self-understood, is the word that crashes into my mind—as if they had been the birthright of every German for generations.

Louis Ferdinand is not quite at home in this brash new world of the Federal Republic. He is wary of the consumer-crazed society and he is baffled by the phenomenon of terrorism. (Posters promising one million marks—about $500,000—for information leading to the apprehension of members of the Baader-Meinhof gang are in every public building. At the small Bremen airport no fewer than eight armed security personnel scrutinized my luggage.) He is also puzzled by Germans and foreigners who charge that the German police have exploited the fear of urban terrorism and acquired frightening new powers, including the most comprehensive data bank in Europe.

Louis Ferdinand is offended by the vehemence of anti-German

critics in this century. He is one of the very few people who defend Kaiser Wilhelm, a man about whom his one-time chancellor, Von Bülow, has said, "In peace, the Kaiser was a warlord; in war, he evaded making decisions; in defeat, he fled." A more compassionate assessment comes from the military historian, Sir John Wheeler-Bennett, who called Kaiser Wilhelm a blunderer incapable of conciliatory moves, hurtled along by imperialists in his entourage. Wheeler-Bennett was the Kaiser's weekend guest in 1939 and found him "a charming, humorous and courteous old gentleman— though full of guile." Louis Ferdinand's defense of his grandfather is understandable; he was the Kaiser's favorite grandson. He is disturbed by theories such as the one developed by historian William Shirer that characterize nazism as a logical outgrowth of Prussianism. Louis Ferdinand prefers to think of nazism as an aberration, something that could have occurred in any country given certain circumstances.

Louis Ferdinand has been lucky. The collapse of the monarchy allowed him to study at a university instead of a cadet school; his grandfather saved him the humiliation of quitting a dueling fraternity; the relocation order from Henry Ford kept him from marrying a publicity-hungry actress; he did not have to commit himself totally to the Resistance because his father was still alive. How many young and able-bodied Germans—or Europeans for that matter—could have spent the last three years of World War II on an ancestral estate in a peaceful province, playing the organ in a tiny church on Sundays, and looking after crops, and rejoicing in children borne by a loving wife year after year?

He is a lover of music, a devoted family man, a practitioner of the art of *Gemütlichkeit*, a believer in the fundamental goodness of humanity. He is a man of impeccable intentions. At seventy-one, Louis Ferdinand is still the young prince in search of truth and beauty, a replica of himself in the 1920s. He has remained innocent, unsullied by cynicism. Unlike others of his generation in Germany and elsewhere, he has kept the faith of his youth: democratic humanism. All of his life he has believed in the invincibility of an elusive, poetic goodness that informs and improves mere existence. That such a credo, once revolutionary for a Hohenzollern, nowadays strikes his fellow Germans as vague and pietistic as well as obsolete, does not disturb him. Like so many Germans, he looks back upon his student days as his personal golden age; he calls the day of his Ph.D. examination one of the most glorious in his life.

Like Thomas Mann's celebrated hero Tonio Kröger, Louis Ferdinand is both a patrician and a rebel, yet drawn ultimately to the "bourgeois love of the human, the living, and usual. It is the source of all warmth, goodness and humor." Like Tonio Kröger—Mann's alter ego and a symbol of German duality—Louis Ferdinand has always stood between two worlds, attracted by the faraway and the unconventional but loyal to the circumstances of his birth. His great talent lies in his ability to resolve for himself conflicts between the elite and the masses, between patriotism and internationalism, FDR and Henry Ford, Christian Democrats and Social Democrats. He has escaped the torment of these conflicts through conviviality and—another device of both Mann and Germany—through absorption in music.

In his old age, he has even reconciled himself to his royal heritage. He has strongly disapproved of his son's marrying commoners, and now upholds the medieval principle of *Ebenbürtigkeit*—eligibility due to equality of birth—a principle that forces a prince who marries below his station to forfeit his right and his children's right to the throne. Louis Ferdinand quotes his grandfather: "A good horse-breeder does not mix thoroughbreds with percherons." He hopes that his favorite grandson—the orphan of his third son who was the only son who "married right" and was his designated heir—will carry the Hohenzollern tradition into the future.

It hardly seems to matter that the Prussia whose virtues he now extols no longer exists on the map, its territory divided as spoils of war among three Communist states, its capital Königsberg (where the kings of Prussia were once crowned) now called Kaliningrad after the U.S.S.R.'s first president, its people fast disappearing in the melting pots of the two Germanies.

Could a rebel prince have successfully opposed Hitler? Of all the might-have-beens in Europe, Louis Ferdinand's is the most tragic case—not for him personally, for he never burned with the desire to reclaim the throne—but for the world, which would have taken an imponderably different shape had he been called upon to rule.

The Operatic King
Umberto of Savoy

First Citizen:	*For mine own part,* *When I said banish him, I said 'twas pity.*
Second Citizen:	*And so did I.*
Third Citizen:	*And so did I; and, to say the truth, so did* *very many of us. That we did, we did for* *the best; and though we willingly consented to his* *banishment, yet it was against our will.*

Coriolanus

On a recent tour of Portugal, a busload of Communist Party members from Tuscany decided to look up the last king of Italy: Umberto II, who ruled for thirty-four days in 1946 and left the country after the monarchy was terminated by referendum. "Let's tell a thing or two to the old fool," said the man who proposed the visit, and the crowd roared its assent. "But will he agree to see us? worried one comrade. "He won't keep us out," joked another, "after all, aren't we his subjects?"

The Portuguese driver knew the address. At the gate, a few words of Italian sufficed; the tourists were swiftly ushered into Umberto's presence.

They were greeted as brothers and sisters from Italy. Umberto was delighted to find out that they were from Tuscany, several of them vintners. He praised Tuscany's incomparable wines and cited the incontestable superiority of food grown and prepared under the blessed sky of Italy. Conversation was spirited. The host was witty and voluble; everyone laughed and took photographs. The visitors emerged from the meeting shouting, "Long live the king!"

They were not converted to the monarchist cause. They did not revise their Marxism by one iota. They merely surrendered themselves to the instinctive awe felt when encountering royalty— in their case, the head of the House of Savoy, rulers in Italy for a thousand years.

For non-Italians it is not easy to be admitted to Umberto's presence. My letters from the United States go unanswered. Even with his unlisted telephone number, I cannot get past the chambermaid and the caretaker, who either have me hold the line for minutes on end or suggest that I call again some other time. One of Umberto's aides-de-camp regretfully informs me that His Majesty will not be available for the next few weeks. Pleading a bad connection, I say I cannot hear him and that I will call again. When I try to get through to Umberto himself, I fail ignominiously.

A telephone call from one of Umberto's relatives does the trick. Several days and several phone calls later I hear a *basso romantico* on the other end of the line. "Your name is not entirely unknown to us," says the voice. "His Majesty has granted you an audience. His Majesty receives all the visitors he can. Such is his wish; such is his pleasure. So for you, Monsieur, it will be tomorrow, at six in the evening, at Villa Italia."

The voice belongs to Count Dino Olivieri, who just celebrated his ninety-fourth birthday and is the doyen of Umberto's court-in-exile. He began his career at the age of sixteen, serving Umberto's mother, Queen Helena. He has devoted his entire life to the Savoys.

There are four aides-de-camp who take turns attending their king. Two of them are always in Cascais, the resort town some ten miles from Lisbon where Umberto has been living since 1946; the other two are in Italy where their families live. One aide-de-camp is usually at Umberto's side, accompanying him to dinners, other formal events, and on his frequent trips.

In his book *Secrets of the Gotha*, aristocrat Ghislain de Diesbach condemns the Savoys as "impecunious, restless, greedy and parsimonious, driven by ambition." He dismisses Victor Emmanuel II, the first king of united Italy, as ignorant, vulgar, and wholly occupied with the pursuit of women of the lowest social strata. His son Umberto I did not represent much of an improvement but he at least preferred ladies of nobility. In 1900, he was assassinated by anarchists and was succeeded by his son, Victor Emmanuel III, known as the Tom Thumb of royalty. Diesbach describes him as jealous of his tall, dashing son Umberto II, called by Dolores Del Rio "the most handsome man in the world."

Not many Italians love the Savoys. Originally rulers of the mountainous dukedom of Piedmont in the northwest, they acquired a royal title by taking over the island of Sardinia in the eighteenth century. First dispossessed by Napoleon's armies, they later profited from the reactionary settlement after Napoleon's banishment—the Congress of Vienna regarded Piedmont as a buffer state between Austria and France—and then from the revolutionary tide of the *Risorgimento* that liberated Italy from Bourbons and Habsburgs, and, finally, from the temporal rule of the papacy. Military victories by Garibaldi and France's Emperor Napoleon III gradually annexed all of Italy to Piedmont and made Victor Emmanuel II king of a unified Italian state in 1861.

After being told that Turin, in Piedmont, would not do as the capital of all of Italy, the Savoys moved to Rome. But like Julius Caesar and other conquerors of the Eternal City, the Savoys never quite felt at home there. They were regarded as intruders and, despite their illustrious ancestry, not quite on a par with Roman aristocracy, the presumed descendants of the patricians of ancient Rome. The simple Savoy taste in cooking and in women was ridiculed. "That shepherdess" was one of the more polite references by Roman aristocrats to Queen Helena, wife of Victor Emmanel III and daughter of the king of Montenegro, a small and underdeveloped mountain state across the Adriatic Sea, now part of Yugoslavia.

At first "eternally opposed" to the incorporation of the Papal State in Italy, the pope excommunicated, then merely snubbed the Savoys. It took the dictator Benito Mussolini, the son of a blacksmith, to negotiate a settlement between Italy's two monarchies. Romans trace the papacy's unwillingness to help the Savoys in 1946 to the papal humiliation three-quarters of a century earlier. Pope Pius XII liked Umberto personally, and when his cardinals asked what he was going to do in the referendum, he replied, "I am a monarchist." But the pope's praise was faint in the midst of a frenzied political campaign during which Umberto's supporters promised aristocratic titles, medals, and honorific positions, and his opponents threatened both civil and international war. "The Church has an unfailing instinct for scenting a winner," I once heard a Roman declare on his terrace overlooking St. Peter's Basilica. "The Holy Roman Catholic Church always gives in to the stronger party. That is the secret of her survival."

The monument the Savoys left to Rome is the memorial of Victor Emmanuel II, "the Father of the Nation." Erected shortly before

World War I, it is designed to overwhelm, towering over Papal Rome and invoking Imperial Rome. Its white marble, imported from the north, glares—in contrast to the pastel tones of travertine Rome. It is the tallest, bulkiest monument in the city, with huge heroes and horses. To this day, Romans cannot forgive the Allies for leaving it intact in the bombing raids of 1943.

Monarchists defend Victor Emmanuel III by asserting that it was his constitutional duty to appoint Mussolini in 1922, that as a constitutional monarch he is blameless for what followed, and that he tried his best to signal his desire to switch over to the Allies but that the Allies were unsympathetic and unresponsive.

During his nearly half-century reign, Victor Emmanuel III always swam with the tide. His supreme objective was to stay on the throne. His one emotional moment came when Mussolini gave him the title emperor of Ethiopia. He needed a stool to mount his steed, but there was a conqueror's glint in his eyes—the blue eyes of an Aryan, he once assured Hitler—when Germany and Italy launched World War II.

When the Axis powers began to lose on the battlefields, Victor Emmanuel III adopted neutrality. He refused to assist the anti-Fascists, but he chose to fight the Fascists over trivial issues: he would not permit Mussolini's henchmen to wear their black shirts in his presence, and he protested when Parliament failed to ask for his "royal and imperial approbation" before giving Mussolini the title of First Marshal of the Empire. Toward the end, he was proud to have admonished American and British officers arriving in army fatigues to come back properly dressed to meet a king. They acceded to his wish.

Umberto was disingenuous when during the campaign in 1946 he declared that the people's enthusiasm for fascism had "forced" his father to appoint Mussolini as premier. Apart from the exaggeration, Umberto misjudged the mood in a country where a sizable portion of the population actively turned against the Fascists and had no patience for people such as the Savoys, whose anti-fascism consisted of private grumbling and symbolic defiance.

"Umberto is the victim of his father's dry, legalistic thinking," declares a close relative who asks not to be identified. "Victor Emmanuel III was a most distant, cold man, shriveled up inside—the pitiful product of a military education. The need to repress his feelings was drilled into him. Thus he could not understand feelings, his son's or his people's. Had he abdicated earlier—for instance, in 1943, right after he finally stripped Mussolini of power—Umberto would have had time and opportunity to prove himself, and the nation would have accepted him because he was not burdened with any link to fascism.

"Instead, Victor Emmanuel fled Rome and set up a powerless charade of a government and a fully functioning court in the south. He thought that the capital is where the king is. He wanted to preserve what he believed had to be preserved at all cost: the principle of legitimacy. He was a courageous man, and in both world wars he went to the front lines, braving gunfire. But he was afraid of the fate of a Wagnerian martyr; the prospect of the Germans immolating him in Quirinale Palace frightened him. What mattered to him most was the orderly transfer of authority, be that from him to Umberto, which he kept delaying, or from monarchy to republic, which he privately predicted. He could never understand why Italians interpreted the flight of the Savoys from Rome as an act of cowardice. There is no question that had one Savoy, Victor Emmanuel or Umberto, stayed behind in Rome, Italy would be a monarchy today."

When arrive at Villa Italia, at six p.m. sharp, the aide-de-camp on duty is Count Solaro di Monasterolo. He meets me on the marble steps of the mansion, built with definitive Renaissance simplicity and proportion. It is all rectangles and triangles, no chubby angels floating in niches or ceramic tiles of turquoise and yellow. A classical restraint curbs Italy's earthy excess. The colors, freshly painted, are beige and white, and the roof tiles are terra cotta. Villa Italia was a gift from Umberto's supporters, given shortly after his arrival in Portugal.

Count Monasterolo is in his seventies, slim and smooth. His small silver moustache has an upward curl—a replica of the moustache that once adorned Victor Emmanuel III. He is a craftsman in courtesy. With waves of his delicate hands and a staccato assortment of *tout droits* and *à gauches* and plenty of *s'il vous plaîts*, he leads me through a foyer and an antechamber to a large room where, he whispers, His Majesty is waiting for me. We cross expanses of Persian carpets; tall double doors, composed of rows and rows of flawlessly mitered moldings, open and close noiselessly.

Umberto greets me with a firm handshake and a cascade of Italian words. I apologize for not knowing his language. He motions for me to sit down on the couch across from him and switches immediately to English, fluent but Italian in its inflections. His hands are always in the air; his gestures are elaborate but carefully tailored.

He is totally at ease, and gives the impression of enjoying himself hugely. At seventy-four, he looks a decade, perhaps a score, younger. He is bald, and has an ivory complexion, lustrous brown eyes and sensual lips. He has the long, bony face of Titian's silky princes. He wears an immaculate dark gray pinstripe suit, a striped shirt and a blue silk dotted tie. His slender six-foot frame is gracefully recumbent, his legs crossed. Portraits of ancestors and pictures of cities they once ruled are displayed around the room. The furniture is antique; the curtains of pale brocade; porcelain vases and silver objets d'art lie about on tables and cabinets of gleaming wood. Amber is the dominant color.

"The Portuguese," he begins, "are such nice people, such gentle people. In 1946, Portugal was the only country that would let me enter. One doesn't forget that kind of thing. The Portuguese have always been especially kind to me. During the 1974 revolution, officers from an army unit stationed nearby came to see me. 'Call us right away if someone gives you problems,' they said. I thanked them but also told them that no one would give me trouble. Indeed, no one did. I was not worried for a moment. I knew everything would turn out to be fine. It was a real revolution yet no one got killed. The Portuguese are not impulsive as we Italians tend to be.

"I love Cascais. It's a quiet place where everyone knows everyone else. And I am so grateful for the view of the Atlantic Ocean."

Umberto's mansion is on a street that runs along the seashore. It is called *Estrada da Boca do Inferno*—the Street of the Mouth of Hell. It sounds like a name Dante, another exile, might have invented for a banished king. But in fact the street is named after a cavernous opening in the ground, partially covered by boulders that produces a frightening rumble when waves surge over it at high tide.

"From the window of my study," Umberto says, "and from nearly all the windows of this house, I can look at the sea and watch its many moods: the calm and the storm, sunny days and foggy days. The sea is never the same. I am fond of watching ships, of walking on the beach, of talking to fishermen."

Local people tell me that Umberto often spends a full day out on the sea in a small and not always seaworthy boat that belongs to a fisherman he knows. He frequents a Cascais bar and will talk with anyone who walks over to him. He is well-liked, unlike other nonreigning royalty who have lived in the area at one time or another but never mixed with the locals—Henri, the count of Paris, who still owns the cattle farm he ran with his family before he was allowed to return to France; Juan Carlos, now king of Spain, who maintains a villa in nearby Estoril; Romania's ex-King Karol, who eventually married his lifelong companion Elena Lupescu, and who was ostracized by the rest of the local royalty—except for Umberto. Even Portugal's own nonreigning royal family, the Braganças, keep to themselves.

Tourist brochures describe the Cascais area as a favorite of royalty and bullfighters, and many American visitors ask their travel agents to arrange meetings with both. "It's easy enough to get someone who can act like a bullfighter, but kings are hard to find," explains one hotelier. Once a group of air-conditioner salesmen from the United States insisted that a king be brought to a cocktail party they were giving. So the hotelier called Umberto, and told him he needed a king. Umberto obliged, and gave the Americans a good time.

"Umberto is one of the people," the hotelier declares. "He appreciates the same things we Portuguese appreciate: friendship, the sea, good food. He likes Portuguese fish dishes, but my God! how he loves sweets—cakes, ice cream, bonbons. Just like a Portuguese!"

Everyone in Cascais knows Umberto, at least by sight. Some call him plain *Senhor*; most refer to him as His Majesty, or king. He doesn't seem to care how he is addressed. His Portuguese is excellent, and he loves to talk—about friends, movies, food, wines—anything but politics.

Umberto used to grow the most beautiful roses in Italy. He is heart-broken that roses do not do well in Portugal. He is not sure if it is the soil, which is different, or the cold winds, or perhaps the humid air and the salty spray of the Atlantic. Umberto plants annuals; his beds of petunia and geranium are the finest. He has the assistance of an elderly gardener, but he prefers to do the yardwork himself. He recently broke an arm in the process. "But that is life," he says. "I am not discouraged." Years ago, he imported many seeds and seedlings from Italy. Again and again the plants wilted and withered. The Atlantic wind burns, singes—so different from the gentle Mediterranean breeze.

"I am so busy," he says, "I wish I had more time. I have so much correspondence. Then I have visitors, oh so many visitors, primarily from Italy and from Italian communities everywhere in the world. I don't like to say no to people who want to see me. This morning, for instance, I met with about 100 Italian university students who were on their way home from a tour in Cuba. They were leftists, I suppose, but I didn't ask—I don't like to—and they didn't say anything political. Some of them talked about their fathers or grandfathers meeting me or my father back in the old days. Even young people like to remember, don't you agree? I was with them for most of the morning because each student wanted to speak with me, and each wanted a photograph with me, too. It was very sentimental. These young people were so nice, so kind. They called me Your Majesty. In Italian, it's easy; it comes naturally. And, you know, I *am* a king."

Umberto laughs, and his laugh sounds like part of an aria. It goes on for several seconds; he seems reluctant to return to words.

Umberto loves to travel. He goes everywhere in Western Europe and has visited Yugoslavia, even the Soviet Union. He has been to the United States many times, and met with President Eisenhower, Cardinal Spellman, Governor Rockefeller. Everywhere he goes he wanders into the Italian communities and talks to all kinds of people. But it is forbidden for him to enter Italy. He often takes flights that stop over in Rome, but the Italian government will not permit him to leave the aircraft. He looks at the tarmac, the hangars, the olive trees in the far distance.

"My son Victor Emmanuel and I are the only Italians forbidden to step on Italian soil," he says matter-of-factly. Asked about the possibility of a return for him, he replies, "Monarchy is a good thing, isn't it? Why should people put an end to a good thing? Look at Juan Carlos in Spain. That's a lovely restoration for you. But the poor fellow has his job cut out for him. Spain is fortunate that he is so talented. He is doing well, don't you Americans think?"

Umberto's bullishness on monarchy may reflect his devotion to the virtue of being positive. At weddings and christenings of fellow royalty, Umberto is always a most cheerful guest, everyone's favorite Uncle Beppo. He is close to the younger generation; if requested, he offers them encouraging advice. He takes offense at nothing. One of his friends, an aristocrat who has seen better days, tells me, "Umberto is a most sensible man. He doesn't argue with history; he doesn't allow useless regret to drag him down. On the contrary, he makes the best of being out of power. He reads books and talks to people from all walks of life. At heart, he is what the French call a *flâneur*, a spectator of life. He realizes that as king of Italy, he could not be as free with his time. He doesn't believe that he will visit Italy ever again, but he will not say that."

Umberto has never abdicated, and he continues to encourage his followers. During the most recent presidential crisis, he cabled members of the Italian Senate to tell them that he was available and ready to serve as president of the Republic.

He is an Italian citizen, a fact noted in his Portuguese passport, which is made out to one Umberto Sarre (the ancient seat of the House of Savoy, Sarre is the name Umberto likes). Border police often stop him. "If you are an Italian citizen," they, being logical bureaucrats, ask, "why do you travel on a Portuguese passport?"

"Should I tell them that I am king of Italy?" Umberto muses. "Should I explain to them recent history? I don't. I say something about the complexity of life and I laugh. Eventually, they laugh with me, and they let me pass. They are nice people, too."

Umberto's laugh is operatic, and accompanied by a sort of a chuckle. That chuckle has been his trademark all his life. In the 1930s and '40s, it prompted his enemies to name him "the laughing fool of Europe." The Umberto chuckle is a resonant chortle. It is uninhibited and frequent, sometimes occurring between subject and predicate. Although his speaking voice is a deep baritone, his chuckle is strictly soprano. He ends up not so much speaking as chanting. His is a rhythm of permanent merriment. Our conversation strikes no sour notes. Umberto appears to be a man without bitterness, but perhaps his secret is Pagliacci's: as he smiles, he is weeping inside.

Those who know him well insist he says nothing nasty about anyone. People he dislikes he will simply not discuss—Mussolini or the Nazis, for instance. He refuses to discuss Italian politics during and immediately after World War II. This reticence keeps him from working on his memoirs. "I would have to disclose things about people, many of whom are still alive," he says.

With an offer to do any favors for me in Portugal, my audience with Umberto abruptly ends. He shakes my hand several times. "So nice of you to come to see me," he says, "come again please. We'll talk again." He accompanies me to the door that seems to open by itself. Count Monasterolo greets me. I hear a snatch of the royal chuckle, then the door closes, and Count Monasterolo asks me how I found His Majesty.

"Charming," I say, "charming."

He smiles; he has heard the same comment hundreds of times. "Please sign the guest book," he says, extending both arms to show me the direction.

The page I sign is filled with mostly American addresses, many Italian-American names. "Americans like His Majesty," Count Monasterolo whispers. Then, with a graceful motion of his hand, he shows me the way out. From the door he waves goodbye, both hands in the air.

Many Italians, and not only monarchists, are convinced that monarchy would have won in the 1946 referendum had it not been for the machinations of the Communists and the large-scale cheating ignored by the minister of the interior. The vote—12.7 million versus 10.7—was uncomfortably close, disappointing both monarchists and republicans, who had hoped for a more decisive victory than a 53 percent majority. Umberto's supporters variously advised him to demand a recount, to press for another referendum, or simply, to declare the referendum null and void, and call out his loyal *carabinieri*. Another suggestion was to retire to the resoundingly pro-Umberto South and organize his return from there. The Allies warned him: if the monarchy had to be defended by force, Josip Tito's Yugoslavia—then Stalin's ally—might step in and a third world war might break out. Italy's eastern frontier was undefendable, and, in any case, the West had more important problems than shoring up the House of Savoy.

In the opinion of Luigi Barzini, Italy's premier journalist, the West's advice was superfluous. In his book, *From Caesar to the Mafia*, Barzini describes a conversation he had with Umberto a few days prior to the referendum. Barzini predicted that the monarchy would lose because defeat in war always costs kings their throne, because political parties organized by the anti-Fascists were for a republic, and because to the Allies—and particularly to the British— Italy's defeat would not seem complete without a liquidation of the monarchy. Umberto told Barzini that he would not fight for his right to be king. Barzini concluded, ". . . It is this human, modern, reasonable, civilized reluctance to shed his subjects' blood for the sake of his crown that showed [that] the monarchy had lost the old brutal vigor, which, in earlier centuries, had driven so many kings into the saddle at the head of their men, banners flying, drums rolling, trumpets sounding. . . . Umberto was no longer a king who cured scrofula by laying his hand on the sick man's head, or chopped off his subjects' heads either. He was a king who shrank from bloodshed. He was one of us."

To the monarchists and old soldiers and citizens who came to see him, Umberto declared: I don't want a single Italian killed, not even a Communist. Upon hearing the final tally of the referendum, he looked out the window, and then turned to a friend and said, "I think it's going to be a beautiful day." Umberto left Italy without a bitter word. (His father Victor Emmanuel quit in a nasty mood, snarling at the British naval officer taking him to Egypt: "Now that the Allies made Italy a republic, every Italian will want to be president of the Republic, and that means communism.")

Family squabbles have long plagued the Savoys, contributing to the demise of the monarchy. When Crown Prince Umberto married Princess Marie-José of Belgium in 1930, the European press spoke of a brilliant dynastic match uniting the Houses of Savoy and Saxe-Coburg-Gotha. The bride was the daughter of King Albert I of Belgium, the richest monarch in Europe, and the wedding festivities, lasting a full week, are remembered as the last lavish royal wedding on the continent. But Marie-José also inherited the Wittelsbach predilection for eccentricity from her mother, Elisabeth of Bavaria. She was intense, impetuous and headstrong and had political ambitions. Umberto was easygoing, light-headed, and spoiled. According to Domenico Bartoli, their biographer, Umberto and Marie-José were separated by "a profound dissimilarity in character, an irreconcilable contrast in tastes, likings and sympathies." They lived together only for a short while, and later only for the sake of Catholic and dynastic propriety—and for procreation: they had four children.

Marie-José openly despised Mussolini; Umberto's disdain was less vociferous. She was rebuffed in her attempts to join forces with the anti-Fascist underground, and in 1940 flew to Berchtesgaden to plead with Hitler to spare her native Belgium—a move variously interpreted as folly and treason. When the postwar struggle began between monarchists and republicans, Marie-José was observed rushing up and down the streets of Rome at night tearing down promonarchist posters. Umberto had frequently made snide comments about the Fascists, but always quietly. He refused to wear their black uniforms; the Fascists retaliated by instructing the press not to call Umberto tne Hereditary Prince and to drop hints that there was another candidate for succession. A thick dossier was also assembled on Umberto's amorous involvements with people of high social standing—both women and men.

When the referendum sealed the fate of the Savoys, Marie-José hoped that as a republican and as a Belgian she might be permitted to stay in Italy. It was a bitter disappointment for her to learn that she too had to leave. She accompanied Umberto to Portugal, and fell critically ill. A blood transfusion of the wrong blood type left her partially blind. A few months later, she left for Switzerland, finally freeing herself of her husband.

For the past twenty years, Marie-José has been working on a history of the Savoys. If the book will be a sympathetic account, as she has promised, it will be a final act in her life of fealty to the impractical and the self-defeating.

It is doubtful if Italian monarchism can survive Umberto. His only son, born Prince Victor Emmanuel in 1937, weakened his standing by his marriage in 1970 in Las Vegas to a commoner, Marina Doria, a former Italian water-ski champion. Their first and, to date, only child, Emmanuel Filiberto, was born in 1972.

Prince Victor Emmanuel is an impulsive young man who inherited his father's good looks and his mother's difficult character. A pilot and yachtsman, he lives in Geneva and is employed as a consultant to an Italian helicopter industry. Gossip columnists and left-wing journalists charge that as a close friend of the shah of Iran he received a helicopter and small arms concessions some years ago. In exchange, Victor Emmanuel reportedly tried to convince his sister, Maria Gabriella, to marry the shah.

Last year he was involved in a tragedy. Details of the incident which occurred on Cavallo, a tiny French island between French Corsica and Italian Sardinia, are still murky, but some facts have been established in court: there was a group of vacationers high on cocaine, an altercation in a restaurant, the spiriting away of Victor Emmanuel's cabin cruiser, a warning shot fired by Victor Emmanuel. The bullet wounded a German tourist, who nearly bled to death. Four months after having his right leg amputated, he died of complications resulting from the wound.

Victor Emmanuel has admitted that he fired what has turned out to be the fatal bullet, and he spent fifty days in a Corsican jail while his family and lawyers tried for an out-of-court settlement. Frantic attempts to hush the press and to buy off the German tourist's family—the compensation paid was reportedly between one and five million dollars—earned the prince additional adverse publicity. He was released on his own recognizance, but the victim's sister, a former Miss Germany, has launched an international campaign to protest the decision, citing the intervention of the pope, the Belgian royal family, and Valéry Giscard d'Estaing.

Umberto will not discuss his son's conviction even with friends. Victor Emmanuel is not his only child with difficulties, though. Princess Maria Pia, the eldest, is divorced from Prince Alexander of Yugoslavia, a cousin to the claimant to the Yugoslav throne by the same name. Princess Maria Gabriella gave Umberto a series of headaches: after a number of amorous escapades, covered extensively by the press, she married Jewish-born Robert de Balkany, a wealthy divorcé who is a real estate speculator headquartered in Paris. The youngest princess, Maria Beatrice, is now married to an Argentinean diplomat, but Umberto strongly disapproved of her first marriage to Italian film star Maurizio Arena, a lower-class divorcé. Umberto disregarded suggestions that he confer a title on Arena, just as the queen of England did when her sister, Princess Margaret, married Tony Armstrong-Jones. Arena complained that upon marrying Maria Beatrice a "thousand years of history fell on my shoulders."

Umberto is typically Italian in his dedication to family ties. He attends memorial masses for both his father, who died in Egypt in 1947, and his mother, who died in France in 1952. He maintains diplomatic relations with his estranged wife, and he speaks to his children by phone several times a week.

The Savoys are well off; Victor Emmanuel III had a multimillion dollar life insurance policy, and a private estate worth approximately fifteen million dollars. The Italian government seized the estate, but Umberto succeeded in recovering four-fifths of it in courts.

Ever since 1946, monarchist strength in Italy has been declining, though Umberto's stature has steadily increased. But the consensus is that he would not get more than 10 percent of the vote in another referendum. Most of those who voted for him thirty years ago have died, or changed their views. Former monarchist strongholds in

Piedmont and the South now usually vote Communist. Mafia leaders are prominent members of Italian monarchist councils.

In Portugal, Umberto has become a footnote to Italian politics. He does not figure in any of the coalition combinations Italians specialize in. In a country that relishes conspiracies—real and imagined—there are not even rumors of monarchist plots. Umberto is a melancholy anachronism, a postprandial topic, a trill in the baroque of Italian life. His exile may one day inspire a Fellini film. For Umberto and Marie-José, the Savoy dethronement was tragic, but in a typically Italian way Umberto has become an actor in that tragedy, or rather, tragicomedy. A patrician incapable of self-defense, an aged playboy uselessly wise, he is an operatic king who is playing himself. Superbly.

The Sadness of
Dom Duarte João

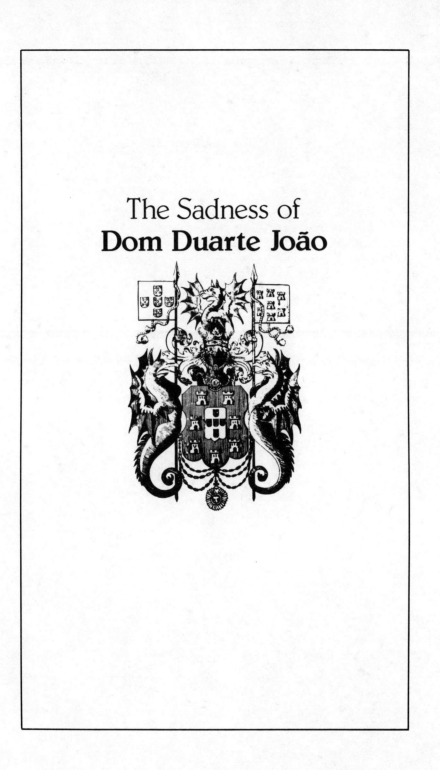

'Tis no sinister nor no awkward claim,
Pick'd from the worm-holes of long-vanish'd days,
Nor from the dust of old oblivion rak'd

King Henry V

At thirty-three, Duarte João, the duke of Bragança and claimant to the throne of Portugal, is the youngest European pretender. His ideas have the fragrance of the Middle Ages; he is part of the quixotic minority that retains faith in Portugal's African destiny, a faith that present-day Portugal has surrendered. He is a patriot, and takes pride in his country's ancient windmills and terraced vineyards, rococo fortresses and huge fish feasts.

He is a gung-ho helicopter pilot, but what stir his soul are the fabled machinations of Jesuits and Jews. He envies the power of freemasons; heretic is a word he uses often. He is a guardian of Old Europe, who mourns the decline of civilization—the ancien régime of inherited rights and obligations—and resents the gains of "hustling classes" and "pushy nations." He grieves over the loss of the Catholic Church's passion to redeem and rule. "What has happened," he asks, "why have disunity and decadence set in? Why, why, why?" He looks for an explanation that ascribes a simple motivation but traces an intricate, long-range strategy. He believes in conspiracy theories arching over continents and centuries. He would like to launch his own conspiracy, but he has not found allies and has not defined his cause. His enemy is not just the United States or an international liberal cabal of financiers and intellectuals, but time itself. He would like to undo centuries. But he is weighed down by his dynastic inheritance: the Bragança kingdom was one of those absurd places Candide or Gulliver might have visited.

He is an avid reader of history, geography, zoology, and anthropology. A restless man, he travels a great deal and enjoys talking to people of all classes. He is impulsively generous, and has surprised everyone by becoming the chief lobbyist for refugees from Portugal's former African holdings. He has pulled strings, cajoled banks and governments, pressured international organizations, and overcome the apathy and hostility of the mainland Portuguese, and to date he has obtained loans to finance the resettlement of 20,000 families in various Latin American countries.

"He is really a very good boy," says his Aunt Isabelle, the countess of Paris and wife of the Bourbon claimant to the French throne. "He may not be the smartest man in Portugal, but what he really lacks is plain good luck. Who needs superior intelligence? Look at my dear husband Henri—he is very intelligent, no doubt about it, but of what use has that intelligence been to him? I wish Duarte well, and what I wish him most is luck—luck in finding a good wife and a good profession."

"He is a sweet fellow," says one of his cousins. "He hasn't had much luck with girls but perhaps it is because he is too anxious to get married—and to the right kind of girl. He has all kinds of strange ideas and expects people to agree with him. Unfortunately, he is very thin-skinned. His feelings were really hurt when Princess Anne of England snubbed him at the wedding of his cousin, Dona Maria da Gloria, to Prince Alexander of Yugoslavia. It was partly because of his strange theories and partly because she didn't care for him as a man. I am sure that Duarte would make a dutiful husband, but I guess that is not what girls, even princesses, look for these days. He is just not with it, I'm afraid."

Duarte João reads the newspapers but has no great interest in politics. It is the past that enthralls him. His voice trembles with bitterness when he discusses Pedro I, his great-great-grandfather, responsible for "the tragic severance of Brazil from its Portuguese motherland." The first emperor of Brazil, Pedro I "hated the Church with all his heart" and "deserved to be driven out of his realm." He was "a terrible monarch, a veritable disaster, the extravagant adulation of the Brazilians notwithstanding." Had it not been for his "impetuous" and "misguided" decisions, "Portugal and Brazil would still be one, and Portugal would be a great power." He repeats the phrase "great power" slowly, lugubriously. He strokes his chin, recently cleaned of a beard. "Oh, my poor little homeland!"

Portugal is a provincial country, off the main highway of European thought and action, where people eat and sleep well and where nothing of great importance ever seems to happen. Lord Byron, coming from faraway England, looked at the verdant hills, the olive groves, and grape arbors, and pronounced the land "a glorious Eden." Spain's Miguel Unamuno found the people "tender and smiling on the outside, but tormented and tragic underneath." Visitors from the United States and France have called the Portuguese hardworking and hospitable, but dull and bourgeois.

Once, Portugal occupied center stage in world history. In the sixteenth century, its graceful caravels sailed around the globe exploring oceans and islands, and setting up intercontinental trade routes. Portugal, with naval bases in the Persian Gulf and China, India and the Red Sea, had built its overseas empire before France, before Great Britain, before the Netherlands.

A Florentine countess I met in Lisbon remembers a dinner she once had with a Portuguese poet. They held hands and ate sea trout with chestnuts in a tiny restaurant in the old Lisbon harbor. Afterward, they went for a walk by the seashore.

"We were a great nation once," the poet said.

"So were the French and the English," came her gentle rebuke.

"Yes, but we Portuguese cannot forget our past; that's all we have that's precious."

"But there is a life to live," the countess suggested, "there is the sweetness of the moment, and, thank God, we are young."

"My tears mingle with the brine of the Atlantic," the poet declared. "We are a people of sadness."

Portugal was launched as an independent nation eight centuries ago by a feudal lord, Count Afonso Henriques. His father, a French adventurer, was a descendant of the kings of France, and his mother was a bastard daughter of King Alfonso VI, the great Spanish warrior against the Moors. Lands with much stronger claims to autonomy—Wales, the Ukraine, Macedonia, and Bretagne—have failed as independent states while Portugal, somehow, has survived.

Portuguese architecture blends Versailles with Fez; the instinctive native baroque triumphs over the classical restraint of the Italian Renaissance and the austere rigidities of Spain. Coral roots, elephant tusks, and seaweed festoon Gothic arches that soar toward heaven; sailors' memories of Chinese pagodas and Hindu temples are transformed into Bavarian castles. Moorish tiles are everywhere; the Portuguese call them azulejos and proclaim their Portuguese origin.

Where does Iberia end and northern Africa begin? Do the

symmetrical, endless arabesques reflect the imperialist theology of the medieval Church or the resolute anti-imagism of Islam? In Morocco, the word symbiosis is used to explain the confluence of factors at work among Muslims and Christians and Jews in North Africa and Western Europe and the Near East. In Spain, tolerance is ever a rare commodity, and proprietary pride can be extravagant. The Portuguese have a painful awareness of their marginality, an almost colonial consciousness of dependence on stronger, richer cultures. But the result is self-deprecation not haughtiness, playful imitation rather than adherence to any national canon.

The Portuguese royal house has somehow remained distinctly Portuguese despite marriages to Bourbons and Habsburgs and the importation of Germans, Spaniards, and Italians. Listed in the annals of royalty as the House of Saxe-Coburg-Gotha-Braganca, or simply Bragança, and dating to 1640, it is traced to a bastard son from the previous house, which in turn descended from a bastard son of the preceding house. Voltaire said of João V, who ascended to the throne in 1706, "This monarch's gaieties were religious processions; when he took to building, he built monasteries; when he wanted a mistress, he took a nun." The great liberal of Portuguese history as well as its great despot, Marquis of Pombal rose to the post of prime minister in the eighteenth century. In charge of maintaining a supply of women for his king, he was also a disciple of the Enlightenment, and worked to discourage the Inquisition, expel the Jesuits, and abolish slavery. A few years before the French Revolution of 1789, he was fired by a new ruler, a pious queen who tried to reverse the effects of his reforms. In 1807, the Portuguese court surprised Napoleon's small, easily defeatable invasion force by fleeing to the Portuguese province of Brazil in ships provided by the British navy. ("Don't go so fast," Queen Maria told the British admiral. "People will think we are running away.") Besides accelerating Brazil's development as the first independent state in Latin America, the royal exodus helped to modernize Portugal. Under the tropical sun of Brazil, the House of Bragança recovered the vitality it had lost in Europe. According to Brazilian historian Sergio Correa da Costa, King João VI, "flabby, apathetic and spineless," threw off "his burden of melancholy" in Brazil and felt kingly for the first time in his life. He fought wars and expanded his realm; he learned to ignore his demented mother and to dismiss from his mind a wife who slept with everyone else but only rarely with him. It is not absolutely certain that her two sons—the good Pedro and the handsome Miguel—were his. But, as genealogists say, what matters is the acknowledgment of paternity, and João VI acknowledged them as sons.

The British liberated Portugal in 1811 but João VI kept postponing his return home. Finally, with a liberal revolution in Portugal threatening to unravel the monarchy, he left Brazil in 1822. Da Costa writes: "The Braganças, who had disembarked upon the white sands of Rio as an absolute monarchy, founded on divine right, returned to the Old World humanized, liberalized, aware of the essential rights of man. The king, once a divinity, arrived in Lisbon a crowned citizen."

When handing over the South American regency to his elder son Pedro, João VI admonished him: "If Brazil breaks away from Portugal, don't let the crown fall into the hands of an adventurer but put it on your own head." In a ceremony reminiscent of Napoleon's coronation, Pedro soon proclaimed himself emperor of Brazil. Like Napoleon, Pedro was a genius who shaped rather than fought the revolution. As the crown prince, he joined the freemasons and conspired to rise to the post of grand master. He was the best horseman in Brazil and the country's legendary lover, the champion of independence, and the hero of the liberal revolution.

In Portugal, events took an unexpected turn. Pedro's younger brother Miguel led a revolution against his father to restore the absolute monarchy and cleanse Portugal of freemasons and other heretics. King João won the struggle and banished Miguel. Upon João's death, Pedro, who was declared king of Portugal, made a surprising offer to his brother in Vienna. Provided he marry Pedro's daughter, upon her reaching maturity (she was nine at the time), Miguel could return to Portugal as a regent. Miguel accepted the offer but, once in Portugal, canceled the liberal constitution, and instituted a reign of counterrevolutionary terror.

Furious with Miguel and regretful for his own foolish offer, Pedro handed over his empire to his five-year-old son and in a version of chivalry otherwise unknown in European history, renounced his claims to the thrones of Portugal and Brazil, and offered his services as a general to his daughter, Queen Maria II, then twelve years of age. Like the Spanish civil war a century later, the Portuguese war of succession became a European battle between progress and reaction. Napoleon's veterans and freethinkers of many nations signed up in Pedro's recruiting centers in London and Paris. Legitimists, mostly French, swelled the ranks of Miguel's army.

In 1834, the liberals won. Soon afterward, in the pink palace of Queluz where he was born, Pedro died of tuberculosis at the age of thirty-six. Pedro's generous last will and testament was denounced by liberals as a sellout: the will provided for a general amnesty, permission for Miguel's men to stay in Portugal, and a large pension for Miguel. But Miguel and his descendants were forbidden, on pain of death, to set foot in Portugal again.

Miguel set up an exile court in Rome where the pope, incensed by Pedro's closing of convents and his links with freemasonry, recognized Miguel as the legitimate king of Portugal. Miguel died in 1866 in Austria, a bitter recluse.

Then came an unexpected reconciliation, a grand Bragança gesture. Manoel II, great-great-grandson of Pedro I, made peace with Miguel's son, also called Miguel. Manoel II was the last king of Portugal. He survived an assassination attempt that claimed the life of his father and his older brother. Two years later, a naval mutiny forced him into exile, and a republic was declared. In 1912 in London, Manoel II, then nineteen, named his cousin Miguel II as his successor in case he died without issue, which he did, in 1932. In 1920 came another abdication: Miguel II surrendered his rights to the throne in favor of his second son, Duarte Nuno (the first son had married a commoner).

Born in Austria in 1907, in the castle of Seebenstein, Duarte Nuno was educated in Germany, Luxembourg, and France; his interests were flying and agriculture. In 1942, he voyaged to Brazil to marry his cousin, Princess Françoise Orléans-Bragançá, a sister of the countess of Paris. She was the great-grandaughter of Pedro I; thus the two rival branches of the Bragança dynasty were once again united (Duarte Nuno nevertheless continued to condemn Pedro as a "foreigner" and identified himself as a Miguelist dispossessed by Pedro and his descendants). With World War II approaching Austria, Duarte Nuno took his wife to the safety of Switzerland, where all their children were born—Duarte João, Miguel, and Henrique.

After World War II, in which Portugal maintained a precarious neutrality, Dr. Antonio de Oliveira Salazar initiated an open door policy for deposed royalty. Under his protection, claimants to the thrones of France and Spain, as well as the former kings of Romania and Italy, took up residence in Estoril, near Lisbon. Salazar was neither a monarchist nor a republican, but an ultraconservative ersatz sovereign, and as a quaint and out of the ordinary as the Braganças.

In 1950, after the French Parliament abrogated its Law of Exile, Salazar instructed the Portuguese Parliament to study the legality of the ban on Miguel's descendants. Parliament did as told, and ended by repealing the law with the unanimous vote customary under Dr. Salazar. A few weeks later, Duarte Nuno and his family stepped on Portuguese soil for the first time. By order of Salazar, no publicity accompanied their repatriation.

Salazar did not permit the return of the Braganças' considerable private wealth, nor was there any compensation paid. Instead, the government set up a family foundation with the official objective of keeping the historic Bragança properties intact. In effect, the foundation, which still exists, owns the Braganças; it authorizes members of the family to use certain palaces and other properties. The Braganças charge that their monthly stipends do not even cover their basic needs.

In 1957, Salazar raised monarchist expectations by declaring that justice was owed "to those who led the nation through eight centuries of history" and "that there may come a time when the monarchial solution may become a national solution. Whether the House of Bragança is considered merely as the repository of a historical heritage or whether the possibility of future services to its and our homeland is borne in mind, it should be distant from a political leadership which might divide instead of unite the Portuguese people."

Salazar's statement, however hedged with diplomatic ambiguity, signaled to the nation the strong likelihood of a Bragança restoration. Confirming that impression was a parallel development in Spain, initiated by Francisco Francq. Salazar was among a small group of people first informed by Franco that Juan Carlos would become king. At the same time, Franco told Salazar that restoring the monarchy in Portugal would be the best guarantee of stability and a means of ensuring continuing cooperation between the two countries. The two Iberian dictators, who seldom ventured outside their peninsula, met at least once a year for a ritual boar hunt. The cunning, taciturn economist and the stiff, haughty soldier were famous for sharing a brand of authoritarianism that had become alien to the rest of postwar Western Europe.

As the years passed, however, Salazar did not renew his interest in the Braganças. There was no attempt to groom Duarte Nuno or his eldest son. Salazar never met any of the Braganças, and did not think that they were up to ruling Portugal. He thought that "there have been too many Bragança marriages between cousins."

"Salazar had the mentality of a prudent book-keeper," says a veteran observer of the Portuguese scene. "He figured out everything in cruzeiros and pounds sterling. He calculated that setting up a royal colony in Estoril would bring in money. After inviting foreign royalty, he couldn't very well keep out Portuguese royalty. But he made sure that the Braganzas would not challenge him, and he kept them off balance by holding in abeyance the issue of their family property."

"Salazar was an egotist who had to have everything revolve around his person," Duarte João says. "As a man of humble origins, he was jealous of our lineage and glamor. Unquestionably he exploited monarchist sentiments—I would say that every third Portuguese is a secret monarchist—and he was clever enough to let the monarchists believe that in his heart he was one of them. Well, he duped many people. He played a role similar to Charles de Gaulle, who also preempted true royalty—my uncle Henri, the count of Paris."

Under Salazar, monarchists were politely but firmly discouraged from organizing themselves; they were told not to give large receptions and not to refer to Duarte Nuno as Royal Highness in public. Interest in the soft-spoken, retiring Duarte Nuno steadily diminished. After his wife's death in 1970, he lived alone in the cavernous palace of San Marco, in the ancient town of Coimbra. He contemplated history under the Renaissance archways of his eighteenth-century palace, tended his cactus collection and took long, solitary walks in his garden, which was maintained by the government foundation. By inclination and perhaps by an agreement with Salazar, he stayed out of politics. He was a courteous old gentleman left behind by time. His death in 1978 was hardly noticed in Portugal.

Duarte Nuno's eldest son and heir, born in 1945 in Bern, Switzerland, is boyishly clumsy. Duarte João wants to do great things; he wants to be worthy of his illustrious ancestors. He introduces himself by his first name, Duarte, then adds, with a tense little throat-clearing cough, "I am, you know, the duke of Bragança." His followers call him Royal Highness, occasionally Your Majesty, for he is King Duarte III by formal monarchist calculation. Others attach to his first name the honorific "Dom"— or Sir—which comes from the Latin *dominus*. His preference is Dom Duarte.

When I meet him he is wearing an inexpensive gray sport jacket that pulls at his broad shoulders, a well-worn plaid shirt open at the neck and beige slacks a bit too large for him. Just under six feet tall, he has a pink complexion and the flat, squarish face of his great-great-grandfather Pedro I—the very man he despises.

He seems a bit unsure of himself. He is that untried, anxiety-ridden prince courtiers in other ages would have turned into an insecure ruler dependent on their advice—a tyrant if pressures got too heavy; a moody sovereign in times of ease.

He concedes that his chances are not good for regaining the throne of his ancestors. He puts his hope in the unforeseen and the invisible. The Monarchist Party, legal since the 1974 revolution overthrew Salazar, receives about 5 percent of the total vote. But Duarte João contends that 40 percent of the people are latent sympathizers with the monarchist cause. "Portugal is such a secretive country," he whispers, "and monarchism is a secret of many people.

"Portuguese monarchists are pessimists. So they stay home when there is an election, and expect the worst, like the country going Communist or Spain swallowing up Portugal."

A national sadness afflicts the Portuguese. "It's because we lost eight-tenths of our territory," he sighs, "because we have been reduced to insignificance and beggary after a glorious history of exploration and settlement overseas. We have been thrown out of Africa after 400 years! The status quo cannot continue—not economically and not psychologically. Our national poet Camões called Portugal a nation without frontiers. Now Portugal is all frontiers, no territory.

"Portugal's political destiny lies in its evolving a new relationship with Africa. Africa is the continent most important in Portugal's four centuries of overseas expansion." He predicts that anti-Marxist elements will gain ascendancy in Angola and Mozambique and, eventually, Portuguese people will be invited back and a mutually advantageous alliance will emerge—a much stronger bond than what the French achieved with their former colonies because the Portuguese were far better colonizers than the French or the English or the Spaniards. "In Africa lies the best chance for Portugal, a way out of the malaise the nation has been suffering and a way to guarantee that the Communists stay out of power. And in a new relationship between Portugal and former Portuguese Africa lies the best chance for a restoration of the monarchy."

He lived in Africa for four years—the best years of his life. He liked the tribal system. While doing his stint in the military, he volunteered as a helicopter pilot, a dangerous assignment. He evacuated the wounded in the Angolan guerrilla war that reached its crescendo in the early 1970s. It was called Portugal's Vietnam, and the discontent over the human and material cost led to the Portuguese revolution of 1974. "I felt useful in Africa," Duarte João says, "more useful than at any other time in my life."

He prefers Africans to Brazilians. "Brazilians lack the Portuguese sense of humor," he feels, "and they have no sense of the ridiculous."

"Brazilians are too egalitarian for him," says a Brazilian who knows Duarte João. "He couldn't stand Brazilians telling him off and criticizing Portugal or the Catholic Church. He refuses to understand that we Brazilians went our own way almost 200 years ago because we wanted to and that then or now we wouldn't have any prissy, narrow-minded Portuguese tell us what to do."

Duarte João is a busy young man with a lot of nervous energy and many interests. He spends his mornings at home. After a leisurely breakfast, he writes letters, reads the newspapers and sits in his library with a book. Shortly after noon, he goes to his office in downtown Lisbon to deal with business affairs. He has investments, and is involved in the promotion of Portuguese handicrafts that died out with industrialization. He has dinner in town with friends and usually returns home around midnight.

He heads several philanthropic enterprises, the most important of which is an agency that resettles Portuguese refugees from Africa in oil-rich Venezuela and other Latin American countries. "I will do anything for those refugees," he says. "They have been abandoned and betrayed by Portugal and by the world."

Duarte João participates in Portugal's political life by attending meetings of the Monarchist Party and by addressing civic groups on Africa and two other causes to which he is committed: environmental protection and the preservation of national monuments.

He spends several months a year at a large farm he and his two brothers inherited. The farm, to the north of Lisbon, has vineyards, orchards, and pasture for sheep. Duarte João says that he and his brothers do every kind of farmwork, partly because they like doing it and partly because it is an example to the workers.

"Braganças have a family tradition of marrying late," Duarte João, a bachelor like his brothers, says. He will not necessarily marry a princess, but his bride will be from the aristocracy. He wants her to have a strong Catholic faith and a family tradition similar to his own.

He lives some ten miles outside Lisbon in a tidy little village called San Pedro do Sintra. He has been renovating his seventeenth-century mansion for two years. The walls are freshly painted, and their brilliant white constrasts with the dark carved woodwork of the ceilings, doors, and moldings. The sanded oak parquet and terra cotta tile floors are waiting for their varnish. Here and there are some furnishings, lost in the cavernous halls: oil paintings of ancestors and battle scenes; capacious arm chairs of roughly carved blond pine at least 300 years old, chairs with tooled leather seats and backs, a hulking chest of drawers covered with brass hardware. Duarte João thinks it will be a fine house if the work on it is ever completed and if he finds the money to pay for it. He gets lost as he shows me around. "Let's see," he says several times with a frown. "Let me figure out where we are." He has difficulty finding the light switches.

He was amused when a friend discovered that the mansion he bought had once been used for freemason meetings, illegal of course, and that the elaborate formal garden had been designed for freemason initiation rites. We go from room to room as he searches the wall tiles for freemason symbols which, he explains, are cleverly concealed in village and harbor scenes. He finds two symbols, but there are more, he assures me, many more.

Duarte João checks several built-in wardrobes, looking for something. Finally he finds a corner cabinet with a back that flips open. I peer into darkness; I smell the dank breath of centuries. "Every old house in Portugal has secrets built into it," he says. His mansion has hidden staircases leading to different floors and hiding places between floors that can accommodate a dozen people.

We go up to the top floor, the third, to the library. The shelves are jammed with books in a half-dozen languages: sumptuous Victorian compendia on the East Indies, Latin and French classics bound in leather and printed in the eighteenth century, large Portuguese folios on the fauna and flora of Angola and Mozambique, gold-embossed Spanish tomes about the Americas, a collection of seventeenth-century nautical maps and bound volumes of nineteenth-century Portuguese newspapers. There are also popular novels in paperback and travel guides to dozens of countries. There are many books on genetics and genealogy. "Genes carry our secrets," he says, "but scientists don't want to tell us what they know. They are resisting conclusions which confirm the decisiveness of personal and racial heredity. They want us to believe in the importance of the environment and education, and they don't want us to know what we suspect instinctively: heredity is three-fourths of our character."

The view from the library resembles a romantic painting from the eighteenth century: a high mountain on one side and the ocean on the other, and in between, the red-tiled roofs of a hillside village. The wind from the Atlantic shakes the windows; the air is damp. Duarte João talks about the thick fog that descends from the mountain and hides most of the scenery. "For some reason," he says, "that fog makes me feel sad."

Duarte João's favorite books are history books. He detests the liberals, those nineteenth-century enemies of the Church and royal power. For him, they were the Communists of the day. "Those leftist agitators were articulate and clever," he concedes, "but they didn't succeed completely. The republican tradition is weak in Portugal. The banishment of Miguel and his descendants was in fact a tribute to the strength of monarchist feeling, a proof of how worried republicans were about the possibility of restoration."

Duarte João dines with republicans often; he finds them "amusing." They exchange jokes, and there is no awkwardness. He believes that deep down Portuguese republicans are frustrated monarchists.

He castigates America for abandoning the anti-Marxists of Angola, and for letting the Communists take over. He is absolutely convinced that there was a secret agreement between the

Americans and the Cubans, that U.S.-owned Gulf Oil of Cabinda had been paying Cuba for the mercenaries and Russia for the arms, and that there was enough left in revenues and bribes to pay the Angolan Communists.

The old mansion echoes with his voice, which gets more frantic. "What do you think of the Rockefellers' Trilateral Commission? How did it capture Jimmy Carter so completely? What about the Council on Foreign Relations? Don't you think that these are the organizations which decide everything and rule America, the world?"

Duarte João is in his element. He traces connections and suggests the existence of secret accords going back decades, centuries. "The freemasons are very, very important," he says, "one should study their methods, their master plan. The Jesuits too have a lot to offer. And the Jews, what do you think is their secret?"

The village named after Saint Peter is quiet; the lights are out everywhere. It has gotten chilly. The wind from the Atlantic howls, battering the twisted, unhappy pines. An improbable red moon has risen over the ten-foot walls of the Bragança mansion. "It once belonged to a Jewish family that converted to Catholicism," Duarte João tells me, "but like other converts, they remained Jewish in the depths of their souls."

We take an after-dinner walk—he had a stew of wild boar meat with chestnuts and pickled carrots; I had garlic soup and fish roasted with cinnamon and coriander.

"It's an old, old village," Duarte João says. "Moslem Moors lived here before they were driven back to North Africa. Some of the houses were built in the thirteenth century, and the foundations are even older. Before that, the Phoenicians traded here, and the Greeks. The Romans built an outpost, then came the Visigoths, the Vandals."

The houses and the walls are made of black and green granite, and the lintels are sometimes marble. Stone is forever.

"Who knows how many generations's work lives underneath," Duarte João says, and we both look at the cobblestones of the street, undulating as all the streets of Portugal do.

As we part, I watch a thick fog settling down on the village.

In De Gaulle's Shadow
Henri Bourbon-Orléans

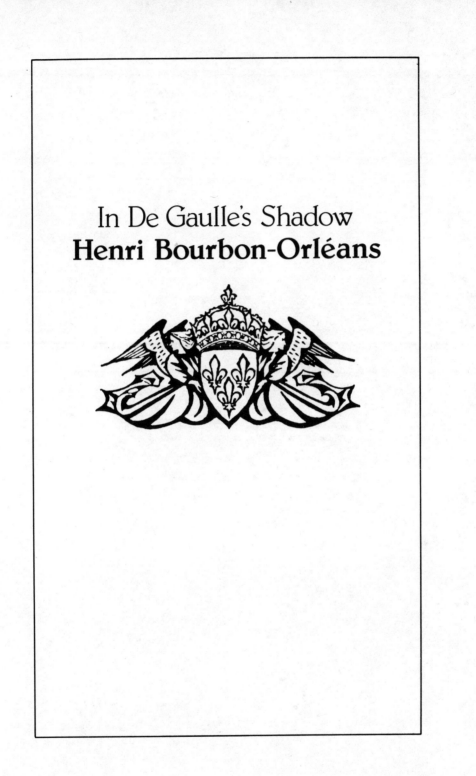

He wills you, in the name of God Almighty,
That you divest yourself, and lay apart
The borrow'd glories that by gift of heaven,
By law of nature and of nations, 'long
To him and to his heirs; namely, the crown,
And all wide stretched honours that pertain,
By custom and the ordinance of times,
Unto the crown of France

King Henri V

The favorite story of Henri Bourbon-Orléans, the count of Paris and pretender to the throne of France, is one told of Genghis Khan, the Mongol conqueror of the thirteenth century. Sitting in his tent, the great khan saw a tiny ant struggling to haul away a seed ten times its size. The seed would not budge, but the ant tried again and again. For the Mongol emperor, as for the count of Paris, the ant and the seed offered a parable of life.

"Failure doesn't bring me down," says the man French monarchists call Henri VI. "One can learn from failures. They teach lessons. My life has had its high points and low points. But I have never changed my mind about what I tried to do. And not once has my morale been broken."

At seventy-one, he is slender, erect, with brisk movements and sharp ripostes. He would still cut a dashing figure in a victory parade on the Champs Elysées.

"I am never discouraged," says his wife Isabelle, a princess of Orléans-Bragança and mother of his eleven children. Her words have the ring of a chanson. "I am even more of an optimist than my dear husband Henri. It's harder for him than for me. He thinks too much. Too deep, too. He worries about things that may go wrong. I don't worry. He is a man of reflection and duty. I am impulsive."

Henri is the doyen of Europe's nonreigning royalty: of all the claimants to imperial and royal thrones, he is the furthest removed from a reigning ancestor; the last king in his dynasty, his great-

121

great-grandfather Louis-Philippe, abdicated in 1848. Louis-Philippe's father was Philippe, the head of the younger, or Orléans, branch of the Bourbons. To this day, many Frenchmen believe in the theory of the Orléans conspiracy: to capture the throne for himself, Philippe paid the mob that attacked the Tuileries and unleashed the Revolution of 1789. Philippe joined the Jacobins, had himself renamed Egalité and, as a member of the revolutionary convention, voted for the execution of his cousin, Louis XVI. His vote sealed the king's fate. But within a year the inexorable logic of paranoia caught up with Philippe-Egalité. He too was guillotined.

His son Louis-Philippe came to power after the revolution of 1830 banished Charles X, brother of Louis XVI and the last reigning Bourbon of the senior branch of the family. Charles X was the vengeful émigré who, returning after the 1789 Revolution and the collapse of Napoleon's empire, exemplified the saying "the Bourbons learned nothing and forgot nothing." People called Louis-Philippe the Bourgeois King because he wore a felt hat and carried an umbrella. He explained that the crown was too hot in the summer and too cold in the winter, and that the scepter was too blunt to be a weapon and too short to be a support. His popularity began to decline after he moved from the upper floors of the Palais Royal—once his father's headquarters—to the Tuileries, the traditional royal residence. He should not have done that, Parisians thought, because the Tuileries were haunted by the ghosts of Louis XVI and his queen, Marie-Antoinette. Indeed, Louis-Philippe had nightmares of St. Denis, the martyred patron saint of French kings usually depicted with his head in his hands.

When the time came for another Paris mob to storm the Tuileries, it did not even occur to Louis-Philippe to call on the army for protection. He slipped out with his wife by the servants' entrance and flagged down a hansom cab. "Where to?" asked the driver. "Anywhere you can," replied the seventy-five-year-old king, who had signed his abdication ten minutes earlier. He found his way to England, where he died two years later under the name "Mr. Smith."

"France is bored," the poet Lamartine summed up the great complaint against Louis-Philippe. "But what's wrong about being bored?" the puzzled king asked his ministers. "Boredom is healthy. I don't understand people who can't accept peace and tranquillity." His descendant Henri would have understood. He knows that

France expects passion, grandeur, and surprise. And had he been able to offer more of each, he might have become president of the Republic, if not king of the French.

"I detest the Orléans," I once heard an aristocratic lady declare. "They are upstarts, typical second sons, a younger branch that tries to make up for what it missed at birth. Unfortunately, we have no real Bourbons left any more—they married one another until they bred themselves off the map. So we have to make do with Henri who strikes a royal enough pose, I guess. But the descendant of Philippe-Egalité and Louis-Philippe that he is, he has never stopped courting the socialists."

Henri was born in 1908 at Nouvrion-en-Thierarche, a castle surrounded by a forest that once belonged to Mary Stuart. He was one year old when his father Jean, an amateur historian and archeologist, moved the family to a large farm near Rabat, in Morocco. Henri was eighteen when his father became the head of the royal house, and both father and son were instantly forbidden to enter France. An edict passed in 1886, fifteen years after the flight of Emperor Napoleon III to England, condemned to exile the heads of the Bourbon as well as Bonaparte dynasties and their heirs apparent.

Henri began his political career at Louvain University in Belgium, where he studied civil rights and socialism. He also spent many nights in his parents' house listening to Charles Maurras, the brilliant writer and passionate monarchist who in 1899 established l'Action Française, a far Right movement dedicated to restoring France to its former glory. In 1931 Henri married his third cousin, Isabelle Orléans-Bragança, a descendant of the kings of Portugal and France and the emperors of Brazil. He asked for her hand in marriage while they were both on horseback during one of the many family hunting parties. She agreed instantly. Due to French governmental pressure, the wedding could not be held in Belgium; Isabelle set herself up in a Paris hotel, exhibited her trousseau and received the best wishes of some 60,000 visitors. A radiant and voluble Isabelle presided over a glittering prenuptial reception in Paris; the Law of Exile kept Henri away.

The cream of European aristocracy attended the wedding in Palermo, Sicily—the French government asked that the event be held as far from France as possible. The festive dinner was in the Orléans family's Palermo palace, part of the dowry of Amélie, a

Bourbon princess of the Kingdom of the Two Sicilies, who had married Louis-Philippe in the early years of the nineteenth century. When Isabelle and Henri honeymooned in Sicily, they were warned to watch out for the Mafia. They disregarded the advice and were well received everywhere on the island. Later, they found out that the royalist-hearted Mafia had decided to be hospitable to the young French visitors.

As a wedding present, their parents gave them a small blue granite castle in the Ardennes, on the Belgian-French border. From their windows, they could see France.

In 1934, Henri founded two journals and wrote a book on monarchy that sold 40,000 copies within a few weeks. With his father's permission, Henri began promulgating his own brand of monarchist thought. Three years later, at age twenty-nine, Henri publicly broke with Charles Maurras, a major move for Henri. The manifesto was issued in his father's name, but the words had Henri's swagger: "I have to dissipate a misunderstanding. There is a confusion in the public . . . which leads one to believe that *l'Action Française* is our interpreter. . . . Only the House of France, of which I am the head, is the repository of the royal doctrine. Only this House is qualified to forecast what tomorrow's monarchy will be."

In 1938, Henri defied the Law of Exile by piloting his private plane to a small airfield in the north of France in order to hold a press conference. The press had been promised a meeting with the countess of Paris, and reporters were astonished when the count of Paris appeared in her stead. Wearing a trench coat, collar upturned, and with a cigarette hanging on his lip, his phrases terse and his insults aimed at the government with a marksman's skill, Henri was an updated image of the handsome young adventurer from Alexandre Dumas's *The Three Musketeers*. He then denounced the Munich accord that France and Great Britain had just signed with Germany. "No concessions can stop Hitler's plan to extend German frontiers," he declared, "only a wall of force can do that."

A year later Henri was rebuffed in his efforts to join the French army. He penned eloquent letters, he pulled strings. But even in wartime, the Law of Exile could not be bent. The French government, however, entrusted him with a secret diplomatic mission: to use his personal contacts with European royalty to find out their intentions vis-à-vis Hitler. His report, which predicted the futility of resistance in Rome, Athens, Belgrade, and Sofia, was ignored.

He enlisted in the Foreign Legion in 1940 as Henri Orliac, a Swiss citizen born in Geneva. A photograph of him, treasured by his wife Isabelle who captions it "my handsome legionnaire," shows a gaunt, bright-eyed soldier in a coarse woolen army jacket a size too large for him—the kind of snapshot displayed in tens of thousands of French homes. But before his basic training was over, France had lost the war, and Henri was demobilized in Marseille. A few days later, his father Jean—a very tall, taciturn gentleman—died, and Henri became the head of the Royal House of France. Jean had had no interest in public affairs; Henri was to devote his life to politics. The father had dismissed any thought of restoration; the son was ready to take on the world to reclaim his inheritance. "Another restless, ambitious Orléans," noted many of his fellow countrymen.

At first, Henri was sympathetic to the government of Vichy that signed the armistice with Germany. He contacted Prime Minister Pierre Laval, who offered him the post of minister of food, an unglamorous wartime job. Henri turned him down and moved to Morocco, then a French protectorate, where he spent the rest of the war on the family farm. His wife continued to produce children— six in the first eight years of their marriage—while Henri was often gone for weeks. He tried to convince the French military governor in Algeria not to oppose an Anglo-American military landing that he had predicted—correctly—but the officers laughed at him. He flew to Rome to consult with the pope, and to Vichy. He advised the head of state, Marshal Philippe Pétain, to transfer the government to North Africa. He attempted to mediate between Charles de Gaulle and Henri Giraud, then competing for the leadership of the Free French. General Giraud reminded him that in Algeria, then part of metropolitan France, the Law of Exile applied. He also offered to use his influence to get Henri a commission in the army. Henri retorted, "The head of a royal house is permitted to hold one of two ranks, either commander in chief or private, second class."

In 1940 and 1941, Henri declined invitations from the Gaullist camp to go to London. He was afraid of becoming an émigré; to his mind, émigrés were the unforgiving Bourbons who returned to France after the defeat of Napoleon I. He had a horror of siding with one political party and thus contribute to what he called France's "infernal divisiveness." Unity had always been the grand Orléans idea, and Henri pursued it. He did not foresee that Marshal Pétain, the hero of World War I, would be condemned as a traitor in 1945— an indictment Henri disagrees with to this day—and that an obscure, lanky officer by the name of Charles de Gaulle would have so much courage, fortitude, and good fortune.

"Had the count of Paris joined me in London in 1940," de Gaulle later confided in his biographer, Philippe Saint-Robert, "he would have become France. Together, we could have done great things."

The gallant musketeer did poorly as a diplomat. His first mistake was to overestimate Vichy's independence from the Nazis. His second was to try to mediate between Vichy, which, convinced that the war was over, sought cooperation with Germany, and de Gaulle's fledgling movement, which refused to accept defeat. Henri was reflective and conciliatory at a time when bravura was needed.

However much Henri sought to represent his heritage, it was de Gaulle who in this century recalled "the Forty Kings of France." De Gaulle was never more of a monarch than when, as a nervous young officer disobeying his commander, he broadcast with a breaking voice his appeal on BBC: "France is not alone. . . . This war is not over with the Battle of France. This war is a world war." Later he pronounced the unforgettable words that would be printed on posters put up in the dead of night: "France lost a battle, but France has not lost the war." Another message, worthy of Racine: "There is every reason in the world to accept Vichy's argument for armistice, except one: honor." Henri's occasional communications, smuggled into France, lacked de Gaulle's verve: "On every occasion act as a Frenchman. By every possible means create opposition to the invaders."

After World War II Henri left North Africa, first for Pamplona, Spain, then for Sintra, Portugal, where he bought a farm. The countess of Paris and the daughters milked the forty cows, and the count of Paris and the boys tended some 150 sheep. The farm was a commercial success, but Henri and Isabelle, both independently wealthy, had motives other than financial. "My children must all have jobs," Isabelle has declared many times. "They have to render service. We must all serve."

In 1948, Henri began publishing a monthly bulletin that soon attracted 30,000 subscribers. After hunting and travel, Henri enjoyed writing most. Composition has satisfied his need for structure and precision; he has always thrived on the discipline of self-editing and solitude. Isabelle on the other hand is an indifferent grammarian and a poor speller—"All Braganças spell badly," she says. She prefers talking and entertaining. In her 1978 memoirs,

Tout M'est Bonheur, she cites two enduring disagreements she has had with Henri since the early days of their marriage. Henri thought silence was golden and maintained "an oyster-like reserve" that Isabelle ascribes to his Protestant forebears—he had a Lutheran great-grandmother. Also, Henri did not like playing second fiddle for a moment—he was resentful when on visits to Brazil and Normandy, he was a mere husband to the Princess Isabelle that people had known since childhood.

When Parliament in 1950 abrogated the Law of Exile (with only the Communists speaking out for its retention), Henri returned home with his wife and eleven children. (The eleventh had been born in 1948; had there been a twelfth, by French custom the president of the Republic would have been the godfather.) They took up residence in an old mansion outside Paris, called *Le Manoir du Coeur Volant*, The Manor of the Flying Heart. The two older boys were soon off to do their military service, and the others enrolled in French schools.

In 1954, Henri met de Gaulle, a bitter émigré from the revolving-door governments of the Fourth Republic. Their association continued through correspondence; two patriots estranged from the politics of the day enriched French literature by exchanging thoughts in exquisite longhand.

Henri's eldest son and the heir apparent, also named Henri, in 1957 married his fourth cousin, Duchess Marie-Thérèse of Württemberg, a German Catholic with a Habsburg mother. De Gaulle wrote to the count of Paris a missive laden with signals of fealty: "The marriage is a reason for each Frenchman to rejoice. But also, *Monseigneur*, because the life of your family is identified with our history; because everything coming from you now is exemplary for our country; because your future and that of Prince Henri and that of your family are bound up with the hopes of France. I salute the union, which God will bless, as a great national event." The wedding, which cost the count of Paris $150,000, was attended by Greek, Danish, Dutch, Luxembourg, and Liechtenstein royalty, and by the pretenders to the thrones of Italy, Spain, Portugal, and Yugoslavia. Notably absent was anyone from the House of Windsor.

In 1958, Henri extended his support to de Gaulle, who was called from his self-imposed exile to save France from insurrection in Paris and guerrilla war in Algeria. De Gaulle's Fifth Republic dropped the previous constitution's stipulation that members of the former royal and imperial families of France could not be elected to the post of the president of the Republic. Henri became a frequent visitor to the Elysée Palace. It was always a tête-à-tête, usually late in the evening. De Gaulle waited for him by the staircase or outside, reserved a special armchair for him and lit his cigarette. They talked of history, of France. "He very much loved to pronounce the word 'king,' which he invested with the content of a ritual," Henri recalls.

De Gaulle dispatched Henri in 1961 on a tour of Libya, Ethiopia, Iran, and Lebanon to explain France's Algerian policy. Henri volunteered to serve as de Gaulle's special representative, or "pro-consul," in Algeria; he was friends with Moroccan King Hassan and Tunisian President Habib Bourguiba, and he had valuable contacts in Algeria from his stays there during the 1920s and during World War II. De Gaulle approved the project, but Prime Minister Michel Debré intervened: "Jamais de la vie."

In 1962, de Gaulle told Henri in strict confidence that he had arranged the direct presidential election so that the head of the royal house might succeed him as president of the Republic. Georges Pompidou, de Gaulle's eventual successor, confided in a close friend: "I know that the general has made up his mind in favor of the count of Paris." But the general changed his mind; in 1964, de Gaulle informed Henri of his decision to run for another seven-year presidential term. He won. In January 1968, in increasing disagreement with the Gaullists, Henri stopped publication of his monthly bulletin, then in its twentieth year. Years later, the countess of Paris explained: "Under de Gaulle, Henri came two fingers close to becoming king. But by 1968, it was all over, finished." In May, the student uprising, supported by the general strike of half of France's labor force, shook de Gaulle's rule. He won one more referendum, but in 1969 lost the next, on regional reform, and he quit. Henri, paying his respects at de Gaulle's grave, was told by de Gaulle's son Philippe: "Monseigneur, my father often told me that if circumstances had been different, he would have been happy to be your faithful and loyal servant."

When Henri's book Mémoires d'Exil et de Combats appeared in April 1979, every newspaper in France carried the sensational disclosure that de Gaulle had once asked the count of Paris to prepare himself for the presidential elections of 1965. In an interview with the newsmagazine Le Point, Henri declared, "At all times de Gaulle desired restoration, I am convinced of it. He thought monarchy was the form of government most adequate for the French people under the present conjunction." In his memoirs Henri quotes de Gaulle as having said to him, "Make yourself known, show yourself on television." But as he told *Le Point*, "It was difficult to get anywhere with de Gaulle. He agreed to favor my accession to the highest position, but he didn't understand that it was necessary to give me the means of getting there."

Few people question the veracity of Henri's account; what is debated is de Gaulle's motive. Those who see him as the man who betrayed French Algeria argue that Henri was another victim of the general's duplicity: he misled Henri, knowing that Henri would trust him as a monarchist. One of the hardliners, writer and politician Jacques Soustelle, contends that de Gaulle enlisted Henri's support in order to neutralize the traditional Right. Others argue that it was all a misunderstanding, that de Gaulle, a man given to historical abstractions, spoke in terms of his wishes and dreams, and Henri, always hopeful and ambitious, thought he was receiving political promises. Debré, a Gaullist of many years standing, told *Le Point* that it was a great pleasure for de Gaulle to receive the count of Paris, "to face a man disengaged from the everyday, with whom he could have a dialogue . . . to whom he could deliver a monologue and be understood."

Henri believes that de Gaulle never forgave him for not joining the Free French in London in 1940, and that de Gaulle could not understand that the same principle he respected in Henri also prohibited Henri from joining him in London: the count of Paris could not be a Gaullist.

"De Gaulle was not my *friend*," he says. "One is friends with people one grows up with, or, to put it in a different way, two young men with hopes they discuss are friends. De Gaulle and I shared some common ideals and I agreed with him on the essentials of his approach to politics. We did at times work together.

"He was brought up in a monarchist house and in a monarchist tradition; he came from a milieu pervaded by the ideas of *l'Action Française*. He had a concept of France that was extremely elevated. He had a great admiration for the monarchy. I believe he was sincere when he wished that France may return to a monarchy. But once he was in power for a few years, he changed his ideas. De Gaulle was deceived and disappointed. He thought that France would be more faithful to him. He didn't realize that power is not faithful. De Gaulle, it must be said, died a sad man, under sad circumstances. I never blamed de Gaulle for my failure to reach the pinnacle of power." To the newsmagazine L'Express, Henri declared: "I have missed my chance. But it isn't in my character to have regrets. The only reproach I can make to myself in this old, infinitely complex story is that I have perhaps sinned by an excess of confidence."

I interviewed Henri in an apartment that used to be his Paris headquarters before he shut it down in 1968. The apartment covers an entire floor of a small apartment building on rue Miromesnil, in a neighborhood the French describe, ever so unlovingly, as bourgeois. The street is narrow, one-way, with boxy, modernistic parking meters in front of houses built in the early 1900s style, when the imitative classicism of the Third Republic curbed the ebullience and ostentation of Napoleon III's Second Empire.

The concierge is an old woman in brown felt slippers who has problems climbing the stairs from her room in the basement. She had a heart operation last year. She admires the count. "He is so gentle, so kind. He asks about my heart condition whenever he comes. He has had three heart attacks himself, may God keep him, such a fine man. All his children are married now—but he lost a son, François, in Algeria. He has thirty-nine grandchildren, imagine that!" She says that things used to be very busy in the building when the count of Paris had his headquarters here. "Now he only comes once a week, to pick up his mail. But no, he hasn't given up the idea of becoming king one day, why should he?"

The concierge has been in charge of the building since 1928, long before the law permitted the count of Paris to live in Paris. Her husband died, her brother died. "But the prince tells me not to worry, he'll take care of me." His photographs, with or without his family, are all around the concierge's dark little cubicle. "I'll die in peace," she says, "in service of the prince."

Henri arrives from his chateau at Chantilly, some thirty miles outside Paris, in his chauffeur-driven Mercedes Benz. He opens the door and shows me in. The apartment is spacious, consisting of some half-dozen high-ceilinged rooms. We speak across a nondescript conference table with plenty of glass ashtrays, the kind one sees in bistros throughout France. But the chairs scattered in the room are covered with crimson velvet.

Henri looks like a man in his sixties rather than seventies, a graying but still battle-ready musketeer, with the alacrity of Athos and the smile of Aramis. He goes hunting—sometimes several times a week—and he is a passionate horseman. He likes hiking, and believes that strenuous physical activity complements his genteel eighteenth-century pursuits—writing memoirs and letters.

He wears an immaculately tailored gray suit with strands of blue, an ink-blue tie decorated with what seems to be rows of tiny Bourbon lilies, and a gray shirt with a touch of blue. His eyes, as every journalist before me has noticed, are azure. Asked to find the Bourbon prince in a room crowded with a hundred strangers, I could pick him out without fail.

He is hard of hearing, but by cocking an eyebrow he makes it clear that he does not appreciate it when I raise my voice. He not so much answers my questions as predicts them. He speaks with Gallic shrugs, purses of the lips, expressive hands. "Would you mind if I spoke French?" he asks, but barely waits for an answer. His English is competent, slightly British, but his French is supple and effortless, the kind that makes foreigners feel that French is the superior language. His words are ready to be inscribed into marble.

He begins, "In the arch of state, the monarch is the keystone, and the monarch must find a formula to satisfy the hopes of his people. But there is no system other than democracy—a popular democracy that is, of course, not a people's democracy East European style. No regime is perfect, but it is helpful when the personality of the head of state is not disputed or contested periodically. The monarch is an arbiter, the incarnation of popular hope and the repository of national legitimacy."

"The French monarchy was the supreme monarchy," writes Sanche de Gramont, the talented interpreter of France, in his 1967 book, *Epitaph for Kings*. "Anyone, anywhere in Europe, who referred to 'the king,' meant of course the king of France." De Gramont quotes Michael Suriano, the Venetian ambassador in Paris, who reported in 1562 that "by unanimous consent of all the peoples, the Kingdom of France has always been recognized as the first and most excellent kingdom in Christianity, as much for its dignity and power as for the absolute authority of he who governs it. . . . It is the oldest kingdom, having begun not much later than 400 years after the birth of Christ . . . and it was the first to embrace the Christian religion . . . which won for its sovereign the title the

131

eldest daughter of the church."

Henri does not seem very interested in the world outside France. "The future of monarchy in Europe?" he repeats my question as if considering it for the first time. "Not much there . . ." he replies, then begins to say something about the great need in Italy for "someone with ideas." He abandons the sentence. "Well, the pope is there." He adds with a broad grin, "The pope always hopes that he will be half a king." He does not claim to be friends with any other royalty, though he was a student at Louvain University in Belgium at the same time as Otto von Habsburg. He is skeptical about European unification. "That is Archduke Otto's cause, not mine." About France today, Henri is reticent. He refers to "different currents of thoughts, conflicting trends." At present there is "an indifference" to the advantages monarchy could offer.

"France is profoundly individualistic," he says, his face showing disapproval as well as pride. "We have not the Anglo-Saxon talent to coordinate." He speaks about "the traditional divisiveness of France," the endless arguments between Left and Right. His disagreement with l'Action Française—which he calls "a Rightist party with extreme Right sympathies"—stems from his refusal to put his stamp of approval on any monarchist party. He has always tried to "gain the sympathy and respect of different parties," and while he thought that l'Action Française represented "a powerful movement with many talented leaders, no one should be in a position to claim a monopoly on the monarchist idea. I address myself to all Frenchmen and Frenchwomen." His protestations notwithstanding, Henri sounds like a politician who would like everyone, or at least a vast majority, to belong to his version of l'Action Française.

Henri has declined to run for Parliament. De Gaulle too once suggested it but understood his refusal. A socialist politician recently wrote an article in Le Monde nominating Henri for the post of the secretary general of the Socialist Party, which is led by Francois Mitterand, de Gaulle's opponent in the 1965 presidential contest. Henri has never been a member of any party, calls himself a centrist and dines with politicians from across the political spectrum. His strategy, though, has been to court the Left and ignore the Right. His critics and enemies have called him the Crown Prince of the Republic, and many of his nonreigning colleagues think of him as a dyed-in-the-wool socialist, if not a Jacobin, a true heir to the regicide Philippe-Egalité. Henri has always calculated that the Right has no choice but to back him—and the Right in France ranges from the money-conscious bourgeoisie to the traditionalists nostalgic for the organic France of the eighteenth century. Rightist France is not the France foreigners love to love. It is the France of chauvinism and xenophobia ranging from just-below-the-surface to the brazen (the tactless young bracket them all as racists). Rightists criticize Henri as a man of the Left but the royalists among them accept him, faute de mieux, as their hereditary king, Henri VI. But some royalists are part of the unspeakable Right that came out of the woodwork during the days of Vichy to assist the Nazis in rounding up Jews and tracking down Resistance forces (Charles Maurras, a member of the French Academy and the most prominent of French monarchists in this century, ended up in jail for collaborating with the Nazis). Henri disowns them.

Henri is critical of primogeniture, and favors an elective monarchy. He cites the example of his ninth-century Capet ancestors who were elected, and later chose their successors. Henri argues that in a modern monarchy, a council of state might be entrusted with the mission of finding the most worthy successor within the royal family. Henri is faced with the problem of his eldest son Henri, the count of Clermont, who refuses to carry the burden of heir apparent. As the count of Paris stated in an interview with the mass-circulation magazine *Paris-Match*, "My eldest son lives in a way which I regret and which is perfectly idle. He has a charming wife and five children, two of whom are handicapped. I don't criticize him for living with someone else. But one does not abandon one's family, especially sick children." Henri puts his hopes in his eldest son's two sons, now aged thirteen and eleven. He spends a lot of time with them, teaching them history. "To die without reaching power doesn't bother me," Henri said in *Le Point*. "But to disappear without being certain who will succeed me is a real anxiety."

"Henri is an authoritarian and an absolutist," says Isabelle, the countess of Paris. Her lovely smile is free of malice. "My dear husband feels that he must decide everything. It's hard on our sons—it is hard to have such a remarkable, formidable father. Our sons respect him but they can't always agree with him. I keep telling them that it's stupid to be afraid of their father—my God, I have known him for more than sixty years—but they are still afraid of him and haven't got the courage to say certain things for fear of his saying 'no' to them.

"But our daughters have it easy. For women, it's always easier to deal with authority. Our daughters twist their father around their little fingers, and I don't mind that at all. Not at all."

In her youth, Isabelle was called the most beautiful woman in Europe. "From the top of the brow to the tip of her nose there is almost no indentation," wrote Geoffrey Bocca in his 1959 book, *Kings Without Thrones*. At sixty-eight, she is chatty, cheerful, and open. She interrupts other people and does not mind if they interrupt her. She is a great-great-granddaughter of Louis-Philippe and the great-granddaughter of Pedro II, the last emperor of Brazil. If she has any pretensions she hides them well. She is funny, irreverent, indiscreet. She would have made an earthy queen of France.

She is a devoted mother to her eleven children—one, François, died for France in the Algerian war in 1960, but he is always counted and mentioned. Two sons married commoners, but the rest of the children allied themselves with aristocracy—a Spanish prince, a German duchess, an Italian duke, a German duke, an Austrian count, a Belgian count, a French countess, and a French baron. Isabelle is an affectionate grandmother to her thirty-nine grandchildren. In addition, she has many visits with nephews, nieces, and more distant cousins. She is the most popular aunt among European royalty.

In raising her children, she had three educational principles she regards as most important: to serve the country, to respect Christian tradition, and to get a job. Her eldest son has had his problems, Isabelle concedes. "He is a painter, but very lazy. He is quite talented though—more talented than my two daughters who are also good painters. But now he is trying to become a businessman. He is setting up a shop. But he is not a good businessman, he doesn't have a head for business. We don't have good businessmen in our family. We Orléans are good workers, we work very hard, we drive ourselves. But we have no brains for business."

The past is of no interest to Isabelle. She says with a grimace, "We cannot re-do history. I guess we had a chance to come to power when de Gaulle became president of the Republic. Of course, I would have been only the king's wife, not queen as Queen Elizabeth of England is queen. A wife. But that would have been fine with me.

It's too late now. It will not happen."

Isabelle takes part in local politics in the small town of Eu, in Normandy, where she owns some property and where she lives. The property, part of her Capet inheritance, has been in the family since William the Conqueror. In Eu, she goes around with one message: "Don't vote for the Communists." She does not mind which party they do vote for; she just wants to make sure they do not vote Communist. "They listened to me," she says with pride. "Unlike other municipalities in the region, Eu did not go Communist."

Isabelle and Henri parted ways quietly several years ago. Henri had been seeing another woman, a secretary according to rumors, but no name, age, or other particulars have surfaced.

According to the story making the rounds among French aristocrats, Henri thought of leaving in his will a substantial sum to his new friend. Henri is a millionaire, owning forests and other country property in addition to real estate in some of the most elegant sections of Paris. He also inherited a large portfolio of stocks and securities. But the Code of Napoleon, which is still in force, does not permit a man to leave more than a small part of his legacy to a woman other than his wife—even if that wife is independently wealthy, as is Isabelle. For that reason, the story goes, Henri has decided upon a separation, which enables him to divide his estate as he wishes. But in *Paris-Match* Henri denied that he is legally separated. "We just don't live together," he said.

Henri permits himself some nasty comments about Isabelle. For instance, he condemned Isabelle's 1978 bestselling memoirs, *Tout M'est Bonheur*, as idle chatter. He told *Paris-Match* that "We never had much to say to each other and much less now. I am an oyster with her because she talks too much and cannot keep a secret."

Isabelle is as loyal as ever, though some people detect a note of irony in her standard reference to Henri as "my dear husband." They remain friends, and see each other regularly. Presiding over a family gathering or attending a state occasion, they provide a romantic tableau of a graciously aging couple—a vision of grace, light-hearted and without regrets that is, one might say, France at its best.

Footnote to a Legend
Louis-Napoleon

Now we go in content
To liberty, and not to banishment

As You Like It

Prince Imperial Louis-Napoleon is 6'3", ten inches taller than his great-granduncle Napoleon I, emperor of France. He has a pale complexion; his hair was blond before it turned silver. He is the chairman of several corporate boards, and a lover of sports—bicycling, car racing, horseback riding, mountain climbing, sailing, scuba diving, skiing, and swimming. He is an art collector; his unique Napoleon memorabilia ranges from Napoleon I's Tuileries furniture to his famous gray riding coat, from David's celebrated full-length portrait of the emperor to a collection of rare nineteenth-century toys with Napoleonic themes.

Louis-Napoleon is dedicated to living the good life. He has an attractive wife and four children—two boys, two girls—who share his enthusiasm for sports; a mansion in the most exclusive section of Paris facing the Arc de Triomphe (the arch was erected to commemorate the great emperor's victories, but the circle, known by the politically neutral name of Etoile for more than a century, is now named after Charles de Gaulle); a nineteenth-century chateau in a thirty-five-acre park in Switzerland (one European country that Napoleon I and III refrained from fighting or liberating); a hilltop villa on the Côte d'Azur; a yacht named Aquila (a reference to the imperial emblem of the eagle); a fleet of automobiles (his first love, at age eighteen, was a red Bugatti); and a large collection of antique and modern guns. He is an experienced pilot, an underwater archeologist with numerous Greek and Roman amphores to his credit, and an explorer of Africa, which he has traversed twice with his wife.

His is a multinational business empire including coffee plantations in Central Africa and the Caribbean. A multimillionaire who greatly increased the wealth he inherited (most of it from his maternal grandfather Leopold II, king of the Belgians), Louis-Napoleon is a contented citizen of France, without political ambitions and preferring anonymity. "I am not a star," he tells journalists and photographers. "We all work." Fearing publicity, he has resigned from such posts as honorary chairman of a charity ball, and though he dutifully attends ceremonial functions marking Napoleonic anniversaries he will make neither speeches nor small talk. "I am just a plain businessman," he tells his friends, "and I am very, very busy with my business."

In a rare interview in the late 1960s, for the private publication of a family album, *Le Livre de la Famille Impériale*, he was asked about the possibility of his occupying the imperial throne one day. The interviewer records that Prince Napoleon was silent at first. "Should one day the majority of my fellow citizens wish that," he finally responded, "I would not escape from their desire. But I will always refuse those who advertise my name and my person for partisan purposes, because in my eyes the name Napoleon is synonymous with unity." In the one press interview he has granted, to the French picture magazine *Point de Vue Images du Monde*, Louis-Napoleon declared, "I would always be ready to do my duty if the majority of France wants me, but I wouldn't ever impose myself by an unreasonable action."

But Louis-Napoleon who considers himself more of a republican than a monarchist, insists on his title. Those who make the mistake of addressing him as His Highness are informed in glacially polite language that Louis-Napoleon is His *Imperial* Highness. He is the head of the Imperial House of France, established by Napoleon I in 1804, which has nothing to do with the Royal House of France that traces itself to Hugues Capet in the ninth century and is known as Bourbon, and, of late, Bourbon-Orléans. Technically, Louis-Napoleon is not a claimant to the French throne; unlike Henri Bourbon-Orléans, he is not a pretender.

Louis-Napoleon obliquely criticized Henri in the interview with *Point de Vue Images du Monde*: "I maintain the traditions of the empire that are just as important as the divine right [of kings]. . . . But I don't have to look behind my shoulders and regret the past. I have a horror of princes waiting for the crown." He has stated flatly that the empire cannot be restored.

He presented his thoughts to the nation in May 1971, when France's daily *Le Monde* asked for his reflections on the 150th anniversary of Emperor Napoleon's death. Louis-Napoleon's thesis is that Emperor Napoleon's place in the national consciousness owes not so much to the military glory he earned, but to the fact that he founded the modern state of France. He explains that the nation is still conscious of the great events of Napoleon's era "not only because Europe and new society remain fundamental objectives, and our institutions are still largely those that he created but, equally, because he proclaimed virtues and principles for which the necessity is as great nowadays as it was in his time. . . Isn't it the state alone that is capable of coordinating and assembling resources and means necessary to undertake this or that particular action indispensable to the development of the country or to its independence? Such a dynamic and active conception of the modern state, the principal agent of society's progress, should be completed by a principle of a limitation of its intervention." Louis-Napoleon declares: "It is beyond doubt that though a centralizer by the requirements of his time, Napoleon would be, by the requirements of our time, a decentralizer."

The essay continues for another 1,200 words. It explores mission and purpose, design and implementation, the roles of youth and the military, the significance of an elite and its interrelationship with the masses, and a Europe of states prior to a Europe of peoples.

Louis-Napoleon is a disappointment. He cannot help his height and nordic looks, but one expects a literary style, a Napoleonic spark. Louis-Napoleon's writing, though, has the analytic lucidity and liturgic solemnity that the French drill into their bureaucrats.

In high school, French children study only the positive aspects of Napoleon's career. For many a teacher of history, the Napoleonic conquests on the continent represent the high point of the curriculum because they form the conviction that France once did— and thus perhaps can again—dominate the world. Those in charge of national education believe that the adolescent months spent on reliving Napoleonic glory plant those memories that ensure the continuity of French civilization.

Louis-Napoleon is a footnote to the legend of the nineteenth century. Tens of thousands of people watched Emperor Napoleon enter the great cities of Europe and pass through its small villages along ancient invasion routes. Who could forget him, the little man in the gray riding coat—not a hereditary monarch, but the son of a poor man, whose invincible army humbled the descendants of Charlemagne?

Of all the nonreigning royalty of Europe, Louis-Napoleon is the one who belies his legacy. In him, the Napoleonic tempest comes to a complete calm; the ambition of conquest is transmuted into the contentment of possession.

His secretariat refused my request for an interview, explaining that "in face of the multiplicity of such applications, the Prince Imperial decided not to accept any, because it is not possible to accept some and reject others. We are sure you understand this position."

I stormed his Paris headquarters on rue Presbourg, a street named after Pressburg, now Bratislava, where Napoleon imposed a peace that deprived the Austrian emperor of his centuries-old title, the Holy Roman Emperor. On one side is Avenue Kléber, one of Napoleon's marshals and on the other Avenue Victor Hugo, the romantic poet who both hated and loved Napoleon. The crescent-shaped neo-Renaissance mansion is on the Étoile, in the center of which the Arc de Triomphe stands, inscribed with Napoleon's victories. A high wrought-iron fence surrounds Louis-Napoleon's property; sheet metal fastened to the fence blocks any view of his garden. I entered the front gate, passed through a cobblestone courtyard, and rang the bell. The voice of a well-educated older lady answered from behind a ten-foot-tall double door. She told me to leave my name and telephone number with the concierge. Then the voice added, "Don't touch anything, because if you do, the police will come immediately. The place is wired." A prim, efficient voice informed me the next day on the telephone that "the prince imperial doesn't give interviews. I hope you understand." Intercessions by relatives and acquaintances were of no use. "He detests being considered a pretender to the throne as well as having to explain that he is not." I also received a warning: "You will be bored. There is nothing there except money." A final letter cited his activity as "very different from those of the royal families" who interested me. The signature was diagonally scribed—a complex, moody, twice-underlined "Napoleon."

By chance I did end up seeing Louis-Napoleon—in a restaurant in Paris. Even the waiter, a savvy old Parisian, did not know whom he served, though on reflection he did recall having waited on the monsieur before. Louis-Napoleon ate slowly and methodically through appetizer, soup, fish, meat, salad, and cheese. He hardly said anything during the meal; his companions, a couple slightly older than he, did the talking. They were drinking champagne.

Several times Louis-Napoleon gingerly turned the bottles in their silver cooler, studying the label with concern.

Born and raised in Belgium due to the Law of Exile, Louis-Napoleon first saw France in 1927, at age thirteen; he was smuggled in by his private tutor in military history, a retired French general, to visit the battlefields of World War I. In 1939, with World War II appearing certain, Louis-Napoleon appealed to Prime Minister Edouard Daladier, as well as to the president of the Republic, to permit him to join the army, the navy or the Foreign Legion. "I have in my Brussels home curio cabinets with military decorations earned by members of my family who served France," the young prince wrote. "Will I be the only Napoleon who never wore the French uniform?" He pledged to undertake no political activity and offered to serve under any name, anywhere. "I ask no other right but that of a citizen, under the equality of the constitution." His fourth letter was finally answered. A curt note signed by Daladier expressed regret that the Law of Exile made the request impermissible.

When France declared war on Germany, Louis-Napoleon crossed into Switzerland and joined the Foreign Legion. Suspecting that he might be a deserter from the regular French army, an officer launched an investigation that blew Louis-Napoleon's cover. The prime minister, to whom the matter was referred, decided to overlook the law, and allowed the Bonaparte prince to join the Legion on the condition that he not receive any promotion.

But like Henri, the count of Paris, Louis-Napoleon was barely through his basic training when France capitulated. Shattered, he returned to his chateau in Switzerland, where an invitation came from Nazi Germany to preside over a macabre event in Paris—a reburial of Napoleon II, the one legitimate son of Napoleon I, by Empress Marie-Louise, daughter of the Habsburg emperor, Franz I. (Napoleon II never ruled. At twenty-one, he died of tuberculosis in Austria, a pallid, tragic Habsburg.) Hitler himself had ordered the exhumation in Vienna and the reinterment in Paris. But Louis-Napoleon did not want to legitimize Vichy or the German occupation of Paris. He declined to attend the reburial that was conducted by torchlight on a bitterly cold December night at the church Les Invalides, the final resting place of Napoleon I. Gallic wit triumphed over a Germanic ceremony aimed at gaining French favor. Graffiti appeared all over Paris the night following the reburial: "We want fewer ashes, more coal."

Louis-Napoleon returned to France illegally, established contact with the Resistance and decided to join the Free French in London. He and three comrades were captured trying to cross into Spain, and ended up in a Gestapo jail in Paris. During his imprisonment, Louis-Napoleon was visited by a high Nazi official who told him of the führer's great admiration for the emperor of France, and suggested that Louis-Napoleon cooperate with the German heir to the Napoleonic quest to unite Europe. Louis-Napoleon refused.

Four-and-a-half months later, Louis-Napoleon was released. He remained in Paris for a few weeks under Gestapo surveillance, then escaped to the countryside and joined the Resistance forces as Lucien Monnier, private second class. During the two years he served as a *maquisard*, he took part in several actions against the occupying power and on one occasion was severely wounded.

After liberation, Louis-Napoleon, by that time a lieutenant, received the Croix de Guerre and the ribbon of the Légion d'Honneur—an institution founded by Napoleon I. Because of his outstanding war record, authorities closed their eyes to Louis-Napoleon's taking up residence in Paris under the name of Louis de Montfort, his last nom de guerre. But he was not allowed to marry in the church Les Invalides. A minor functionary informed him that he and his bride, Alix de Foresta, might be better served by a ceremony "discreet and intimate" in a less famous edifice. The wedding took place in a small village church; the location was kept secret until the last moment to keep away the press.

A year later, with the Law of Exile revoked, the first Bonaparte prince born in France in almost a century was baptised by Apostolic Nuncio Roncalli, the future Pope John XXIII. Next to Prince Charles, dressed in the swaddling clothes once used by Napoleon II, was his sister Catherine, the first twins in the Bonaparte family. "An eagle with two heads," one wit exclaimed. At the baptismal ceremony in Les Invalides as well as at the wedding, there were scores of Bonapartists, most of them uninvited, and some of them shouting *"Vive l'Empereur!"* But since 1939, when Louis-Napoleon ordered the dissolution of the small Bonapartist party because he detected in its ranks an attraction for Nazi ideas, there has been no Bonapartist party in France. Only in Napoleon's birthplace of Corsica is there a movement bearing the name Bonaparte, but its purpose is autonomy for the island.

If being a Bonapartist means belonging to the cult of the great emperor, all Corsicans are Bonapartists. The local anthem "Ajacienne" is an emotional song of praise for Napoleon I. On his first visit to the island as president of the Republic, de Gaulle made the mistake of inviting his audience, as he usually did at the end of his speech, to join him in singing the national anthem, the "Marseillaise." The crowd responded with a spirited rendition of "Ajacienne." De Gaulle did not enjoy the performance.

At the 150th anniversary of Napoleon's death, the president of the Republic made the prefect of Corsica his delegate at the commemoration on the island. A compromise was arranged: the prefect arrived while the band played "Ajacienne" and reached his seat just as the song finished. This way, the prefect did not have to stand in attention as did everyone else—which would have been improper for the representative of the national government. But the center of attraction was Louis-Napoleon who described himself "a pilgrim to the source." Descendants of the great emperor's companions surrounded him. It was an unprecedented reunion—a blend of a spiritualist seance and a Disneyland of the Napoleonic Era. The state dinner was attended by a live eagle, old and infirm, but unmistakably the imperial bird. The Bonaparte bee was imprinted on tablecloths and napkins, and the Napoleonic shade of green reigned everywhere.

In Paris, Minister of Culture André Malraux opened an exhibit marking Napoleon's anniversary. "A nation is a tree," he mused, "but an empire is lightning." The exhibit was mobbed, as was every commemoration event throughout France. Week after week, newspapers and magazines published feature stories and essays on Napoleon. "It's Napoleon to the point of indigestion," L'Express groaned.

There are few Bonapartist political activists, but admirers of Napoleon far outnumber Bourbon loyalists. They read books on the Bonapartes that roll off the presses year after year. "Next to the Bible," one Bonaparte princess told me with pride, "books on Napoleon are the most widely read in the world." Scholars estimate that since the beginning of the nineteenth century, the emperor has been the subject of 180,000 books in various languages. In Central Africa, Jean-Bédel Bokassa had himself crowned emperor in 1976 in a ceremony that was a precise imitation of Napoleon's coronation. In the Caribbean, the best fighting cocks are still awarded the name Napoleon. No dictator since has been so honored.

Many Frenchmen declare that de Gaulle himself was a Bonapartist—in the metaphoric sense of the word. *Bonapartisme* in the French political lexicon means a penchant for extraparliamentary solutions in the name of the people—a dictatorial temperament just a shade less reprehensible than *Césarisme*. In Marxist parlance, Bonapartism is an elegant but nonetheless pejorative term for the cult of personality; in exile, Leon Trotsky called Josef Stalin a Bonapartist.

People continue to brood over Napoleon's career. Military men still marvel at his battle plans. Historians search for the secrets of his rise to power, and mystics apply themselves to the meaning behind the many signs and wonders of his life. (For instance, on the day of his death, the sun sets precisely under the Arc de Triomphe. Another occult fact frequently cited: his nephew Napoleon III planted in his garden in England a shoot of the willow tree that grew over the grave in St. Helena; the tree grew but lost its crown in a storm that gathered the day Napoleon III died, and another storm felled the tree the day Napoleon III's only son died, in an ambush in the Zulu War.)

The Republic of France maintains a slightly greater distance from the Bonapartes than from the Bourbons. While on the map of Paris Napoleonic marshals and victories receive places of honor, no boulevard, avenue or street is named after Napoleon I, II or III. The government sends a lower level representative to attend the annual mass for Napoleon I than to comparable Bourbon ceremonial functions. The commemoration, complete with eagle scouts dressed as Napoleon's grenadiers and cuirassiers, has been used as a means to identify Napoleon I with the military, rather than the national history of France. In 1979, the army chief of staff represented the president of the Republic. The event was officially dedicated not only to the memory of Napoleon, but to all the soldiers who died for France.

But Napoleon I reigns under the dome of Les Invalides, which was converted into a Temple of Reason during the Revolution of 1789 but restored by Napoleon as a church after he made his peace with Roman Catholicism. Thousands of visitors, including foreigners, make the pilgrimage to Les Invalides to circumambulate his porphyry tomb—the color of dried blood, and in the style of a Victorian bathtub. He is the only French monarch to receive such homage.

No French republic has shown interest in repatriating the remains of Napoleon III, who died and was buried in England. Recently, Louis-Napoleon signed an appeal, initiated by Bonapartists, calling for government action, but, despite the current vogue of the Second Empire, neither Parliament nor the Elysée Palace has bothered to react. (Napoleon I's ashes were returned in 1840, under the reign of Louis-Philippe, France's last Bourbon king, who hoped that his gesture, which included a royal shout of *"Vive l'Empereur,"* would win him Bonapartist support. Instead, the emotions stirred helped prepare the way for Napoleon III, who first had himself elected president of the Republic and then, four years later, was crowned emperor.)

Although de Gaulle privately praised Louis-Napoleon's rush to join the Resistance, and contrasted it favorably with the equivocation of the count of Paris (who set himself up in Morocco), de Gaulle had no personal or political interest in the head of the House of Bonaparte. His greetings to Louis-Napoleon on family occasions were noticeably cooler than similar messages transmitted to Henri, and the polite handshake granted to Louis-Napoleon at ceremonial functions contrasted with the long, intimate conversations and correspondence he maintained with Henri.

"The two Napoleonic empires are mere episodes in French history," observes Pierre Pujo, editor of the royalist weekly *Aspects de France.* "Both periods were unhappy for France. The first Napoleonic venture issued forth from the Revolution of 1789 and ended with the defeat at Waterloo; the second began with the revolution that overthrew Louis-Philippe and ended with the defeat at Sedan and the Commune of Paris in 1871. Both empires brought misery and suffering to France, and both concluded with foreign armies occupying France."

Pujo and other Bourbon loyalists consider the two Bonaparte emperors usurpers, and products of the Revolution of 1789—the original sin as defined by the French Right. They dismiss Louis-Napoleon as a man of no consequence and Bonapartism as a cult of a few hundred sentimental army officers and provincial eccentrics. In practical political terms, both families are described as marginal, one of those lethal, polite French words. But French history is one of grand surprises, of spectacular comebacks, and Bonapartes in particular have a habit of returning from exile: Napoleon I stormed France from the Island of Elba and nearly succeeded in securing a

147

second tenure for himself; Napoleon III failed twice in coup attempts before seizing power. The Bourbons, on the other hand, did not try as hard. The brothers of Louis XVI claimed that their right to the throne was God-given and felt that the nation owed them their restoration.

Members of the Bonaparte family have little use for Bourbon pretensions. "The count of Paris is a fool," one Bonaparte tells me. "He thinks that there will be a Bourbon restoration. He really believes in it. He does not realize that the days of the monarchy are past. But there is absolutely no hope for the monarchy in France or elsewhere. Juan Carlos is an exception, a miracle. Spain is such a special situation.

"France is collapsing. There was a ray of hope under de Gaulle; now we are back where we were before him. But if France is to be rescued once again, it will be saved by a strongman who will do it on his own, like de Gaulle, and not by a Bourbon like Henri who believes that France should submit a request that he be her savior. Henri has been waiting for such a call all his life."

Louis-Napoleon and Henri know one another. They say they have no objections to being invited to the same dinner party, yet sensitive hosts and hostesses always ask them if they mind. "There is no rivalry between us," comes the standard response from both. "We are good friends." But frequently if both are invited to a gathering only one will show up. If their paths do cross, Louis-Napoleon and Henri shake hands and exchange a few words—as do their wives who patronize the same hairdresser in Paris, on rue de St. Honoré. Isabelle and Alix speak highly of each other, but they do not get together on their own, and neither has the other's telephone number.

Alix comes from an old aristocratic family from the south of France, originally Italian, raised to the ranks of French nobility in 1651 by Louis XIV. The de Forestas have been fiercely loyal to the Bourbons, and, at the time of their daughter's engagement, the word was that count and countess de Foresta were opposed to the match with a Bonaparte prince. In her preface to *Le Livre de la Famille Impériale*, Alix does not write of her parents' feelings. Instead, she plumbs a more distant past: "It pleases me to imagine that the sweet Clotilde of Savoy, Princess Napoleon and my husband's grandmother, should have come to a secret understanding in the other world with the tender friend of her adolescence, Natalie de Foresta, my great-aunt. Didn't the two of them guide our steps and hearts so that I, a descendant of a legitimist family, would become on a lovely day in August 1949 the wife of the head of the imperial family of France?"

It is Princess Alix, rather than her husband, who takes an interest in promoting the Bonaparte tradition. She helps researchers and exhibition organizers. Gossip has it that while Louis-Napoleon, apprehensive about revolution and expropriation, insists on keeping most of his collection of Napoleon memorabilia in safe Switzerland, Alix, outgoing and ambitious, would like to have the fabulous relics seen by as many people and in as many exhibitions as possible.

One hundred twenty-five years after Napoleon's coronation in Notre Dame, and after subsequent alliances of Napoleon's four brothers and three sisters with the reigning families of Europe, the Bourbons and Bonapartes are no longer incompatible. In fact, Henri and Louis-Napoleon are third cousins: Louis-Philippe, the last king of the French, is great-great-grandfather to both. Yet the relationship is not mentioned in the Bonaparte family album, which merely states that Louis-Napoleon "descends, along several lines, from St. Louis and Louis XIV."

Another fact that neither Bonapartes nor Bourbons advertise is that the handsome businessman Prince Charles, Louis-Napoleon's eldest son and heir, has married an authentic Bourbon princess, Beatrice, from the branch of the family that reigned in the Kingdom of the Two Sicilies—an ancient Bourbon realm that King Victor Emmanuel, with the assistance of Napoleon III, absorbed into Italy in 1861. The alliance between the renascent Kingdom of Italy and the Second Empire of France was sealed by the marriage of Prince Napoleon-Jerome-Charles-Paul, nephew of Napoleon I and grandfather of Louis-Napoleon, to Princess Marie-Clotilde, daughter of Victor Emmanuel II.

It is believed that Charles and Beatrice, both in their twenties, lived together for some time without the benefit of priestly blessing, even after the birth of their first child.

But monarchist publications, eager to record the date of Prince Charles's marriage and the particulars of the new generation of Bonapartes, have been unable to obtain information. His interest in adapting to the contemporary world notwithstanding, Louis-Napoleon does not approve of his son's trendy ways. Harsh words are said to have been exchanged between father and son, and the affair has reinforced Louis-Napoleon's determination to stay out of the limelight.

But if Prince Charles angered his father, he was fulfilling a Bonaparte tradition. In the nineteenth century, no other European dynasty showed more of a preference for siring illegitimate children than Napoleon I's immediate family and descendants. As a result, Burke's authoritative almanac of royalty notes with British dryness, "Louis-Napoleon and his two sons are indeed the only living legitimate male descendants of the progenitor of this House, Charles (or Carlo) Bonaparte."

Some of the illegitimate Bonapartes were acknowledged. The most prominent among them was Count Walewski, who was Napoleon I's son by a Polish beauty, and who served as Napoleon III's foreign minister. Others spent their lives noisily claiming to be Bonapartes, and still others hinted at their origins and cultivated a resemblance to one of the Napoleons.

The twentieth century demands proof; under the bright lights of its media, everything must be perfectly clear. But the nineteenth century—the century of declining blue bloods and rising impostors—preferred twilight, and cherished its illusions. No newspaper exposé or blunt query could threaten an aging countess thriving on mere allusions to her origin, or a gentleman with exquisite manners but no visible source of income who seemed to be forever stroking a tobacco-brown goatee à la Napoleon III, or a solitary soul who brooded day after day at a particular cafe table and took long walks with one hand slipped into his coat.

The nineteenth century was an age of fantasy, of lace and brocade, of sweet cheap patchouli and cool lavender. It was an age of ambition and caprice. Napoleon I carved out of Prussia the Kingdom of Westphalia and gave it to his youngest brother Jerome, Louis-Napoleon's great-grandfather. Twenty-year-old Jerome proceeded to set up a court in which the ladies served as his harem. For additional supplies, he relied on the local theatrical company, stocked by actresses recruited in Paris. The one pretty woman he neglected in his kingdom was his wife Catherine, daughter of the king of Württemberg. She, however, was in love with him—Jerome was a slender, charming youth with dark romantic curls and a winning smile.

After the collapse of Napoleon's empire—and with it the end of the Kingdom of Westphalia—Catherine was delighted to take Jerome back, secured a pension from her family and set up house in Rome. In exile, Jerome consented to fulfill his conjugal duties; he fathered Prince Jerome-Napoleon, who strongly resembled his Uncle Napoleon I, and who led a French army to liberate Italy of Austrian yoke and then conducted peace negotiations with Emperor Franz Josef on behalf of his emperor, Napoleon III.

Historians no longer hesitate to say that Napoleon III was *not* the son of Louis, Napoleon I's brother and king of the Netherlands. Napoleon III was the son of a Dutch naval officer, a favorite of Queen Hortense. And Queen Hortense was the daughter of Josephine, Napoleon I's first wife and true love, but by her first husband, a royalist marquis guillotined in the Revolution of 1789.

The Bourbons claim that their forty kings and their reign of a thousand years is France, Eternal France. But Napoleon, symbol of youth and revolution, is an indispensable ingredient of the French mystique. The Bourbons may represent historic legitimacy, but France still lives under the law fashioned by Napoleon I.

Splendor was defined for Europe not only by the Sun King, Louis XIV, but by the two meteoric Napoleons: the obscure lieutenant from the provinces who crowned himself emperor, and his heir who, two revolutions and three Bourbon kings later, made Paris the City of Light and the capital of Europe. In Versailles and in the Tuileries, Bourbon France laid down the standards for European monarchy. But Napoleonic France offered the romance of opportunity. Under the Bourbons, France became the supreme monarchy. But in the dreamer's dictionary, Napoleon is the synonym for ambition and courage.

A Bonaparte princess attending the annual mass on May 5 for the repose of the great Napoleon's soul in Les Invalides was once astonished to note in the crowd someone she knew by sight from her neighborhood. She asked the man, a balding bank teller dressed in his Sunday best, why he came. "I admire Napoleon more than I admire any other person," he replied, and then added, with all the pathos he could muster, "He is France."

Everybody's Cousin
Czar Simeon of the Bulgars

O that I were as great
As is my grief, or lesser than my name!
Or that I could forget what I have been!
Or not remember what I must be now!

King Richard II

In the genealogical charts of European royalty, Czar Simeon II is the missing link. He connects the Russia of the Romanoffs to the Portugal of the Braganças, the Bourbons to the Napoleons. A second-generation Orthodox, he bridges the gap between Roman Catholic and Protestant dynasties. His blue blood is just about an equal mix of German and Latin.

Except for his friend and former neighbor in exile, Leka, king of the Albanians (who is second-generation royalty and not related to any of his colleagues), Simeon is a cousin to all reigning and nonreigning monarchs in Europe.

He has the unique distinction of being equidistant from the two French dynasties: he is third cousin to both Henri Bourbon-Orléans, the count of Paris, and Louis-Napoleon, the prince imperial. Simeon is also third cousin to Henri's wife, born Isabelle Orléans-Bragança, whose great-grandfather was Pedro II, the last emperor of Brazil. Portugal's Dom Duarte João, the duke of Bragança, is also a third cousin, through his great-great-grandfather Louis-Philippe, king of France.

Simeon's father, Czar Boris III, was first cousin to Archduke Otto, current head of the House of Habsburg. Their mothers were sisters, princesses from the House of Bourbon-Parma, which ruled the Duchy of Parma until 1859, when Victor Emmanuel II incorporated it into Italy. (The Bourbon-Parma connection also makes Jean, grand duke of Luxembourg, Simeon's first cousin once removed.) Italy's last king, Umberto II, is Simeon's uncle. Umberto's wife, Queen Marie-José—sister to Leopold III, former king of the Belgians—is Simeon's fifth cousin.

Simeon is the scion of the House of Saxe-Coburg-Gotha that

traces itself to the tenth century and that ruled until 1918 over a small, impecunious German duchy centered around the town of Coburg, now in northern Bavaria and near the East German border. Headquartered in a rat-infested medieval fortress surrounded by a double ring of fortified walls, the dukes of Saxe-Coburg-Gotha were in great demand by other dynasties and acquired a reputation in the nineteenth century as the royal stallions of Europe. The Romanoffs were stalked by anarchists; the Hohenzollerns were suspected of assisting German imperial schemes; the Bourbons, diminishing in number, preferred to marry among themselves; the Savoys were not prolific; the Habsburgs were too frequently afflicted with mental disorders—and so the search for a dynastically correct marriage often ended up in small German courts, and among them, the ramshackle Duchy of Coburg was favored above all others. When the Congress of Vienna restored normalcy after the Napoleonic shake-up of thrones and frontiers, Saxe-Coburg-Gotha ruled over four German duchies and the kingdom of Saxony, and by the end of the nineteenth century they were in possession of four additional thrones: Belgium, Portugal, Great Britain, and, finally, Bulgaria. The Coburgs boasted: "We reign over half the world."

Queen Victoria of England and her Prince Consort Albert—first cousins—both issued from the House of Saxe-Coburg-Gotha. Simeon's great-grandfather Augustus was their first cousin, which means that Queen Victoria's descendants, five of whom head nonreigning royal houses and five of whom reign in Great Britain, Spain, Denmark, Sweden, and Norway, are Simeon's fourth or fifth cousins, and often along more than one line of descent. They include Grand Duke Wladimir Romanoff, Prince Louis Ferdinand Hohenzollern (as well as his late wife Kira, born a Romanoff grand duchess), King Michael of Romania (whose wife Anne, born Princess Bourbon-Parma, is Simeon's first cousin once removed), King Constantine of Greece (whose wife Anne-Marie, born a princess of Denmark and sister to the reigning Queen Margrethe II, is Simeon's fifth cousin), and Prince Alexander Karageorgevitch of Yugoslavia (whose wife, Dona Maria da Gloria of Orléans-Bragança, is Simeon's third cousin once removed).

"European royalty is one big family," says Simeon with a broad smile, and that family interconnectedness is his favorite argument for monarchy. "We can cut through formalities and awkwardnesses because we are all relatives and have known one another all our lives. When the head of a powerful country can approach the head of a small country by saying, 'By the way, Uncle, couldn't we settle this little problem between us,' the situation lacks the ominousness of a prime minister talking to a counterpart he barely knows. And of course, we all speak many languages. It's easier for us to settle disputes."

Simeon never misses a royal get-together. "Oh, Simeon is a very good cousin," I heard repeatedly. Simeon is not discouraged by the example of World War I when monarchs who were first cousins fought each other. "Those empires fell apart internally," he declares, with a touch of impatience in his voice. "The political leaders, economic rivalries and restless minorities all *demanded* a collision. The system *had* to collapse.

"I cannot defend foolish kings or an absolute ruler such as the old emperor of Ethiopia. Absolute anything is awful. But to write off a political force as old as monarchy is silly. In this age of provinces such as Quebec and minorities such as the Basques demanding independence, no old system, no traditional political idea is dead. We witness so many absurd things. Why not a return of the monarchies?"

Czar Simeon is just under six feet tall—slim, athletic, and dapper in a starched Spanish manner. He has blue eyes, a long, thin nose, and a pink complexion. A narrow ribbon of meticulously trimmed beard frames his face—no moustache—making him look like a Velázquez portrait.

When he speaks about international affairs, his abstractions and absolutes have an unmistakably Germanic stiffness. But he is a devotee of the French cult of *lucidité*. "I am Cartesian," he says, "rational analysis is my thing." He smiles at his Americanism. His English is French-accented; although when he is at loss for a word he resorts to French, he enjoys colloquial American expressions, many of which he learned at Pennsylvania's Valley Forge Military Academy where he was Cadet No. 6883 in 1958-59.

The loss of his throne depresses Simeon—it is not the kind of experience one forgets, even if it happens when one is nine years old. Training and breeding triumph over momentary weakness. Surrender is unthinkable. Having studied "kingship" and "statecraft"—he pronounces these words slowly, with an etymologist's fondness—as well as genealogy, Simeon is determined to be optimistic about restoration.

"A shifty Balkan type," says one observer who also knew his father and grandfathers. "Like his cunning father Boris and his secretive grandfathers Ferdinand and Victor Emmanuel, Simeon will never tell you what he really thinks." He is a smooth, fast, and compulsive talker. He is glad to be interviewed, but would rather make proclamations than answer questions. His arguments are often confusing. He gives a five-minute lecture on the importance of the monarch in modern society and the usefulness of his training and background. Then in a quick aside, he declares himself an ideal candidate as Bulgaria's ambassador to the United Nations. One moment, he is a conventional anti-Communist émigré from Eastern Europe; next, he reveals his offer to the People's Republic of Bulgaria to assist its new embassy in Madrid. He shifts his ground with splendid ease. Had he been allowed to reign, he would have been another in a long line of elusive royal foxes the Balkan admires as much as its roaring lions who have made Balkan history an alternation between sly submission to the stronger power and reckless rebellion against it.

When speaking of battles and armaments, Simeon sounds like a professional soldier. But he projects a convincing image as a businessman *au courant* with market indicators and investment trends. He is also an historian, a critic of contemporary politics, and a student of jurisprudence.

He is at his liveliest when conversation turns to Italy and his Italian connections; his mother Giovanna, who lives near him in Madrid, is a daughter of King Victor Emmanuel III, and his paternal grandmother, Maria Louisa, was an Italian princess. He travels on an Italian passport that the Republic of Italy offered him and his mother in 1946, after declining their request for political asylum.

"I feel uncomfortable about my Italian passport," he says, his expression prim. "I always advise Bulgarians to take up the citizenship of the country that receives them, and not to remain refugees." The tension on his face eases. "I hate the word refugee. But I feel awkward taking up citizenship abroad. So I accepted the offer of an Italian passport made out to Count Rylski, an alias my father invented. Rylski was the famous mountain monastery where Bulgarian culture and identity survived during the Ottoman rule.

"A passport is a piece of paper, really." He thrusts his hands in the air, palms upturned, in the classic Italian gesture of submission to life's absurdity. "A new passport does not mean a change of allegiance. For practical reasons, I don't want to travel under my own name. As Rylski, I am anonymous, and I can keep the low profile I prefer." A broad smile settles on his handsome face. "I love traveling and meeting different kinds of people."

Abruptly, he adds: "I would be glad to serve my country as its U.N. ambassador." He cites his knowledge of eight languages—Bulgarian, French, German, Italian, English, Spanish, Portuguese, and Arabic—and his extensive international connections. "I think I would do well as a diplomat." As royal daydreams go, a U.N. ambassadorship must be one of the most innocuous.

A few minutes later, he stresses his availability as a monarch. "If called upon to rule, I shall serve Bulgaria. I see myself as an alternative." He contends that in 1968, under the influence of Alexander Dubcek's liberalization in Czechoslovakia, there was some talk of restoring the monarchy in Bulgaria. And, in 1956, during the Hungarian revolution, there were "echoes" in Bulgaria; the monarchy was mentioned as "a possible Third Road—neither communism nor capitalism." Back in 1950, the Communist regime of Bulgaria considered him—at thirteen years of age—enough of a threat to dispatch gunmen to assassinate him in Egypt, a clumsy plot foiled by the Egyptian police. A mimeographed information sheet issued by his secretariat quotes him as declaring, "Exile, provided that one has the power to return, is the best school for a king." In 1955, when Simeon turned eighteen, a *Te Deum* was celebrated in a Madrid church, and the king addressed Bulgarian monarchists in the presence of three members of the Spanish cabinet. The declaration, circulated to the press in English as well, stated that the Bulgarian constitution was still in force today as it expresses "the unshaken will of the Bulgarian people towards the rights which they hold sacred." Simeon concluded: "I am still invested with the mission assigned me by Providence."

Several times during our conversation, Simeon points out that he has never abdicated. His palace, surrounded by a fifteen-foot stone wall in an exclusive section of Madrid, befits a reigning monarch. A policeman guards the gate, and sturdy wrought-iron grills protect the windows.

The two spacious reception rooms have Persian carpets, Louis XIV furniture, and family heirlooms in silver, bronze, marble, jasper, and porcelain. The walls are covered with oil portraits of

Simeon's parents and grandparents, as well as of more distant forebears. "Much of this was inherited from great-aunts and great-uncles," Simeon says, "and some I picked up in antique stores. Wherever I go on the continent, I am always searching for historical mementos." He points to a two-foot-high silver tankard with medals of all the kings and dukes of Germany. Gothic lettering around the bottom identifies the tankard as a present to Otto von Bismarck on the twenty-fifth anniversary of his appointment as the imperial chancellor of Germany, in 1896. "Don't ask me how much I paid for it," Simeon says with the wink of a smart buyer's pride, "I don't remember. But it was a bargain." He shows me a magnificent oversize volume bound in blue leather embossed with the heraldic fleur-de-lis of Bourbon France. It is a commemorative album from 1886, presented to Princess Clémentine on her eightieth birthday by a Belgian infantry regiment that bore her name; Princess Clémentine was the daughter of Louis-Philippe, the last king of the French, and her son was Ferdinand, the first czar of the Bulgars, Simeon's grandfather.

Simeon can identify some of the faces in his portrait gallery only with the help of the *Almanach de Gotha*, that invaluable compendium of monarchial information that was issued annually in the small Duchy of Gotha from 1764 to 1944. He owns a complete set.

His wife, a Spanish heiress of aristocratic ancestry, is referred to as Queen Margarita. Their four sons are listed on the royal stationery as princes of Tirnovo, Preslav, Panagyurishte, and Vidin—historic towns of Bulgaria—and their daughter as princess of Bulgaria. The sons are all named after national heroes of Bulgaria: Kardam founded the Bulgarian state in the eighth century, Kyril converted the Slavs to Christianity, Koubrat was the first khan of the Bulgars in the seventh century, and Konstantin-Assen was the great conqueror king in the thirteenth century. The daughter has "a typically Bulgarian name albeit pagan," Kalina. A French relative describes the children as poised and well-mannered—typical Spanish aristocrats.

The children do not speak Bulgarian. "I don't have the patience to teach them," Simeon says sheepishly. He plans to send the two oldest boys, aged seventeen and fifteen, to an Israeli kibbutz he has visited where good Bulgarian is spoken. "My sons will surely pick up Bulgarian there," Simeon says, "and they would be welcome and absolutely safe. Jews remember the rescue activities of my parents

*Archduke Otto von Habsburg wearing traditional
Hungarian dress suit on his eighteenth birthday.*

Emperor Franz Josef with his grand-nephew Karl, the last ruler of the Austro-Hungarian monarchy, and Karl's son, Archduke Otto.

Otto, an exile in America, 1940.

Professor Habsburg, currently a sought-after lecturer.

Louis Ferdinand and Kira bow to guests on their twenty-fifth wedding anniversary in 1963.

Prince Louis Ferdinand Hohenzollern in the 1970s.

The prince, with ancestral Zollern Castle in the background.

Crown Prince Umberto
in military uniform.

Crown Prince Umberto marries a Belgian princess,
Marie-José, in 1930.

King Umberto in 1964.

The Portuguese royal family in 1967. Left to right: brothers Miguel and Henrique; head of the family Duarte Nuno; mother Françoise, born Orléans-Bragança; eldest son and current pretender Duarte João.

Two of Duarte Nuno's sons admire his portrait.

Manuel II, the last king of Portugal, with his fiancée, Princess Augusta Victoria, and her father. Manuel lost his throne in 1910.

Henri Bourbon-Orléans, the count of Paris, 1955.

Henri and Isabelle in the 1950s.

The count and countess with their eleven children.

Opposite: Eldest daughter Isabelle, in front of a portrait of her father as a hunter in Morocco.

Louis-Napoleon, the prince imperial, and his wife, Alix, attending a 1968 mass for the repose of Emperor Napoleon III's soul.

Queen Giovanna, Simeon's mother.

Czar Boris, Simeon's father.

Simeon (left) with a classmate at Valley Forge Military Academy, 1959.

Czar Simeon II of the Bulgars and his queen, Margarita, visiting Chicago in the 1970s.

Opposite: The wedding of Crown Prince Constantine and Danish Princess Anne-Marie, 1964.

President Eisenhower greets Princess Sophia, now queen of Spain. Her mother, Queen Frederika, and her brother, Constantine, stand in the background.

Constantine of Greece with LBJ.

Olympic gold medal winner Constantine in 1966.

King Karol and his son Michael, in 1930.

New York Governor Averell Harriman receives ex-King Michael in 1956. Michael was participating in a three-month training course for aircraft industry executives.

Michael and Anne, sailing.

Michael, 1948.

Michael, 1957.

Karageorge, founder of the Karageorgevitch dynasty, became prince of Serbia in 1808.

A 1932 portrait of Yugoslavia's last king, Peter II.

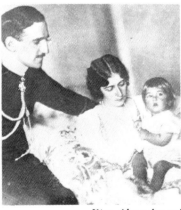

King Alexander and Queen Marie with their son, Crown Prince Peter, 1924.

Prince Alexander, claimant to the Yugoslav throne, and his wife, born Princess Maria da Gloria Orléans-Bragança, in Chicago, 1978.

King Leka on a military exercise near Madrid. He was expelled from Spain in 1979.

King Leka with his queen, Susan Cullen-Ward, and his mother, Geraldine.

Queen Geraldine with Crown Prince Leka shortly after their flight from Italian Fascists in 1939.

Grand Duke Wladimir, claimant to the Russian throne,
in front of a portrait of his great-grandfather, Czar Alexander II.

during World War II. When I was in Israel some years ago, David Ben-Gurion received me to offer thanks to my family. He wore a necktie for the occasion, and I was told that it was in my honor and one of the very few occasions in his life that he wore a tie.

"But," Simeon adds, evenhanded diplomat that he is, "I have good friends in the Arab world as well, including Jordan's King Hussein, who decorated me with the Order of Al-Nahda." Simeon speaks colloquial Arabic, learned in Alexandria during the five years he and his mother lived there after their expulsion from Bulgaria.

The information sheet issued by his secretariat stresses the illegality of the plebiscite that led to Simeon's banishment in September 1946, at the age of nine. It cites the mass executions of army officers, intellectuals, and other personalities, including his Uncle Kyril, the regent. In his occasional messages that appear in publications of the 50,000 Bulgarian émigrés throughout the world, Simeon speaks of "the tragedy of the Bulgarian people" and reiterates his unswerving opposition to the Communist regime.

Simeon says that he is careful not to use "ugly words" against the government in Sofia, or in Moscow, and his restraint is noticed in those capitals. "I never insult them," Simeon claims, "because I don't want to have to take anything back. My hope is that my message will get through, a message which I convey discreetly." He repeats the word 'discreetly.' "I would like to see the government improve conditions in Bulgaria."

Recently Simeon was visited by two Communist journalists from Bulgaria. "At first, I thought it was a joke," he says. "But then I realized that they really wanted to speak with me. We got along well. They were surprised that I am not the monster they had expected. They called me Mr. Simeon, and we talked about Bulgarian literature and arts most of the time. They were also surprised that I keep up with Bulgarian developments. I read Bulgarian daily newspapers and periodicals, and an occasional novel.

"The monarch's role is moderation," Simeon says, "to be above parties and politics, and to avoid becoming a political leader. A monarch must have everyone's ear. It is his job to calm people, to lessen friction. As Louis XIV, the Sun King of France, once said: 'Control your rage and don't give offense.'"

An encounter with Communists is a test for a monarch who must, by definition, be a king of all his subjects—including republicans and members of the extreme Left which, in Simeon's case, banished him. A meeting with a symbol of the pre-Communist regime is also a demonstration of de-Stalinization: these days journalists are trusted—in fact, commissioned—to interview émigrés, once the ultimate traitors. Official publications may still refer to Simeon as "the monarcho-Fascist wolf in the Coburg lair," but on an unofficial level relations can be correct, even cordial. The king is pleased because such a contact suggests that he is still taken seriously; he is a factor. The journalists are happy because meeting an ex-king is a great story to tell colleagues.

In Burke's reverential volume, *Royal Families of the World*, published by Burke's Peerage Ltd. in 1977, Simeon is characterized as "an ardent believer in democracy," whose dream is "to return to Bulgaria as king and be remembered as 'The Pacifier.'" When in 1972 Spain normalized relations with Bulgaria—Spain needed Bulgaria's vote in the U.N. Security Council on the Gibraltar issue, and there was the possibility of Bulgaria buying Spanish oranges—Simeon did not fight the inevitable. "Establishment of diplomatic relations between two countries is a necessity," Simeon notes dryly. "I accepted Spain's decision—not cheerfully but as a pragmatist. I phased myself out of representing Bulgaria in Spain ceremonially."

Simeon did not dispute Bulgaria's demand that he stop flying the Bulgarian flag over his house and that he surrender his diplomatic status—privileges granted by Generalissimo Francisco Franco, who in 1951 had invited the Bulgarian royal family to Spain (Franco also supplied a house, two cars, and five servants). "I don't like to embarrass anybody," Simeon says, "and I am grateful to Spain. What's more, I indicated my readiness to assist the Bulgarian embassy in establishing itself in Madrid. I have lots of contacts here, of course, which could be useful for Bulgaria. But the Bulgarian government didn't respond to my offer.

"I have an Oriental's concept of time, which is also very Bulgarian. I can wait and wait and wait. No regime is forever, and radical changes happen when one least expects them.

"I believe that geography alone is eternal. As Morocco's King Hassan once said to King Juan Carlos of Spain, 'Policies and alliances change, but there will always be fourteen kilometers of sea between our two lands.'

"Thank God we have non-Slavic Romania between us and the Russians. Without Romania as a buffer, Russia would have swallowed us up long ago. We would have been absorbed because of the closeness in language, religion, and sentiments—regardless of the Hun blood we have and much that is non-Slavic about Bulgaria."

Had Simeon been allowed to reign, or, rather, to reign in a country farther from the Russian border, he would have become a welcome visitor to world capitals, a sought-after middleman, and a maker of long speeches at the U.N. General Assembly. He would have known, better than anyone else, how to praise Russian heroism and progress in Moscow, American know-how and sincerity in Washington, the luminous spirit of France in Paris, the greatness of the Arabs in Cairo, Riyadh, and Damascus, and the Jewish attachment to history in Jerusalem. In him, the Third World would have had a traveling salesman to promote the notion of redistributing the wealth of the great industrial nations; he would have been the first European head of state to learn Chinese. He would have been a nonaligned king, if not the king of nonalignment.

Bulgarian monarchy was a casualty of the rival totalitarianisms of Hitler and Stalin in the 1940s; the independent Bulgarian kingdom was a product of the balance-of-power diplomacy that characterized the period preceding World War I. The practice of dispatching dashing young German princes to fashion modern kingdoms out of backward Balkan lands was fanciful, arrogant, even absurd; the motivation was a typically nineteenth-century blend of faith, greed, and intrigue. The Balkan peninsula was Europe's untamed frontier; to promote its stability and progress was the mission in which England, Russia, Germany, France, Italy, and Austro-Hungary were rival sponsors. The young princes were to prove themselves, but they ended up being bored. Instead of the Germanic ideal of a duel, the Balkan offered furtive encounters in the mountains, knifings in taverns, ambushes in the dark. The towns belonged to shifty merchants and suspicious minorities; the villages were fortresses of the family. Life in the Balkan lacked the choreography of Western civilization; wealth was rare, and either ostentatious or hidden—it did not sponsor arts and letters or gentlemanly living.

The Central European investors and entrepreneurs who followed in the princes' footsteps found themselves outsmarted by the natives and by local conditions. The pious hope of Great Power diplomats and Balkan revolutionaries was that under the command of former Prussian army officers the new nation states would join the family of civilized Europe, and that the region, after living with Ottoman brutality and torpor for more than four centuries would become imitations of Germany, France, and England. But local wars erupted instead; autocratic regimes gained the upper hand; and the Balkan became a metaphor for fragmentation and tension—as well as the theater of two world wars.

Each Balkan land cherishes the memory of a great conqueror, and two, Bulgaria and Yugoslavia, are also drawn irresistibly to the heir of Byzantium, the great Slavic Mother Russia. Simeon II was named after Simeon I, a tenth-century monarch whose Great Bulgaria incorporated most of the peninsula. The most unforgettable conqueror was Alexander the Great, yet his Macedonians formed the only nation on the Balkan never recognized in modern times as an independent entity.

Glory and prosperity have eluded the Balkan. Bucharest has acquired a Parisian sheen and Athens a Levantine cosmopolitanism, but Sofia, Belgrade, and Tirana have never amounted to more than dull provincial capitals lacking aristocracies of the blood or the spirit.

Under its three modern kings, Bulgaria's tiny intellectual elite mimicked Paris, Berlin, and Moscow; the great masses of people seemed unable to rid themselves of the debilitating memory of servitude to the Turks. There was no age of intellectual achievement to look back upon with pride, no admirable personalities other than warriors and revolutionaries. Violence, police brutality, dictatorship, and banditry seemed endemic. Bulgarian politicians usually ended up victims of knives or bullets. But millions of farmers, hard at work on small plots of lands nestled in lovely green valleys, continued to produce the finest tobacco and attar of rose, and perhaps the tastiest melon, eggplant, and tomato on the continent. Not surprisingly, the notion of a Green International—to rival the Red International of the Bolsheviks and the White International of reactionaries—came from Bulgaria, from the prototypical peasant movement of Eastern and Southern Europe called the Agrarian Party and finally disbanded by the Communists. The great Agrarian Party leader, Alexander Stambuliski, pushed through the first land reform in the Balkan. In 1921, after visits to East European capitals, he declared: "Our Green International will ultimately free Russia from the Soviets. At least, it is destined to free farmers elsewhere from the unjust restrictions placed upon them by the manufacturers and capitalists." In a coup d'état, tacitly supported by Boris III and led by army officers, Stambuliski, Bulgaria's only Agrarian prime minister, was murdered.

German princes did not take root in Bulgaria. The first, Alexander of Battenberg, was selected as prince of Bulgaria in 1879 because he was the favorite nephew of Alexander II, Czar of All the Russias, a relative of the British royal family, and, of course, a German. He had also fought in the Russian army that liberated Bulgaria. But he would not heed the advice of Otto von Bismarck, the German chancellor, who warned: "If you wish to remain in Bulgaria, give yourself up to Russia unconditionally." Bismarck vetoed Alexander's courtship of Princess Victoria, daughter of Germany's Kaiser Friedrich and granddaughter of Britain's Queen Victoria, because Bismarck feared that Russia would interpret such a marriage as a political alliance with Germany and a challenge to Russian ambitions in Bulgaria. Prince Alexander could not keep the Russians happy; then—as now—they looked upon Bulgaria as their outlying province forever indebted for the military assistance rendered against the Turkish oppressors. The coup d'état that banished Alexander after seven years had more to do with Russia's hostility than dictatorial rule.

The next prince of Bulgaria was found by a search committee of three commissioners that combed European courts. The Russians vetoed a proposal to unite Bulgaria with Romania under King Karol I. For six months the search committee could not come up with a candidate acceptable to Russia.

It was over a marble-topped restaurant table in a Viennese beer hall that someone recommended Prince Ferdinand of Saxe-Coburg-Gotha. Next day, the commissioners offered him the crown. Ferdinand graciously accepted the honor, and the Bulgarian national assembly elected him unanimously in 1887. "If I am only the flea in the ear of the bear," he said referring to Russia, "the experience ought to be none the less amusing."

Ferdinand was spectacularly ill-suited to rule Bulgaria. The French consul, Maurice Paléologue, wrote of him: "Refined to excess, enamored of art and given to whim, very proud of his origins, as disdainfully aristocratic as a prince of ancient German blood can be, he has come to live in a primitive and rough country without tradition and without culture. After twenty years of rule, he has become attached neither to the people nor the country." Ferdinand was delicate, wore sumptuous furs, and collected jewelry. He sheltered himself in his rose garden both to breathe in its scents and to entertain ladies with his versions of Arabian nights stories. "My Bulgarian wolves" was his mockingly affectionate term for his subjects. He was disappointed by their refusal to share in his ambition to build a strong kingdom, a Prussia of the Balkan. Consul Paléologue observed: "The Bulgarians do not care to form a kingdom. . . . They are also profoundly egalitarian and democratic; they know that a sovereign court would cost them dearly, and they are not at all impressed by monarchial trapping."

Ferdinand did not keep court, detested Sofia, and flaunted his title, the Czar of the Bulgars, in the drawing rooms of civilized Europe. The refusal of European powers to recognize his title did not bother him; he was a czar, and he had a realm, however modest, that he could call his own.

Simeon professes great admiration for Russia because Russian troops helped Bulgaria win independence from the Ottoman Turks in 1878 and because Soviet leaders are pursuing objectives established centuries ago. "They are the true heirs of the czars," Simeon says, bowing his head. "They are achieving more or less bloodlessly what the czars tried to do with wars. There is no improvisation in Moscow. The strategy has not changed from the days of Peter the Great.

"Bulgaria must learn to live with Russia. Russia is the vastest country in the region and sentimentally Russia means a lot to us. But I am troubled by the unfortunate hatred Bulgarians have developed for Russia in these past thirty years of Communist rule. It will take time to reeducate our people."

If Simeon's praise for Russia appears fulsome, he is only following in the footsteps of predecessors who always tried to accommodate the giant neighbor. (Boris's father, Czar Ferdinand, however, made one huge error: in 1914, he sided with the Germans and against the Russians. He was forced to abdicate in 1918.) Simeon's hero is his father, Boris III, whom Winston Churchill called the Fox of the Balkan. Simeon cites with pride the World War II *bon mot* about Czar Boris: his people are pro-Russian, his army is pro-German, his diplomats are pro-British—and he alone is pro-

Bulgarian. Boris, surrounded during World War II by German armies and their allies, had no choice but to join the Axis. He permitted the Germans to use Bulgaria as a base for operations against Yugoslavia and Greece. He also took advantage of the war and occupied Macedonian and Thracian provinces long claimed by Bulgarian nationalists. But Boris refused to provide troops against Russia. In August 1943, Hitler summoned him to Berchtesgaden, but Boris was again evasive about increasing Bulgaria's contribution to the war. The meeting was stormy. Three days after his return to Sofia, Boris collapsed and died. Many of his subjects believed he had been poisoned. The Communist government, anxious not to make a martyr of Boris, refused to reveal details of its investigation.

It was in that fatal year for Hitler, 1943, that Simeon, then six, became czar of the Bulgars. When Hitler offered to serve as his guardian, Queen Mother Giovanna fled with Simeon first to neutral Turkey, then to Syria, which was already under Allied control. After the Germans retreated from Bulgaria and Bulgarian armies joined the Russians to fight the Nazis in Hungary and Germany, Giovanna returned home with Simeon. But the regency under Boris's brother Kyril was short-lived. Relying on the Red Army and on their own well-organized goon squads, Bulgarian Communists gradually took over the country. They executed the three regents, eight of Boris's closest advisors, and approximately a hundred politicians. In 1946, the Communists held a referendum, and a republic was declared.

Simeon, his mother, and eight retainers were allowed to leave the country. The Communist regime claimed it gave the royal family twenty million dollars for its properties, but Giovanna's story of arriving in Egypt with two hundred dollars seems more credible. In Alexandria, Giovanna joined her father, Victor Emmanuel of Italy, but until his death in 1947 the Bulgarian royal family was the poorest of European exiled royalty. After the legal battles with the Republic of Italy ended, Giovanna received one-seventh of her estimated fifteen-million-dollar inheritance.

In the 1950s, Simeon attended the University of Madrid, studying law and political science, but he was not an eager student. He also spent one year in an American military school, acquired a reputation as a fast skier, a good dancer, and a jet-setter and, for a few years, appeared to be favored by the Swedish royal family and its three princesses, his fifth cousins. But in 1961, Simeon married Dona Margarita Gomez-Acebo, a nonroyal Latin beauty, daughter of a Spanish financier executed by the Communists in the first months of the Civil War. She was one of the wealthiest women in Spain.

Simeon receives me in his library, a large, elegant room with nineteenth-century furniture, dozens of antique silver objects, and vintage oil paintings. The centerpiece is an elaborate traveling case that once belonged to great-great-grandfather Louis-Philippe, France's last king, banished in 1848. (Among other toilet articles in the case are a gold toothbrush and different seals for different moods.)

The books are in many languages: multivolume sets of Balzac, Conrad, and Mann; tomes on the histories of Bulgaria, France, Spain, Italy, Germany, and Russia; commemorative albums on the great battles of World Wars I and II; the commanding generals' accounts of German, British, and American military campaigns.

"I don't read these," Simeon says, "but I love books. Unfortunately, I have no time to read. I am a businessman, a jack-of-all-trades. I have always found one job a limitation. I can produce more when working for several companies. I provide consultation, I am a member of various corporate boards. I have financial interests in banks, hotels, and the production of television sets. But I suppose my keeping busy—very, very, busy—is part of a defense mechanism. I want to erase the impression that a king is a parasite and that an exiled king is even worse than that." A smile flickers across his face. "And since I married money—blue blood with money, to be precise—I want to prove that I don't just sit around, doing nothing. In fact, I have very little leisure time. I do a bit of skiing, and once or twice a year I go hunting, but I usually combine those activities with business." He gives his itinerary with gusto—Switzerland last week, Germany this week—he speaks as if his bags were packed to fly to the other end of the earth.

"Simeon has a nose for investing in the right kind of business enterprise," says one of his relatives. "Somebody has even suggested—and only half in jest—that he should be put in charge of all royal investments. Royalty Incorporated, we could call it."

For an investor Simeon has an unusual apocalyptic vision. He says he is terrified by what has been happening in Iran, and thinks that Saudi Arabia is the next target for insurrection and chaos. He fears that if Iran goes Communist, World War III will follow because the West cannot survive without Iran's oil, or Saudi Arabia's. "What I fear most," he says, "is what's called in billiards a *carambole multiple*—several balls hitting one another in rapid succession—China's new *Drang nach West*, the financial crisis gripping the United States and Western Europe, and Russia's insatiable appetite for conquest in the Third World."

But Simeon hedges his bets on the decline of the West. He believes that Russia is running headlong into a terrible crisis with its mounting economic problems, an inevitable conflict with China, and the unresolved tensions with minorities. This build-up reminds him of the one that led to the collapse of the czarist system in 1917.

"But the Communists are realists. Before a collapse they might just find it expedient to withdraw from Eastern Europe.

"In Bulgaria and elsewhere, Communist regimes are most unpopular, and consequently people tend to idealize the past," Simeon continues. "My father left an aura of popularity, and Bulgarians remember his wisdom." To be remembered with kindness back at home is another émigré myth that cannot be surrendered. "Should a power vacuum develop in Bulgaria, monarchy has a chance to return because people may want someone who stands for a lot of things—a man without hard feelings and without a desire for revenge. A man for all seasons. I am available."

King with a Sporting Chance
Constantine of Greece

Now my charms are all o'erthrown,
And what strength I have's mine own,—
Which is most faint

The Tempest

"Exile is a Greek habit," observes King Constantine II, who left Greece twelve years ago. "And a Greek royal habit, too. As is return to the homeland." He cites the example of his grandfather, Constantine I, who was forced to abdicate in 1917 because of pro-German sympathies (his wife was Kaiser Wilhelm's sister) but staged a triumphant reentry three years later—only to be banished again after two years. He died in exile in 1923. A military dictatorship toppled his son, George II, who returned home after ten years of exile in London to reign for five years and was then driven out once more, this time by Italian and German invaders. He died two years after his return to his country, which had been ravaged by Nazi occupation and subsequent civil war. Only the first king of modern Greece, Otto, never returned after banishment. The choice of the European powers in 1829, the seventeen-year-old Bavarian prince arrived in Greece aboard a British ship with 3,500 German soldiers and administrators ready to civilize the former Ottoman Empire province. He lasted eighteen frustrating years, and left unloved. He took his crown with him as a souvenir.

Of the three other kings of modern Greece, George I, son of a Danish king and the first of Constantine's dynasty, reigned for half a century until a madman assassinated him in 1913; Alexander I, picked by politicians who disregarded the monarchic law of succession, died in 1920 of gangrene resulting from his pet monkey's bite; and Paul I, who shared exile during World War II with his older brother George II and son Constantine, died in 1964.

"Mind you," Constantine says, "my predecessors were sent into exile by revolutions, never by the people. The people of Greece are monarchist in sentiment. The politicians are however . . ." His voice, a commanding baritone that befits his powerful physique,

173

fades out, and his eyes search the room for a suitable adjective. "Well," he finally announces, "the politicians are a different matter."

Sitting at ease in a leather swivel chair in his London office, he relates an incident that occurred last year in East Berlin where he attended a sporting event. He was about to go downstairs to check out of his hotel when a flustered desk clerk warned him by telephone that a large group of Greek Communist tourists had just entered the lobby. Constantine had a plane to catch. As he walked through the crowd with his suitcase, he was instantly recognized. The Communists jumped up to shake his hand, shouting "Constantine, Constantine" in their excitement. Some of them even kissed him. "But aren't you Communists?" he asked them. "Yes, of course," one of them replied, "but we are Greeks traveling abroad, and we are happy to run into another Greek."

"Those Communists reacted spontaneously," Constantine says. "If they had known in advance that they were going to meet me, or if they had five minutes to discuss what they should do, they might have reacted differently. But we Greeks are such an emotional people, and our politics are so very emotional.

"Take for instance the debate over the new constitution after the 1974 referendum decided in favor of a republic. When the new draft constitution was presented to Parliament, it had a clause forbidding my return to Greece, similar to the Italian legislation which keeps King Umberto abroad. But the cruelty of the clause upset members of Parliament, and some 100 or 150 people from various parties—and not all of them monarchists, by the way—spontaneously decided that they would change the constitution. It was an impulse, and they acted on it. They filibustered, and when around four in the morning they saw that many of those who were for keeping me out of the country went home to sleep, they demanded a vote, and they won. I had nothing to do with the action, and I learned about its details only a few days later. As a result, I can return home anytime I wish. I can run for a seat in Parliament. I can be president of the Republic. I can do anything I like. It's all quite normal. I carry a Greek passport. I even won a court case concerning my house and other property in Greece, and I am paying my taxes in Greece."

But Constantine's status is not all that normal. Should he suddenly land in Athens, the government might or might not arrest him. Many Greeks believe he would be sent out on the next plane.

Others argue that the democratic government of Greece could not and would not do anything. "The issue is academic," says one man who has been seeing Constantine regularly over the years. "He won't go back to Greece because there is nothing for him to do there anymore. He would be bored in a few days. He doesn't even have a house in Greece to go to. Would he stay in a hotel?"

Constantine has reached a satisfactory financial settlement with the republican regime. The compensation he has received is rumored to be around $30 million, and he has retained the services of one of Greece's smartest investment counselors. He is regarded as one of the richest of Europe's nonreigning royalty. One inventory, drawn up by the junta of the colonels after he left the country, included 30 cars, 27 yachts, 17,500 rare books, 12,000 paintings, 200 Byzantine icons, 900 other works of art, and a large estate near Athens worth four million dollars. He owns some property abroad, and purchased a $600,000 villa in a garden suburb of London.

His London headquarters is in a nineteenth-century townhouse on Grosvenor Street, just around the corner from Claridge's, the favorite hotel of royalty for the past fifty years. The directory in the foyer lists no one on the top floor, but evidently not for security reasons. A knowledgeable Londoner and friend of Constantine's explains that the problem is one of semantics. Should the sign read "The Offices of Ex-King Constantine"? "The Bureau of Royal Greece in Exile"? For reasons not entirely dissimilar, newspapers in Greece do not cover Constantine's activities, no matter how newsworthy. He has become a bit of an unperson.

His bureau consists of a suite of five rooms. He has two secretaries, part-time, and an aide-de-camp, a handsome, dapper general who is described as "a carpet for the king to walk on" or, as "the only man in Greece who resisted the colonels." When the junta's men pointed a gun at him, he drew his revolver but was overpowered.

The rooms are spacious and very quiet—a contrast with the typical exile organization's cracked linoleum floor, its beat-up desks competing for space with stacks of old newspapers and the ex-minister of agriculture shouting at the one bilingual secretary.

But Constantine's headquarters is not elegant. Most of the furniture is barely respectable. Constantine's office, carpeted and wallpapered beige, looks temporary—a refueling stop, a waystation. Maps of Greece and the Mediterranean cover the walls. A critic explains, "He would like people to forget that the royal family always asked for more money and that his sister Sophie took a dowry of $300,000 from the Greek treasury when she married Don Juan Carlos, the man who later became king of Spain."

The journey to London began on the morning of December 13, 1967, when Constantine activated his plan for a coup d'état. His objective was to topple the dictatorship of Colonel George Papadopoulos, whose original supporters had been about equally divided between traditional rightists favoring the monarchy and young zealots opposed to Constantine as part of the decadent Athens Establishment.

Constantine flew to a small town called Kavalla, but the military officers and people throughout the country who he thought would support him did not respond to his call for unity. There was confusion. People outside Kavalla and its environs did not hear his broadcast. In a BBC interview later, Constantine expressed regret that he had not addressed the masses directly in a large town such as Salonika, where he would have had a radio station at his disposal. He realized that when he finally said a few words to the people assembled on the town square of Kavalla "there was complete and total contact . . . they knew what I was standing for, and I knew what they wanted, and this would have happened the same way in Salonika and would have happened all the way down into Athens. . . . Equally, the navy and the air force were 100 percent on my side at the beginning."

By evening, Constantine had called off the coup because he feared fighting between military units, and he did not want bloodshed. "My ideal aim is to build my country and not to destroy it," he told BBC. He flew to Rome because he thought that in exile he could bring world attention to the necessity of restoring democracy in Greece. "When we left, of course it was very sad because we had failed from a military point of view," he told BBC. "But at least I felt happy knowing that the Greek people knew what I stood for, they accepted it, they wanted it, and in history we will always be closer and closer together."

"I could have stayed king," Constantine says to me. "The colonels wanted me to stay. But I have some very definite ideas about democracy, and I will not deviate from my ideals."

The royal rhetoric: the easy way rejected, victory even in defeat.

"Constantine had everything going for him, but no military coup in Greece has ever succeeded when launched from the provinces," says a veteran of the Greek officer corps whom I suspect of having done more than an academic study of coups. "You have to stage your coup in Athens or not at all, and all you need is a few good friends.

"The time to get started is between two and three in the morning. You don't need tanks; tanks are good for intimidation—later. Your military unit should be compact—between thirty and fifty men— and you should send them to take over the radio, the prime minister's office, and a ministry or two. To arrest the prime minister, you need a jeep with an officer and five soldiers. Not even his neighbors should know what happened. Everywhere, you point a gun and tell the few sleepy guards that you have come to take over on the king's order. The guards will not take any chances.

"When you take over the radio station, you must have your tape all prepared. You broadcast martial music at six a.m.—that puts people on notice that a coup is on. Then you broadcast the king's proclamation, and by the time people finish their breakfasts, they can go out to the street and demonstrate in support of the coup. By ten a.m., it's all over.

"You may move tanks around Athens in the early afternoon just to show force. But it's really the initial impact that does it."

Why didn't Constantine do that?

"It's the old story of having the wrong people around you. Constantine is a man of average intelligence. Not bright, not dumb. A nice average human being can do well on the top, but only if he is properly advised.

"His people had the staff officer mentality; they thought they needed tanks, a heavy force, numbers, and fire power. So they went to Kavalla, up north, where the bulk of the army was stationed, because of the tension with Turkey over Cyprus. Those staff officers didn't realize that there is no need for a superior force to stage a coup. You don't need tanks to take over a radio station guarded by twenty soldiers maximum. But you must have a powerful radio station to address the nation and you must have the tape ready while the king is busy talking to people someplace else. Constantine wasted time having his proclamation taped *after* the coup began, and it was a fatal mistake to take the tape to Thessaly, a small military radio station with a very limited range. Hardly anyone heard his message.

"A field officer or an intelligence officer understands what small numbers can do, and knows the principle that size of force must be relative to the target. He also knows that no Greek soldier would fight another Greek soldier or take responsibility for bloodshed. In Athens, Constantine's people wouldn't have had to kill anyone. In a properly managed coup, nobody need get hurt.

"Constantine could have done it easily. The colonels would not have been able to do anything. The army wouldn't have sided with them—and certainly not after they heard the news of the takeover on the Athens radio. Constantine would have been the hero."

Opponents of the junta either blamed the CIA for not backing the king's coup or blamed Constantine for botching things—just as they had blamed the CIA and Constantine for organizing, or at least tacitly approving, the colonels' seizure of power eight months earlier.

After the collapse of Constantine's coup and his flight to Rome, the junta promptly appointed a senior army officer as regent and proceeded to devise a new constitution to reduce the monarch's role to a purely ceremonial function. "This was the CIA advice to the colonels," one loyal supporter of Constantine's contends. "The CIA was anxious for the colonels to deemphasize the antidemocratic nature of their rule and thought that cutting the king down to size might help that." One of the authors of the constitution on the other hand insists that they felt that curbing the king's power was a necessary step toward restoration, and that insulating him from politics would have been to his advantage once back on the throne.

Constantine refused to accept the new constitution. He nevertheless continued to draw a tax-free allowance of $50,000 a month. The junta also paid his 150 servants to take care of the Royal Palace. Constantine maintained contact with the colonels through an aide, who shuttled between Athens and Rome, where Constantine kept a low-profile exile in a four-bedroom villa. He was reduced to one car, a blue Mercedes, and a court consisting of two aides and one lady-in-waiting for his wife Anne-Marie, born a Danish princess. Except for attending sporting events, the royal family, which includes three small children, lived a secluded life.

Rome society was disappointed. The royal couple did not go to parties, and failed to display any joy of life. Constantine danced badly, they observed, and when he made a pass at a woman, he did not follow it up. Anne-Marie was found to be short-tempered, vain, and spoiled; she couldn't get over having been the youngest and prettiest of King Frederick IX's three daughters. They were both poor conversationalists, it was decided, and, worst of all, they showed no inclination to learn Italian, nor any appreciation for Italy.

Time magazine called Constantine "lonely" and caught him in the act of pouring his own drink in Rome's Eden Hotel. "I never had a chance to pick up a bottle for myself before," *Time* quoted the king of the Hellenes.

The West European press thought that Constantine carefully avoided giving the colonels a pretext to cut off his allowance and perquisites. His supporters on the other hand called him "prisoner in exile." In the rare interview he granted to BBC, Constantine proposed that while some of the colonels' motives "were probably good ones, the way they went about it was wrong." He said he had not opposed the colonels' coup at its inception because of the immediate civic strife and bloodshed that would have resulted, and, later, he hoped that he could "guide" them toward democracy.

In June 1973, three Greek admirals raised the standard of the revolution against the tyranny of the colonels. The attempt failed, and the men asked for asylum in Italy. Constantine remained silent. He refused to speak to newsmen or to show his face to the crowd of photographers shaking the bars of his villa's wrought-iron fence. "I don't want to offend the army," he told antijunta politicians pleading with him to speak up.

The colonels charged that Constantine had masterminded the attempted coup and sought to establish a "royal dictatorship." They had been looking for a way to get rid of the king's shadow: Greece was still a monarchy and the king's photograph adorned the walls of government offices, including Prime Minister Papadopoulos's. Whatever his relationship with the colonels, his person represented democratic legality and a dangerous rallying point for opposition. One interpretation of the unsuccessful coup—rated as one of the most inept in the long history of Greek coups and countercoups— was that the colonels themselves had encouraged it in order to have a pretext to sever ties with Constantine.

After Constantine refused to move to Switzerland (the colonels having long felt that an Italian exile, just across the Adriatic from Greece, was too close for comfort) and refused to take a vow of political silence, the colonels stopped his allowance, confiscated his property in Greece, and organized a plebiscite on the monarchy, which they of course won. After six years in Rome, Constantine decided to leave for London. People speculated that it was because of family ties—both Constantine and his wife Anne-Marie are great-great-grandchildren of Queen Victoria and thus cousins to both Queen Elizabeth and Prince Philip—or because he intended to capitalize on British solicitude for Greek democracy, a tradition going back to the days of Lord Byron. "I leave Italy because I can't pay my rent," Constantine explained. He told the press that he was looking for "a decent job" to support his family. "I have no specialization," he confided in a reporter friend in a Rome bar. "What about journalism?" he asked, "can one make a living?"

Five months later, the colonels were thrown out of power. The revolution promptly restored the old constitution, but with one significant difference: the new prime minister of national unity, Constantine Caramanlis, submitted to a referendum the question of the form of government. Caramanlis, regarded as a leader of conservative (i.e., royalist) elements, did not appear to be anxious for a restoration of the monarchy. Some people thought that he wanted to placate the Left and that keeping Constantine out of the country was a cheap price to pay for a national unity government. Others suggested that he had not forgiven Constantine's father, King Paul, for dismissing him as prime minister nearly two decades earlier. Or, perhaps, he wanted no rival as the savior of Greek democracy.

Outside observers agree that in the campaign preceding the referendum Constantine was the best spokesman for the monarchist cause, and that his press conferences and messages made more of an impact than all the propaganda efforts on his behalf. (His enemies spread the rumor that the shah of Iran, a close friend, was Constantine's financial angel.) His slogan was "Crowned Democracy"; he proposed a Scandinavian-style system; his posters cried "Eagle, come home!" He said he had changed, that in exile he had become a sincere democrat. He conceded previous mistakes, such as the dissolution of Parliament, which many Greeks believe had paved the way for the colonels.

Working against him were charges of collusion with the dictatorship—he had signed some 200 emergency laws submitted to him by the colonels—and the unpopularity of his mother, Queen

Frederika. As a granddaughter of Kaiser Wilhelm, Frederika was accused of having been a spy for Germany, and many Greeks were firmly convinced that smart, greedy, pushy Frederika, rather than Constantine or his father Paul, ruled the country. The most effective weapon in the antimonarchist campaign was a poster with Frederika's picture captioned, "I am coming!"

All the major political parties declared themselves against Constantine's return. Despite pressure from both sides, Prime Minister Caramanlis stayed out of the campaign and, to this day, has kept his vote secret. But the abstention of the man who became a symbol of democracy was perhaps as damaging to the monarchist cause as the others' opposition. Royalists have compared his role to that of Pontius Pilate.

Constantine's final appeal was moving. "The great dream I have always cherished is to live in my homeland," he told the nation in a television address. "Whoever knows the bitterness of having to live in exile will understand me." He concluded, "I am at the service of Greece. Whatever may happen, I will serve and support Greece with self-sacrifice and with worship. It is my place and my house, the Fatherland and the home of my children. There are the tombs of my father and my ancestors."

Constantine's handsome face, so very Greek with its round features and soulful dark eyes, made a favorable impression. He might not have a drop of Greek blood—his ancestors were Danish and German—but Greek is his best language, he was educated in Greece, and he is the most Greek of all the kings of modern Greece.

But Constantine lost: 69 percent voted for the republic, 31 percent for the monarchy. The bulk of the monarchist vote came from rural areas, from women and old people. After 111 years, the House of Schleswig-Holstein-Sonderburg-Glucksburg was succeeded by a democratic republic. *Burke's Peerage* summed up the feeling of Britons when it called "Constantine's embarrassing closeness to politics" the principal reason for his defeat. *Le Monde* characterized Constantine as "more seductive than able" and contended that he neither deserved the throne nor knew how to defend it.

"He is gutless and inept," bristled one journalist the junta had expelled from Athens. "Had he ignored his advisors always advising caution and had he come out against the junta earlier and stronger, he would have won. He can only blame himself."

This was the sixth such referendum in Greek history. Three of them were won by the republic, three by the monarchy.

"Considering that we had only a few weeks to prepare a campaign and that we had virtually no money," Constantine says, "we didn't do badly." He charges that the democratic government acted unconstitutionally by putting only the form of government to vote, rather than the entire constitution. He was not informed properly· he learned about the referendum from a visiting journalist. He points out that the government refused to let him go home to campaign in person and that only at the very last minute was he permitted to address the Greek people on television.

Of all the nonreigning royalty in Europe, Constantine is the most confident about his return to the throne. But neither he nor his followers will hazard a guess as to when that might happen. His enemies and critics disagree that he has any chances at all. But "disagree" is an understatement, a pallid Anglo-Saxon word that does not convey the roar of Greeks debating in a coffeehouse, nor reflect the passionate loyalties and hatreds, often maintained through generations.

Constantine himself believes that Greece is drifting toward the Left, that under the current regime the country lacks direction and purpose, and that sooner or later Greeks will peer into the abyss of anarchy and withdraw, calling on him to restore stability. "The sentiment for monarchy is growing," he declares. He cites complaints about the inefficiency and waste under the republic: Prime Minister Caramanlis had an entourage of sixty people on his state visit to Paris, while he, Constantine, used to take no more than six. He charges that the government is spreading a dangerous euphoria about the importance of Greece's joining the Common Market instead of preparing the civil service and the people for higher standards of efficiency and productivity.

"Constantine is a fool, an idiot," I heard a Greek student in New York sputter. "He let the colonels take over because he thought that they would do things he wouldn't or couldn't do—such as repression of the opposition, restoration of the power of the Church, a return to the so-called ancient virtues. When Constantine realized that the colonels were inept and brutal, and would be thrown out of power sooner or later anyway, he tried to step in and to lead the countercoup to save his skin. But he fouled up his countercoup. He deserved to lose. Good riddance, I say, and may he never go back to Greece."

"Constantine is not a bad fellow, but his mother, Queen Frederika, was a Nazi, and has been a terrible influence on his life," a soft-spoken middle-class Greek in her fifties comments. "Fortunately, she now lives in India, far away from her son, and she spends her time contemplating her previous incarnations. His father, King Paul, was nice but weak. The only strong thing he did was to drive his sports car like an absolute maniac. With such parents, what do you expect of an only son?"

"Constantine didn't have a chance to prove himself," suggested an old companion of his, now in the diplomatic service. It took two weeks to arrange a meeting with him, through an intermediary, a childhood friend of his, a good friend of mine. The first appointment I set up he could not make; he canceled the second at the last minute. He finally succumbed to my telephone calls, and we met on the street and walked over to a dingy bar of his choice. He claimed that he barely knew Constantine—which our mutual friend dismissed as utter nonsense: the king trusted him; he was involved in one of Constantine's coup attempts; he sees the king at least once a year. He discounted Constantine's role in the 1973 countercoup against the colonels. Did Constantine know about the countercoup, I asked. "Everybody in Greece knew about the king's coup for months. You sense when a coup is on its way. Greece is a small country, and people know when the time is ripe for a coup and where it will come from." He said he had no idea of what Constantine may be doing now. "Is Constantine still in London?" he asked me with a perfectly straight face. After some coaxing and prodding and quite a bit of Scotch, he finally hazarded a judgment: "Constantine reigned for three years, and he was just getting his ideas translated into action. He is a decent man but unlucky. Fate sent him the colonels to mess up everything." He blurted out that it might prove "embarrassing" for Constantine to return home now or in the near future. He would not elaborate. "Please understand," he pleads, "I am a civil servant. I can't talk about such things. Not even as a private citizen. It's all very complicated."

"In exile, Constantine has conducted himself with dignity," notes a Greek law professor, a monarchist. "No scrapes, no scandals. That's important for the future. But his unwillingness to speak with the press since the referendum works against him. Silence is golden, but it can kill a politician. If he stays silent, he will be forgotten."

He should stick to his sports," advises an Athens intellectual. "He shouldn't try to be a politician. He will always be outsmarted. Greek politicians are much too clever for him."

Perhaps there is something in that. Constantine, forty and a strapping six-footer, is the only Olympic gold medal winner modern Greece has produced—in sailing. He is also a third degree black belt in karate. A Briton tells me, "He knows sports, and what's more he knows that in sports what matters is who gets there faster or who gets the puck or the ball. Not who you are. You can't pull rank when you compete in sports. I say that's what's great about sports: it's true democracy."

"I am very competitive," Constantine admits. "I like winning, and I never really liked sailing for the fun of it only." He credits Danish yachtsman Paul Elvstrom, an Olympic gold medal winner in 1948, 1952, 1956, and 1960, as responsible for his triumph in the Rome Olympics in 1960.

"Sailing is for the young," Constantine declares, "I am too old for it." There is no regret in his voice. He still looks and speaks like a champion. In 1972, he entered the pre-Olympics in sailing and qualified as number six in a field of sixty-four. The next Greek ranked number forty. "I did it in order to prove to myself that I could still do it," he explains. But he did not enter the Olympics which, unlike the pre-Olympics, are not held on an individual basis, because he would have had to represent the Greece of the colonels.

He has not sailed since 1972 because, he found out, he cannot keep up with the faster reflexes of younger people. "You must see every tiny ripple, any turbulence, any darkening of the water that comes before a turbulence, and react to it right away so you gain a foot or more over your opponents," he says. "I am now forty and cannot do that as well as a twenty year old. Elvstrom, who is now almost fifty, told me that on one occasion recently, he capsized. Imagine that—a four-time Olympic champion capsizing! It's tough. So instead of sailing, I play golf, have taken up tennis and squash, and do a lot of horseback riding. I keep myself in good shape."

He is also very busy with politics. But he eschews publicity and declines interviews. The audience he granted me is the first, or so I am told, granted to a journalist since 1974.

Still, he cannot help getting into the limelight. During a private visit to New York in 1978, he telephoned some old friends on the Senate Foreign Relations Committee "just to say hello." They insisted that he come to Washington. Constantine says that he had not intended to visit Washington because he did not want to give the impression of lobbying with Americans on his own behalf. But his friends—Senators Jacob Javits, Claiborne Pell, and others— prevailed upon him to join them for what they said would be a small, private lunch to talk about old times.

Constantine was astonished to find that almost the entire Foreign Relations Committee had showed up, and that the senators used the occasion to solicit his views on the arms embargo to Turkey, which President Jimmy Carter had asked them to lift. First, Constantine assured the senators that he was not sent by the government, that he represented nobody but himself. Then he proceeded to deride Carter's request that Congress remove the "humiliation" of the arms embargo, originally imposed after Turkey invaded Cyprus. Turkey is the aggressor in Cyprus, Constantine held; its army of occupation uprooted 250,000 Greeks. If the embargo is lifted, the Turks will be encouraged in their resistance to a fair, negotiated settlement in Cyprus, and in the upcoming municipal elections the Greeks will vote Left—and anti-American. Moreover, the region will drift toward more instability. Didn't Jimmy Carter get 90 percent of the Greek-American vote by promising in unequivocal terms that he would keep the arms embargo? America must keep its word and Americans must learn not to make hasty, ill-considered moves in a region steeped in historical animosities and possessed of great complexities.

"I turned around the vote in the Foreign Relations Committee," Constantine says, "and at a time when the Greek government had given up all hope."

He impressed his American hosts with his straightforward, unpretentious manner. He never put on the airs of a monarch, yet he was a king.

But, Constantine insists, he wanted no publicity on his achievement, and he was "mortified" when, attending the session of the committee a few hours after the lunch, Chairman Frank Church identified him in the audience and the committee gave him a standing ovation. His protestations about not wanting publicity, however, strike observers as a bit exaggerated, even disingenuous. Constantine, after all, seemed eager to relate the details of the story to several newsmen, and to all his friends who came to see him. A few months later, after more White House maneuvering and the beginnings of the ayatollahs' pressure on the shah of Iran, the Carter administration succeeded in its efforts to lift the arms embargo to Turkey. Constantine nevertheless had the satisfaction of having been proven right in his dire prophecies about the continuing stalemate in Cyprus, the leftward lurch in Greece, and the descent into regional instability.

Constantine travels all the time. He is active in the International Olympic Committee and attends conferences on sports, particularly sailing. He and his wife Anne-Marie often fly to Spain, France, and Germany for a dinner party, a country weekend or a sporting event. Their hosts are usually royalty or aristocracy, not jet-setters. In England, too, they are sought-after guests in upper-class circles; their presence is regarded as an ornament to any party. A few times a year they are invited by the British royal couple for a meal or tea or a hunt, but the relationship is not a warm one; Prince Philip is said to dislike Constantine. "Constantine reminds Philip of his Greek ancestry, which is of course really German," says one insider. "Even when Greece was a kingdom, Philip avoided going there. He has a thing about wanting to be considered 100 percent British."

At least twice a year, Constantine and Anne-Marie go to Denmark and stay in one of the spare castles belonging to Anne-Marie's older sister, Queen Margrethe II. Anne-Marie is sweet and charming, pretty with small features and strong blue eyes. "There is a deliberate simplicity about her," one observer notes. "She is a typical product of Scandinavian royalty: cheerful, low-key, contemporary, and democratic to the point of being middle class. She is a good mother and doesn't gripe about the muddle Constantine got himself into. She is good for him."

They chose to live in London because unlike Rome, which they found "chokingly provincial, really awful," London is an "exciting, truly cosmopolitan city, with great theater, opera, music, and restaurants, and with everyone important passing through at one time or another." Constantine says that there is a constant stream of visitors to his house and his office, and his telephones never stop ringing. On St. Constantine's Day he received hundreds of cables, letters, and bouquets of flowers. Greeks from all parts of the world sent him their best wishes. He was on the telephone from six in the morning until midnight.

Constantine says that the Greek government does not disapprove of contact with him, and that among his visitors are diplomats and other government officials. Constantine stresses the normalcy of his position. But the salient fact is that contact with him has to be kept confidential. It is as if he did not exist. When Greece learned from the BBC and the foreign press of his intervention in Washington in the Turkish arms embargo debate there was not a word about it in the Greek papers. There is no censorship in Greece; it is not illegal to write about Constantine. But somehow writers and editors prefer not to mention him.

While Constantine's opponents are outspoken, his friends are evasive, diffident, and elusive. A favorite theory of theirs is that the leftist cycle of Greek politics, unchecked since the revolution of 1973, is now nearing completion, and when Greece faces its next great crisis—a threat from the Left—Constantine will be the man to turn to. Another apocalyptic scenario sees him returning after Turkey defeats Greece and humiliates the army; in the ensuing chaos and desperation, Constantine would serve as a symbol of unity. But Constantine knows that the wisdom of "time is not ripe" is a recipe for endless delay, and that it is up to him to prepare his passage home.

The Greeks invented exile so that there could be a return; the sweetness of the homeland is increased by the bitterness of exile. The tension between the two yields one of the basic dialectics of Greek life and letters, and creates additional fissures and contradictions that impress outside observers as chronic instability. Confined in exile, or confined at home, Constantine would be bored, an ex-champion. The rules of the game demand that he prove his cunning in plotting his return. He has a sporting chance.

Refugee from Eastern Europe
King Michael

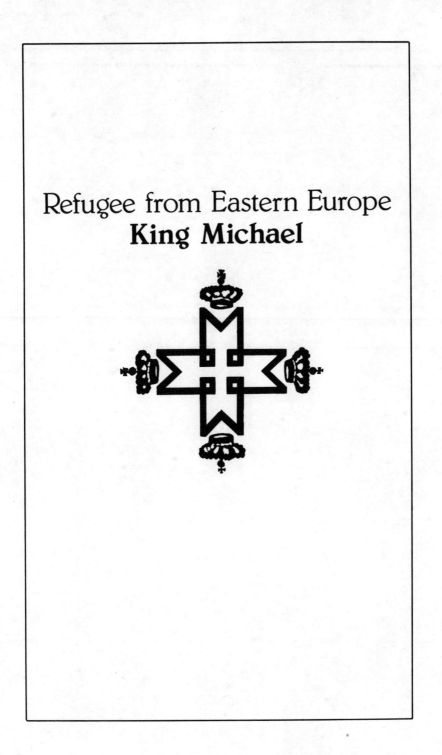

What must the king do now? must he submit?
The king shall do it: must he be depos'd?
The king shall be contented: must he lose
The name of king?

King Richard II

In the garage of King Michael's house in the Swiss township of Versoix, a few miles from the old League of Nations headquarters in Geneva, stands a U.S. Army jeep, built in the Dearborn plant of the Ford Motor Company in 1942. A leather case in its glove compartment contains a copy of a letter, signed in 1944 by Brig. Gen. C.V.R. Schuyler, American Representative of the Allied Military Armistice Commission for Romania. "The transfer of title and ownership," the letter says, "is duly authorized in recognition of the generous assistance His Majesty King Michael gave in the betterment of the plight of Allied Air Force personnel" captured in Romania during World War II.

When the Communists forced him to abdicate on December 30, 1947, the jeep was part of a three-car caravan of Michael's personal effects. "It's my favorite car," Michael declares, "the others are for transportation." He points to two Volkswagen beetles in the immaculately clean garage. The jeep shows only 52,300 miles; the seats were recently reupholstered with authentic khaki canvas. "I love this jeep," Michael says, and for the first and only time during our conversation of several hours, there is a sparkle in his eyes. He wipes an invisible speck of dirt from the hood. "I take care of all the repairs and maintenance myself. It's in excellent condition. I have replaced the carburetor and painted the body twice. I am a born grease monkey, you know." He emits a sound that is a cross between a grunt and a giggle.

Michael is 6'3", broad-shouldered, thickening in the middle. His hands are as large as shovels, and thick-fingered. As he speaks— reluctantly and with a slight slur—he seems to want to hide his hands; they seem to get in his way.

As a youth he was unusually handsome; throughout Romania schoolgirls cut his picture from magazines and carried them in their handbags. Pregnant peasant women stared at photographs of him in stores and railway stations in hopes that their children would look like him. He resembled his father, King Karol II, but had none of Karol's rakery and swagger. Now he looks a decade younger than his fifty-seven years. There are furrows in his forehead, but he has kept a hint of his bashful smile. He is gawky in a boyish way.

"Michael is not unlike the storybook king who was handsome, loved by his people, but unhappy," wrote Simon Bourgin, an American correspondent for *Time-Life* in Bucharest in 1946. "Despite the castle at Sinaia, the automobiles, the speed boats and the El Grecos, Michael is a lonesome young man. As each month goes by, he finds himself more and more isolated from his people. At least figuratively, he is a prisoner in his castle."

For all his links to the Court of St. James—he resembles his cousins George VI and the duke of Windsor, and his blue eyes are those of Queen Victoria, his great-great-grandmother—Michael is a refugee from communism. He is one of the more than three million East Europeans who fled to the West during the Cold War, in the quarter-century between the end of World War II and Henry Kissinger's promulgation of detente.

Lost to him in the 1940s—needlessly, foolishly, and perhaps irretrievably—was the land where, up to his twenty-sixth year, his life had a purpose and the people were his people. He carries wounds that never heal. Still burning in him is the helpless rage he felt as he watched the Russians violate the terms of their wartime alliance, while the Western powers, sealing the fate of his country, acted as bystanders and hypocritical counselors.

It was Andrey Vishinsky, Russia's deputy foreign minister, who arrived in post-World War II Romania to pick a prime minister. "I want Groza," he declared. Petru Groza, the head of a supposedly non-Communist party was in fact a Communist stooge—or anyone's stooge, if the price were paid. He said he was the wealthiest landowner in Transylvania; he boasted of the illegitimate children he had sired; he made passes at his colleagues' wives, visiting newspaperwomen, anything in a skirt. As a cabinet minister in 1920, he built a large villa in what was his hometown's public park. He explained: "It shows that I am a poor man—I don't even own the land on which to build a house."

Michael detested Groza, and wanted an independent-minded

premier, but when he appealed for support in Washington and London he got none, though the three Great Powers had agreed at Yalta to share responsibility for liberated countries. So he accepted Groza under protest. "When I later told Groza to resign, he refused," Michael recalls. "Then I refused to have anything to do with the government thus rendered illegal. I went on strike. I didn't sign decrees. Nothing. The Russians sent me threatening notes and sent complaints to the United States and Britain. Finally, the Russians dispatched to Bucharest Vishinsky, and the Americans dispatched Averell Harriman. To fix things up, Harriman thought we ought to have elections. I privately warned him that elections must be properly supervised, otherwise the Communists, with the help of the Red Army, would take over. Harriman ignored my warning.

"There were no more than 1,000 Communist Party members in Romania at the end of the war, yet the Americans insisted that they be brought into the government coalition. It was useless to try to convince the Americans that Communists have a different concept of democracy and that Russians do not have the same respect for agreements as Anglo-Saxons.

"In a Communist system, you cannot tell what is legal and what is not, and there is no respect for the constitution. I don't call it legal when your telephone is cut off, a regiment of soldiers point their guns at your house, and you are asked to sign a document of abdication that claims that what you are doing is of your free choice.

"The West abandoned Romania as it abandoned the rest of Eastern Europe. At Yalta and in Tehran, Winston Churchill and Franklin Roosevelt handed us over to the Russians. We didn't know it at the time, so we tried to put up a fight to keep our independence. But without Western backing, it was a futile struggle. We were betrayed."

Michael's voice is flat, drained of indignation. This is an argument he has made many times since he arrived in the West in January 1948. He speaks as if to himself. He sits motionless, ramrod-straight in a frayed, overstuffed armchair; his enormous hands are poised on his knees.

"I have no regret over what we did," he says. "We did what we could, and I don't know what else we could have done, and I don't think we could have carried on much longer."

Many officials in the State Department and Whitehall thought that the Romanians were getting what they deserved: a dictatorship of the Left and a red terror of social justice, following various dictatorships of the Right and a frenzy of class privilege.

Romania's reputation as undemocratic goes back to the days of Michael's father, Karol II, whom the Cambridge historian of Eastern Europe, Hugh Seton-Watson, characterized as "superficially brilliant and basically ignorant, gifted with enormous energy and unlimited lust for power, a lover of demagogy, melodrama and bombastic speeches." After marrying Princess Helena of Greece (a sister of George II) and siring Michael in 1921, Crown Prince Karol abandoned his wife, a strikingly beautiful woman with whom he had once been passionately in love. He went to live with Elena Wolf, better known to the world as Magda Lupescu. (A West European newspaper once mistakenly called her Magda, and the name stuck, because "Magda" offered a flavor of sin and intrigue. Lupescu was simply the Romanian translation of Wolf. She preferred to be addressed as Madame Lupescu.)

She was a shrewd, seductive femme fatale—a redhead with a snow-white complexion. During World War I, she consorted with army officers—it is not clear whether she sold her favors or merely offered them—and one of her friends went as far as marrying her. She was emphatically "common." She boasted that only she could satisfy Karol's sexual appetite and strange whims.

The blatancy of the liaison shocked Romanians who, though proud of their Latin worldliness, prefer secret vices quietly pursued. In 1925, responding to court pressure and popular demand, Karol renounced his right to succeed his father, King Ferdinand, and moved to Paris with Mme. Lupescu. After Ferdinand's death in 1927, Michael was declared king. He was six years old.

But regencies traditionally generate uncertainty. In 1930, Prime Minister Iuliu Maniu, a statesman committed to land reform and social justice, took it upon himself to interpret national sentiment by offering the crown to Karol on the condition that Mme. Lupescu stay in Paris. Karol promptly accepted the deal and returned to Bucharest. Wildly enthusiastic crowds greeted him; hopes for a new Augustan Age arose.

Three weeks later, Mme. Lupescu rejoined King Karol II, and Queen Helena donned a widow's black veils to shield her from a mocking world—she still wears them. Maniu was discredited, his democratically elected government fell, and Romania slid into ten years of Karol's rigged elections and anti-Semitic riots.

In 1940, a mob surrounded the Royal Palace and demanded that the king hand over his mistress. In a few days, the Iron Guard—first supported, then criticized by Karol, and subsidized by the Nazis throughout—forced his abdication, citing his pro-British sentiments and Mme. Lupescu's Jewish father.

Karol asked for asylum in Germany. The Führer said, "All right, but I won't take the woman." Karol left Bucharest for Switzerland on the royal train, a saloon car and eight cars packed with his possessions. Mme. Lupescu was with him. In the Transylvanian town of Timişoara, the men of the Iron Guard waited, planning to abduct Mme. Lupescu when the train stopped to take water. But word reached someone in Karol's entourage, and the train sped through Timişoara. As a precaution, Mme. Lupescu hid in the bath tub and Karol sat gallantly on its wooden cover.

The Iron Guard, army generals, and their German allies calculated that Michael, then nineteen, would be a perfect figurehead king. He was known to be timid and apolitical. He kept out of the murderous power struggle that developed between the officers of the army and the terrorist units of the Iron Guard, which was Eastern Europe's most powerful Fascist movement and the only one with genuine mass appeal. Due to the army's ambitiousness, Romania ranked first among the junior Axis partners in the magnitude of its war effort. At Stalingrad, fifteen Romanian divisions shared the German debacle.

The finest moment in Michael's life—the one glorious, sovereign decision of his reign—came on August 23, 1944, when, at the age of twenty-three, he challenged Romania's führer, Marshal Ion Antonescu. According to Michael's account, he startled Antonescu by offering his own assessment of the military situation, which he saw as critical, and then ordered him to negotiate an armistice with the Allies. The tough old marshal, who had a reputation for standing up to Hitler and earning his respect, laughed. He refused to renounce the alliance with the Nazis. Antonescu claimed that they would withdraw to the Carpathian mountains, an impenetrable citadel. Michael countered that the country would then be destroyed. He saw no course of action save suing for peace. When Antonescu refused, Michael told him that he had no choice but to fire him. Speaking of himself in the third person, as was his habit, Antonescu asked, "Who will replace Antonescu?" Michael said, "You leave me with only one alternative."

"One alternative" was the prearranged signal. An army captain and three guards entered the room and arrested Antonescu. The conspirators then summoned Antonescu's main supporters to the palace. One by one, they came and were arrested and detained in the spacious vault Karol had built for his magnificent stamp collection. Four hours after Antonescu's arrest, Michael addressed the nation on the radio and Romanian troops on the Russian front ceased fire immediately. By eleven p.m., an hour later, enormous crowds were dancing the hora, Romania's national dance, on the streets of Bucharest and shouting, "Long live the king!"

No Romanian resisted the king's command for an armistice. The stunningly simple coup d'état worked, becoming the war's one decisive switch from the German to the Allied side—the Italians and the Hungarians delayed and eventually botched their plans, the Japanese never gave serious thought to abandoning their German ally, and the Bulgarians switched only after Romania, their northern neighbor, greatly diminished the chance of a German reprisal. It was a mighty gamble; Michael caught both friends and enemies by surprise.

The Germans, who had been compelled to pull their ground forces out of Romania, were furious, and bombed Bucharest. Two days later, Romania declared war on Germany, and the Russians were presented with the fait accompli of an independent Romania playing its own role in the war against Nazism.

There are different versions of the drama of August 23, 1944. Rightwingers claim that Antonescu had a much better plan to pull out of the war, and that Michael, overly anxious to please the Russians and jealous of Antonescu, bungled everything. They charge the king with responsibility for the eventual Russian takeover. Official Soviet history barely mentions Romania's joining the Allies, and claims that the Red Army liberated Romania. At the time Romanian Communists claimed that a key Communist leader had swayed Michael; but since 1948, they no longer mention Michael. "I don't accept the king's version and I don't accept his enemies' versions," confides a high-ranking Romanian diplomat who participated in the events. "I think everybody is lying, in different measures, of course. We'll never know the truth—if there is a truth to be known."

The impact of the coup, however, is indisputable: the pro-German regime in Bulgaria fell immediately, and the collapse of the Axis forces in the Balkan and Central Europe was accelerated. According to Seton-Watson, had it not been for Romania's break with Germany, "the losses of the Western armies in France would have been higher, and so would those among the civilian population of Great Britain and the Netherlands from V-bombs." The Russians awarded Michael the Order of Victory—their highest military decoration, given only to people such as General Eisenhower and Field Marshal Montgomery.

"I knew that the Order of Victory was a bribe," Michael now says. "And when I now think of that confrontation with Antonescu, I believe I must have been out of my mind to do it that way. We could have been foiled easily. And I find it astonishing that the Germans did not discover that we had been in touch with the Allies for two years prior to our breakaway. In 1943, for instance, we suggested to the Americans and the British that they stage a massive airborne landing in an area of Romania we'd prepare for them. But we never received a response. Now we know that the West had an agreement with the Soviet Union: no Western troops to be introduced in the Russian sphere of influence. And of course Romania was in the Russian sphere."

In 1945, with Romanian troops fighting alongside the Red Army in Hungary, Czechoslovakia, and Germany, the Russians thought of recalling Karol from his exile in Brazil. As past masters of the imperial game of divide and rule, they wanted to pit the unpopular Karol against Michael, who proved his mettle in the Antonescu affair. Karol, who considered himself the true king, needed little encouragement.

On instructions from Michael, Romania's chargé d'affaires in Lisbon turned to dictator Oliveira Salazar and asked him to block Karol's landing in Portugal. Dr. Salazar first argued that the experienced Karol would be better qualified to cope with the Communists than his young son. The Romanian diplomat cited Michael's courage and popularity, and, in the end, persuaded Salazar to cancel Karol's Portuguese visa.

Finding no other European country to serve as his transit point,

Karol had to give up plans for his second return to the throne. But he never spoke to his son again.

In the early 1950s, he settled in Portugal's colony of nonreigning monarchs, near Lisbon. He ate well and lived lavishly. His one sport was shooting pigeons in a local club. On account of "common" Mme. Lupescu, exiled royalty boycotted him. He left his estate to Mme. Lupescu who, when suspected of having terminal leukemia in 1947, asked that he marry her. He did, investing her with the title princess of Romania. Mme. Lupescu recovered and lived in good health for another thirty years. Karol died in 1953, in Estoril, Portugal.

Mystery surrounds the fate of Karol's fortune. As his abdication settlement, he took out of Romania considerable cash, rare antiques and paintings, and his famous collection of stamps and coins. A beneficiary of the Romanian economic boom of the 1930s, he had millions of dollars in Swiss banks. Yet after the death in 1978 of the childless Mme. Lupescu, the smartest lawyers in Portugal, France, and Switzerland have found nothing of value left.

As legend has it, Michael goes once or twice a year to a certain bank in Zurich and asks for his father's special account. Courteously reminded that the code word is necessary, Michael tries another word every time. He has never hit upon the right word and without it, the bank cannot unlock the account.

There probably is an account; Karol was a man who hoarded his secrets as much as he hoarded his possessions. He hated his son with the rake's hate of the puritan. Michael did inherit half of a villa in the south of France, with years of unpaid taxes and a collapsing roof. The other half went to his half-brother, Mircea, the product of Karol's first and secret marriage to the lovely teenage daughter of a socially prominent Romanian family, Zizi Lambrino.

Karol was an early admirer of Mussolini and saw himself as the savior of Romania. At the same time, he was an Edwardian voluptuary—a disciple of Queen Victoria's eldest son, who in the opinion of Europe, "knew how to live." Karol's misfortune was that he lived in a bloodier age than Edward VII, and he had to contend with Hitler and Stalin. His own subjects, heirs to a tumultuous history of subjugations, saw him as another Byzantine potentate, another Turkish pasha.

Michael does not remember a time when his parents were on speaking terms. "When I needed a mother I had a father," he is said to have remarked once, "and when I had a mother I needed a father." Karol's one favor to his son was his insistence on a strict and democratic education—the best any Balkan king ever had. On Karol's orders, boys representing different ethnic groups and social classes were summoned to the palace to form a school in which Michael was taught like a commoner. Michael liked his classmates and he was well liked among them. The classroom left him with only a trace of the stammer he had had, and his shyness, originally of pathological dimension, diminished. Instead of a hothouse Hohenzollern, he became a natural Romanian.

While some Romanians were confident that their democratic leaders could outfox and corrupt the Russians after World War II, Michael never entertained such illusions. He stayed on because he thought that leaving would be tantamount to desertion—a point impressed on him privately by Winston Churchill at the wedding of Michael's cousins, the then Princess Elizabeth and Prince Philip. Oddly enough, Michael's British relatives advised him to quit Romania as soon as possible. They thought that for the sake of his own safety, he ought not to return to what was, by 1947, a Communist dictatorship. The Russians and their Romanian clients were sure that Michael would remain in London, and were disappointed when he returned home. Nine days after he did, he received two visitors who presented him with an ultimatum. The nominally non-Communist prime minister, Petru Groza, first explained that for Michael, an offer of abdication was a good bargain: he would be allowed to leave in dignity, take his possessions with him, and remain a Romanian citizen. When things calmed down, he might even return for a visit. Groza's partner, the dour Communist Party chief Gheorghe Gheorghiu-Dej, then called the king's continuing presence "an obstacle to the development of communism," and threatened the disclosure of incriminating evidence about Michael's plotting with Fascists as well as other enemies of "the Romania of the People," the United States, and Britain. Michael countered that the issue of monarchy was constitutional and must be decided by the people.

"Not necessary," the Communist boss replied, "since it is clear that the people's happiness would be guaranteed in a people's democracy."

Michael refused to sign the abdication document. During the

half-hour he was given to reconsider, Michael noted that Communist troops had surrounded the palace, and that his telephone had been disconnected. Michael refused again. Groza threatened to arrest all opposition politicians even though bloodshed, perhaps civil war, for which Michael would be responsible, might follow. Michael, wanting no bloodshed, signed the document of abdication, and a few hours later the government announced the establishment of a people's republic.

Michael's departure ended a bizarre ritual of mutual deception—a minuet of Queen Victoria and Comrade Stalin. Prewar politicians who joined the government as Communist sympathizers occasionally signaled to the king that they were playing a game and that in truth, they were on his side. Leaders of the Communist Party, of working class origin, took tea in the Royal Palace and dressed according to the protocol insisted on by King Michael and his mother Queen Helen: tails with white tie or long evening dresses. Michael made speeches written by Communist propagandists, and the people, who believed that the hero who defeated the Germans would keep out the Russians too, applauded with the traditional cry, "Long live the king."

Karol's sister Ileana, wife of Archduke Anton Habsburg, took as her lover Emil Bodnaras, the NKVD-trained boss of the Communist secret police in Romania. A Nazi sympathizer during the war, Ileana used her connection to Bodnaras to advance the claims of her son, Stefan, as a replacement for the obstreperous Michael. Her sister Elizabeth, the divorced wife of George II of Greece, also had a political bed companion, a Romanian businessman with excellent Russian contacts. He managed Elizabeth's considerable wealth in business firms, real estate, and banking interests, forming joint companies with the Russians.

Ana Pauker, the ideologue of the Communist Party, was a frequent visitor to the Royal Palace. She had an illegitimate daughter by French Communist Party chief Maurice Thorez. In the 1930s, she approved of her husband's execution in Moscow as a Trotskyite. "If he was against Stalin," she said at the time, "he was no longer my husband. He deserved to be shot." The daughter of an Orthodox rabbi, she was a big, blowzy woman with a sex appeal that was, as in Mme. Lupescu's case, "common." One of her three villas—she alternated, fearing assassination—had once belonged to Mme. Lupescu. She was also a sparkling conversationalist.

Once, after taking tea with Michael's straight-laced mother, Queen Helen, Ana Pauker asked politely: "Should you dismiss me, or should I leave? I have enjoyed myself so much that I have forgotten just what the protocol is."

When Michael left Romania, an honor guard saluted him for the last time. The Communist-controlled press declared that his abdication was in response to the demands of "patriots." These days Michael is pessimistic in the short term. He sees no discernible possibility of dislodging the Russians from Romania or from anywhere in Eastern Europe. But he is optimistic in the long run because he believes that Communist rule outside the Soviet Union cannot last forever.

He considers Romania's present independent line "a lot of hot air, a tactic designed to win Western favor, trade, credits. Internally, Romania is more Stalinist than even Czechoslovakia." The Romanian balancing act has historical precedents. Descended from the ancient Roman legions but following the faith of Byzantium, Romanians have straddled fences in numerous dilemmas. As vassals of the Ottoman Turks, they were ruled by Greek governors, and they achieved their independence by pitting Russia against the Austro-Hungarian monarchy, France against Turkey. King Karol II was an early practitioner of personal diplomacy, with Romanian neutrality as his calling card in the capitals of Europe. He said he believed that England and France would eventually triumph over Nazi Germany. Yet he was inordinately proud when his visit with Hitler turned out to be successful. In 1938, just before World War II erupted, Romania advocated neutrality with the slogan "guaranteed by London, armed by Berlin." Romanian politicians thought that Germany would protect them against Russia, intent upon taking the border province of Bessarabia, and against Hungary, determined to reclaim Transylvania. On both counts, Karol's hopes proved to be illusory.

Romania is one member of the Warsaw Pact that criticized the Soviet invasion of Czechoslovakia, and Bucharest is the only Communist capital that maintains relations with Jerusalem. President Nicolae Ceauşescu is the leading middleman in this age of middlemen. A proven method of contacting an enemy, in Peking, Hanoi, or Cairo, is to transmit a message through Bucharest. Ceauşescu is dedicated to better relations with the United States, and his appeal for joint ventures in technology is couched in a language of admiration for U.S. know-how. He gives the impression that U.S. assistance to Romania gives heart to all independently minded Communists in the bloc, and that U.S. friendship serves as a protective shield against Russian schemes.

Romanian monarchy would have celebrated its centennial in the 1970s. Its founder was a young officer in the Prussian army, the second son of the head of the House of Hohenzollern-Sigmaringen, a branch of the Hohenzollern family that stayed in the south of Germany and remained Catholic. They were known as Hohenzollern-Sigmaringen after their seat Sigmaringen on the Danube, and they were ignored for centuries as the country cousins of the mighty Hohenzollerns of Prussia, who went north in the fifteenth century.

In the 1860s, the Hohenzollern-Sigmaringen family suddenly found itself at the center of European attention. After Prince Karl was offered the Romanian principalities of Moldavia and Walachia, freshly liberated from Ottoman yoke, his older brother, Prince Leopold, was invited to rule Spain following the expulsion of Isabella II, the fat queen whose unabashed sexual adventures were the scandal of Europe. Chancellor Otto von Bismarck was delighted with the chance to extend the reign of German dynasties to Iberia and the Balkan, and he was furious when the Spanish offer was declined. Bismarck could not accept Prince Leopold's assessment that Spain was far too dangerous a place, and that France threatened the peaceful German emperor, Wilhelm I, with war. But Napoleon III, the emperor of France, had no objection to a lesser Hohenzollern for Romania. He calculated that a German prince there would put pressure on the Habsburgs. Also working in Prince Karl's favor was the fact that his maternal grandmother, Stephanie de Beauharnais, was the adopted daughter of Napoleon Bonaparte, his wife Josephine's daughter from her first marriage.

So the offer of the Romanian throne seemed solid, safe. The twenty-seven-year-old Karl looked up the country in an atlas and was impressed with its strategic location between the Ottoman and Habsburg empires, and between Russians and Balkan Slavs. But as Karl prepared to embark on his journey to the east on a Danube steamer, the Austro-Hungarian monarchy mobilized against Prussia. The German prince had to travel in utmost secrecy through enemy territory; his travel papers made him out to be a businessman bound for Odessa. When the steamer approached Turnu-Severin, the first Romanian port of call, Karl asked to be allowed ashore to stretch his legs. But there was something in his bearing upon stepping on the soil of his future kingdom that made the captain cry out: "By God, that must be the Hohenzollern prince!"

A few days later, upon meeting a delegation of his future subjects, Karl exclaimed: "Now I am a Romanian!" In 1886, a plebiscite declared him reigning prince. Twelve years later, he assumed the title Royal Highness. In 1881, "by unanimous vote of the representatives of the nation," Karl was proclaimed King Karol I. He was an authentic iron man of the nineteenth century—ambitious, wily, hard-working. He modeled his adoptive country after Prussia, and didn't quite succeed. But his reign of nearly half-a-century turned a ramshackle semi-Ottoman province of dissolute landowners, corrupt officials, and abjectly poor peasants into the leading nation of the Balkan Peninsula.

During the Franco-Prussian war of 1870-71, Karol set the pattern for his dynasty by expressing sympathy with his fiercely Francophile subjects, thus siding against his ancestral kinfolk. In World War I, his nephew and successor Ferdinand, who had also served in the Prussian army, was first neutral; then he declared war on Germany. Kaiser Wilhelm called him a traitor and caused his name to be struck from the Hohenzollern family records. In 1940, the Nazis inspired the abdication of Karol II, whom they distrusted. Michael, Romania's fourth and last king, turned against the Germans as soon as the *Wehrmacht's* losses made that practicable.

"Duty to country comes before family feeling," Michael explains, "no matter how difficult that may be. We cannot put personal sentiments ahead of national interests. Romanian kings may be twice German in terms of bloodlines, but twice we went off to fight the Germans.

"I was born in Romania; I am a Romanian. Nothing else matters. And now I am a Romanian refugee living in Switzerland. I get pushed around like any other refugee."

Michael's five daughters don't speak Romanian, much to his regret. The languages his family uses are English and French. Michael's wife, Princess Anne Bourbon-Parma, was born in Paris; her mother is a royal princess of Denmark. Escaping from the Nazi invaders with her parents, Michael's future wife arrived in New

York without money, and worked as a salesgirl. She returned to Europe after the landing in Normandy and enlisted as an ambulance driver in the French army. She was awarded a Croix de Guerre. Anne and Michael met at Princess Elizabeth's wedding in London, decided to get married after a brief acquaintance, and were united in the Royal Palace in Athens in a simple ceremony shortly after Michael left Romania.

"In spirit," Michael says, "my daughters are Romanian and they have been brought up in the Orthodox Church. They can't succeed me because the Romanian constitution excludes women from the throne. I cannot change the law, of course."

The daughters, the oldest of whom is twenty-nine and the youngest sixteen, are not married. Finding suitable husbands is a problem because Michael's modest circumstances do not permit his daughters the kind of lifestyle other princesses enjoy. A Romanian-born American millionaire, Michael Marinescu, gave scholarships to the two oldest daughters, but he died a few years ago. "Should there be a grandson one day, I may designate him as a successor," Michael explains. "But Parliament must consent first, according to the constitution of 1923. Our constitution was often criticized as giving too much power to Parliament. I think it's a good constitution and I stand by it."

On the possibility of his return to Romania, Michael says, "I always hope." His voice is flat; his face expressionless.

"Exile has been a succession of crises," he says, sighing. "I haven't stopped being in crisis since I left Romania."

His first venture, a vegetable and dairy farm outside London rented from a close friend, a member of the House of Lords, did not work out. Michael left England after four years. He then worked for an American aircraft company based in Geneva. He sold Lear executive jets in Europe, but found the European market limited. He also invented, patented, and sold a device that facilitates flying under hazardous conditions. In the early 1970s, he was retained by a Wall Street brokerage firm to sell stocks on commission.

Influential friends, such as his cousin King Constantine of Greece, have tried to help him, but Michael has not been a successful salesman. He is not the outgoing type, and he has not been able—or willing—to turn his royal status to commercial advantage.

"Right now, I am unemployed," he says, "I'm living off

investments and looking for a job. It's hard for a king to find a job. Do you know of anything that might interest me?"

He does not like discussing his status as an ex-king or a claimant. He does not usually receive newsmen and is furious with press accounts that call him one of the richest men in Europe before World War II and the ex-owner of 158 castles. "They must have counted every shed and outhouse to come up with that ridiculous figure," he says. "What rubbish! I was allowed to leave Romania with a few suitcases and some cash."

His circumstances are modest, and people close to him say that he is in serious financial difficulties. The compensation he received from the Romanian government was less than $100,000 and he has not earned much money since. He has not been able to buy a house, and his rented house outside Geneva is the Swiss equivalent of a middle-class suburban home.

"I keep busy," Michael says. "I swim, I do photography. My wife and I wrote a booklet on raising gentians, a dainty little flower not well known in Switzerland. I used to fly a lot; I got my license during the war, and later I got my American license in California when I worked for an aircraft company. Now I don't have much opportunity to fly.

"But there is metalwork. I like working with my hands best." He stretches his hands, examines them quizzically for a few seconds, as if to say: at least I am good with my hands. In the garage, he has a top-quality lathe and other equipment to work with metal. His workbench, tools, and accessories are impeccable. "Oh, I am neat," he says, "I believe one must always clean up one's mess."

There are few Romanians in Switzerland, and no more than 250,000 Romanians live in the West. Michael does not keep in touch with émigré politics or participate in émigré social life.

"There are too many agents sent out from Romania to stir up trouble," he says, "and it's hard to tell who is an agent and who isn't. I don't go to meetings and parties. I prefer to deal with people individually. There are some Romanians who come to see me, even visitors from home. Some I meet with pleasure. Others I am not so happy to see. The other day an industrial worker from Romania walked up to my house and rang the bell. We had a good talk."

Romanian émigrés call Michael a recluse, and many of the more recent arrivals are hardly aware of his existence. Rightwingers who sympathized with the Nazis and form the most vociferous émigré faction call him a traitor—or, at best, a bungler—for switching over to the Russians in 1944. Others criticize him for agreeing to deal with the Communists and maintaining the charade of a monarchy while the press was censored, and opposition politicians disappeared in jails and concentration camps. He should not have opened Parliament, thus lending legitimacy to an election that was rigged, they argue; he should not have countenanced the treason trials of democratic leaders.

Yet another group hostile to him consists of nationalists, many of whom opposed the Nazis and who believe that the Hohenzollerns, as foreigners installed by the Powers, should never have ruled Romania. That the Hohenzollerns are an ill-starred dynasty is one superstition that the Communists have not discouraged. In Romania itself there are no known monarchists among the few people brave enough to signal their dissent in a brutally Stalinist system.

Few émigrés are for Michael. After his expulsion there was an attempt to make him a symbol of resistance to the illegality of the Communist regime. Michael declined, thus alienating many anti-Communists.

"Michael has insulated himself from his supporters," a former ambassador of his observes. "Everybody who wants to contact him must go through his one-time aide, General Petru Lazar, who lives in London, and who built a wall around the king. By refusing to engage in political activities, Michael has gradually lost his reputation and authority. I am for the institution of monarchy, and I used to like Michael. Now I am no longer committed to him, and I'd settle for whatever decision the majority might reach once we have free elections."

In the tense weeks during and after the Soviet invasion of Czechoslovakia in August 1968, when the Romanians feared that they might be Russia's next target, a rumor swept through Romania: King Michael is on a visit to the country, driving his car himself as he usually did in the old days, and touring the places of his youth. He was invited by the government and met with President Ceaușescu, some people said. Others suggested that he came on his own and that the government complied with his request for a visa provided that he had disguised his identity.

No newspaper published a word on the subject. No one claimed to have actually spoken to the king, but there were people who said they had spotted him eating by himself in a quiet corner of a restaurant or walking around one of his palaces. He was seen in places throughout the country, and reports of sightings were so persistent that even skeptical journalists began to lend credence to the story. Everyone spoke about it: Communists and non-Communists, villagers, and townsfolk. Some old people were moved, and remembered the king as a youth and the challenger of the dictator Antonescu. The young and the middle-aged, for whom Michael is part of history, wondered whether his visit might not signal an improvement, if not a drastic change in relations with the Americans. For whatever disappointment Michael had with the United States, he was always regarded in Romania as the man the liberating Americans would bring back to power.

But after leaders stopped issuing patriotic appeals and canceled the special military drills, the sightings ceased as well, as it suddenly became clear that Michael's visit was a canard—and a cunning one. People concluded that the government floated the rumor in order to strengthen the feeling of all Romanians uniting in face of the Russian threat and to suggest a historical continuity between past and present crises of standing up to a Great Power.

Michael frequently travels to England, France, and, occasionally, the United States. He visits relatives, businessmen, officers from Romania's royal army and diplomatic corps. After he left Romania, his uncle, then King Paul of Greece, issued him a Greek passport that was renewed by Paul's son, Constantine. But since the time Greece became a republic, the Royal Greek passport has been invalid.

"There is never any trouble in England," Michael says, "but the French are testy. 'There is no more king in Greece, no more king in Romania,' a border guard lectured me once. 'The authorities that issued your passport no longer exist. Your papers are not in order.' 'You fix it,' I replied, 'what do you expect me to do?'"

Michael offers to drive me to the airport, which is very near his house. It's too cold to use the jeep, so we pile into a red Volkswagen beetle. In ten minutes, we are there.

"You see," he says, "we live near the airport. Just in case."

I finish his sentence. "Just in case you are called back home?"

His smile is melancholy. "Yes," he says, "just in case."

Computing Probabilities
Prince Alexander
of Yugoslavia

Your enemies are many, and not small; their practices
Must bear the same proportion; and not ever
The justice and truth o' the question carries
The due o' the verdict with it: at what ease
Might corrupt minds procure knaves as corrupt
To swear against you? such things have been done.
You are potently oppos'd; and with a malice
Of as great size. . . .
                              Go to, go to;
You take a precipice for no leap of danger,
And woo your own destruction

King Henry VIII

When Queen Alexandra went into labor in July 1945, Yugoslav royalists and Communists anxiously paced corridors—separate corridors—in London's exclusive hotel, Claridge's, which had been declared Yugoslav territory while she and her husband were there. Her husband was King Peter II, whose flight to Britain at the age of eighteen followed the German occupation of his country in 1941, and whose return the new Communist regime intended to postpone indefinitely. Peter's position would be strengthened if his wife bore him a son, while a daughter would further weaken the monarchy.

It was a boy, a crown prince named Alexander, and the godmother who held him at the baptismal fount in Westminster Abbey was Princess Elizabeth, next in line for the throne of the United Kingdom. In a few weeks, though, it became clear that the infant's father was beyond help. The British and the Americans had thrown their support behind Marshal Josip Broz-Tito, a Stalinist veteran of the Spanish civil war and the only resistance leader in Europe who had succeeded in liberating his country from the Nazis. Tito, an ambitious man of obscure origins, was not one to share the limelight with anybody, particularly a young blue blood who had inherited, not earned, his place.

"My father had such a sad life," says Prince Alexander, a soft-spoken Chicago insurance executive and a former ski champion of the British army. "He was deceived by some of the people closest to him.

"He was too good an ally. Unlike Charles de Gaulle, he never disagreed with Winston Churchill or Franklin Roosevelt. He did as they advised him. Perhaps he was too young and overwhelmed by those two powerful personalities, who treated him with so much courtesy and even affection. 'My boy,' Churchill used to say to him, and with feeling. Even after Churchill doublecrossed him, he used to have dinners with Churchill at 10 Downing Street. I remember a photo of my father with President Roosevelt; Roosevelt is leaning on my father. The amazing thing is that my father felt no bitterness toward Churchill or Roosevelt.

"He was too straight. He could not believe that his allies—the mighty American democracy, and his relatives and friends in London—could do him in. But that's precisely what happened."

There is not a trace of pathos in Alexander's elegant, understated British English. He is a serious student of history and a careful judge of character. There are some conclusions he has drawn from his father's example which he keeps to himself.

"He was placed in the limelight at an early age, with neither maturity nor preparations," *The Times* of London concluded in its obituary of Peter.

Peter had done nothing dishonest, nothing wrong. He tried to uphold the constitution and to keep together his Yugoslavia, the kingdom of South Slavs: Serbs, Croats, and Slovenes. His heart was in the right place. He hated the Nazis and, at sixteen, could not understand why Yugoslavia did not rush to the aid of its allies Poland and later Czechoslovakia. Wasn't Yugoslavia the country of valor? He sympathized with the coup d'état that removed the regent, his beloved Uncle Paul, who sought to keep Yugoslavia out of the war by temporizing and surrendering to some German demands, and who was therefore suspected of pro-German tendencies. Yugoslav pride could not swallow Paul's pact with the Axis powers, and the military coup in March 1941, carried out in Peter's name, lined the country up with the Allies.

"Yugoslavia has found its soul," Prime Minister Churchill proclaimed in the House of Commons. Ten days later Germany attacked Yugoslavia. Britain was unable to supply any of the arms and assistance that the anti-German revolutionaries had hoped for, and the Yugoslav capital, Belgrade, earned the tragic distinction as the first civilian target of massive German air bombardment. Some 30,000 Yugoslavs perished in what the German high command called Operation Punishment.

Recent disclosure of British documents confirms what many Yugoslavs have suspected all along: British intelligence engineered the coup. From the beginning, it was a Graham Greene scenario: a young officer imitating King Peter's voice in a radio address, the rebels wasting their time quarreling about assignments, the overthrown leader, Regent Paul, knowing about the coup beforehand and offering to cooperate, Peter sympathetic to rebels but approached by none of them for two days, and, in a final absurdity, the new government soon finding itself obliged to follow Paul's policies toward Germany. "We young officers were misinformed," a coup leader conceded years later in exile. "We thought that Prince Paul was a traitor, but he was a patriot."

Prince Alexander suggests that the British knew they could not generate a militarily significant Yugoslav stand against the inevitable Nazi onslaught, but they were anxious to demonstrate authentic anti-Nazi resistance on the continent in order to mobilize the British public, still wavering, against nazism.

Peter first fled to Greece, then to Britain, where he was warmly received by his godfather, King George VI. Both Peter and the Greek Princess Alexandra he was to marry three years later were great-great-grandchildren of Queen Victoria; they were both second cousins, once removed, to George VI. In London, Peter joined kings and other exiles from Nazi-occupied Europe—Norway, Denmark, Luxembourg, the Netherlands, and Albania. Except for Albania's King Zog, who earned his fame as a high-stakes poker player, they were treated with deference and assisted in their campaigns to organize resistance back home. But they were contentious, and the British were manipulative. In an indiscreet moment Churchill permitted a comment of his to be overheard: "Beggar's opera." He meant it.

At first, the British government regarded Peter as the legitimate representative of free Yugoslavia, and as the symbol of the Yugoslav unity the Nazis tried to destroy by setting up a separate Croatian state. In the guerrilla struggle against Nazi occupation, the forces led by the royalist commander, Draza Mihailovitch, and the forces led by Tito spent a lot of their time vying for Anglo-American support. Between the two groups there was a vicious propaganda war and constant charges of collaboration with the Nazis. The losses they inflicted on one another in addition to the German reprisals—100 Yugoslav civilians for every German soldier killed by the guerrillas—totaled more than two million Yugoslav lives, 15 percent of the population. The rival groups may have killed as many Yugoslavs as the Germans did.

The Allies ignored Peter's requests for support of his man Mihailovitch rather than Moscow's man Tito. Early in the war, the Allies concluded that Tito's partisans were better disciplined and more highly motivated than Mihailovitch's. Nor was Peter successful in convincing the Allies to land in Yugoslavia. According to Peter, Roosevelt was against a landing because he did not want to fight for what he saw as British interests; Stalin objected because he regarded Yugoslavia as within the Russian sphere of influence, and he therefore encouraged Roosevelt in his plans for an Allied landing in France instead. Tito, an obedient Party man at the time, accepted Stalin's argument.

"Churchill alone was strongly in favor of landing forces in the Balkans," Peter wrote in his 1955 memoirs, *A King's Heritage.* "He thought it wise both from a strategic and diplomatic point of view; he saw the Germans would be weak against such an Allied front and at the same time wished to counteract the ubiquity of the Russians in Eastern Europe." Peter did not think that Churchill's motive was to help him. Peter noted that Churchill "was willing to support Tito hoping to make him *his* man and thus ensure some stability in Europe in accordance with traditional British policy." Churchill prevailed upon Peter first to abolish the position of chief of staff held by Mihailovitch, and, later, in September 1944, to appeal to his subjects to rally round Tito.

With liberation in view, there were diplomatic skirmishes over a Regency Council, an institution which Tito demanded, and which Peter called unconstitutional. By March 1945, after two months of negotiations, Peter had given in, because the British and the Americans had privately conceded that he was right in terms of the constitution but that Yugoslav reality demanded a compromise with Tito. In August, Peter dismissed his Regency Council and declared himself "acting king."

But he was not able to return home. In November, Tito's electoral list received a typical Communist majority: an overkill of 90 percent, with plenty of evidence of cheating. The first act of the Constitutional Assembly was to abolish the monarchy and to declare a National Federal Popular Republic. Mihailovitch continued fighting in the mountains; in June 1946, Tito's forces captured him. After a summary trial, he was convicted of high treason and executed. In less than a year, Tito triumphed over King Peter—despite the popularity of the Karageorgevitch dynasty, the close ties between Yugoslav and British royalty, and the personal friendships linking "the brave young king" to Churchill and Roosevelt.

Prince Alexander is a cool rationalist when discussing the fall of the House of Karageorgevitch. He does not brandish the words "traitor" and "murderer"; there is an Anglo-Saxon restraint about him, as well as a Balkan patience to wait for the right moment to disclose fully his position.

"I have nothing against the British *people*, of course not," he says to me in his spacious condominium on Chicago's North Shore. He is relaxed; his hands drape over the back of a comfortable, canvas-upholstered sofa. "I do have a quarrel though with some top advisers to Churchill, advisers who included a member of the British Communist Party and others who built up Tito and convinced Churchill to side with him. Without British aid, Tito could not have defeated Mihailovitch and the monarchy."

Alexander grew up with the story of his father's defeat—at home, among fellow exiles, even with his friends in school and in the army. But the hurt he feels is personal—not one displayed for the benefit of a casual visitor. He speaks about "the curious fascination with the totalitarian enemy" that democratic leaders have. He drops dark hints about that circle of upper-class Britons at Cambridge—the circle Kim Philby, the famous Soviet double agent, came from and whose members secretly dedicated themselves to the Communist cause in the early 1930s.

"The British have always considered the defense of the British Isles their number one priority. Second, they were trying to ease the pressure on Greece—a country important to Britons ever since Byron—and they recognized that resistance in Yugoslavia, cost what it may in lives, would be helpful. In their shoes, I would have done the same. So they encouraged the faction they thought was more effective in guerrilla warfare, and they disregarded the consequences of their choice for postwar Yugoslavia. 'I won't have to live in Yugoslavia,' Churchill once remarked cynically."

Forbidden to set foot in the new Yugoslav republic, Peter first lived in Paris, where French Premier Charles de Gaulle welcomed him as a fellow sufferer at the hands of the Anglo-Saxons. While the British hinted that they might have to impose restrictions on Peter's political activities, de Gaulle even extended him diplomatic privileges. Running out of funds and faced with mounting debts, Peter tried to find a job in the United States. He thought he might become a consultant on international affairs or a middleman between European investors and American bankers. But, as he once stated tearfully, he was not fit for any job other than being a king. He missed his homeland terribly and found life in exile miserable. He kept talking about Yugoslavia—"the richest country in Europe," "a land of indescribable beauty," "immeasurable mineral wealth," "vast impenetrable forests," and blessed with "a hot-tempered people with hearts of gold." He told whoever listened that fate had dealt with him most unkindly: his father had been assassinated when he was eleven; when he reached maturity at eighteen, he ruled for only ten days; he lost his throne at the age of twenty-two.

As a royal orphan Peter was storybook handsome. He cried when his grandmother, born Princess Marie of Great Britain and of Saxe-Coburg-Gotha, told him that he would be called "Majesty." "But I am too young to be a king," he said.

As an exiled king during the war, Peter had a boyish charm. As a dethroned monarch after the war, he aged rapidly. Slight and tense, and with a sharp, birdlike profile, he seemed always to need friends around him, and he felt a compulsion to conquer women he met. People who met him wondered whether he would die of a broken heart or alcoholism. In the mid-1960s, he separated from his wife, who then settled in Venice. Peter traveled aimlessly and fell in with individuals who exploited him as a status symbol. His business ventures, from a plastics factory to a shipping line, from real estate to lecture tours, failed miserably. People were reluctant to rent him an apartment; hotel managers began to refuse him as a customer.

Peter tried in vain to assert authority over a dwindling group of Yugoslavs who still had faith in him. In the dispute between the Belgrade-based Serbian Orthodox Church and the exiled church which refused to accept Belgrade's authority, he kept switching sides. He dabbled in anti-Tito intrigues and hopeless plots. He listened to different advisers, and he was easy to sway.

He died in 1970 at the age of forty-seven of complications resulting from a liver transplant. His death certificate also listed "chronic brain injury," "chronic liver cirrhosis," and a number of strangely inaccurate personal details apparently supplied by his sole executrix and companion of fifteen years, Mitzi Lowe of Los Angeles. The will, drawn up in Los Angeles, stated: "Notwithstanding any other desires of my family, it is my desire that I be buried in the United States of America at Liberty Eastern Serbian Orthodox Monastery, in Liberty, Ill." Peter bequeathed 25 percent of his estate to that church—the one that refused to accept Belgrade's authority. "There are indications that the splinter church had close connections with those around Peter who persuaded him to choose its monastery for his tomb and to bequeath funds supervised by a woman friendly to its ecclesiastical cause," wrote C. L. Sulzberger in his *New York Times* column. "Perhaps the sordid details of Peter's life and death, so intimately connected with possible forgery and falsehood, help explain why monarchy today has little support even among Yugoslavs who disliked Tito's regime."

Most newspapers played up another angle: Peter was the only king ever to die in the United States (in Colorado General Hospital in Denver). In Britain, people were surprised by his refusal of Queen Elizabeth's offer of burial outside the Royal Mausoleum at Frogmore, Windsor, where Queen Victoria is buried.

Peter's son and heir, Prince Alexander, is a pleasant, easygoing, wholesome young man. He does not have a commanding royal presence, nor is he interested in developing one. He is quietly persuasive, and wears the weight of his name lightly, as does his wife, born Princess Dona Maria da Gloria Orléans-Bragança. She is his fourth cousin once removed, and their common ancestors are Pedro I, the first emperor of Brazil, and his wife, Marie Leopoldine, born a Habsburg archduchess and a sister of Emperor Napoleon's second wife, Marie-Louise. Dona Maria is great-great-granddaughter of Pedro II, the last emperor of Brazil, and daughter of Prince Dom Pedro, claimant to the throne of Brazil. She was educated in Brazil, Spain, and France, and has a degree in interior design and architecture. In Chicago, she works as an interior decorator. She is the same height as her husband—a few inches shorter than six feet—and has an attractive face, long brown hair, and a readiness to say whatever is on her mind.

The Karageorgevitches, as they are commonly known, have been living in Chicago since 1976. They are the only exiled royalty residing in North America. They live in a condominium, and own little else. They often eat out with friends, and Dona Maria has a habit of tasting everyone else's food and complimenting the chef on what she likes. They go to concerts and dinner parties, and, during the summer, they share with another couple a lakeside cottage fifty miles north of Chicago. Alexander loves sailing, and Dona Maria is a gourmet cook. Alexander is a middle-level corporate executive whose specialty is the design and administration of group insurance packages. Before his assignment in Chicago he worked for an insurance firm in Buenos Aires. He may be sent to Europe next.

Alexander finds Chicago "a very human city, and thank God for the lake." The Midwestern businessman impresses him. "He gets up very early, is always punctual and eats short lunches. He is a hard worker and when he succeeds, he has no one but himself to thank.

"I intend to climb to the top of the greasy pole. I am pursuing a career in insurance. I am also interested in science and history. I want to work, learn, and travel—and eventually to return to Yugoslavia."

Alexander believes in the superiority of constitutional monarchy, Scandinavian-style, and he is not about to relinquish his claim to the Yugoslav throne. "One mustn't live in a dream land," he says with an easy wave of his hand. "But there is a possibility that things may change quickly and dramatically in Yugoslavia. The name Karageorgevitch still carries a lot of weight. There are serious problems with the federation framework, and the need is for another true Yugoslav, someone acceptable to Serbians, Croatians, and Slovenes. Perhaps Milovan Djilas is the man. He is a Montenegrin, an intellectual, and a man of action.

"I don't know what will happen in Yugoslavia, but one has to be an optimist. I just hope that if a crisis develops with the Russians, Jimmy Carter is not president. Carter would accept placidly whatever might happen to Yugoslavia. Until something really stings this country—the Cuban missile crisis was close, but it happened long ago—nothing that the Russians do will matter. In this unpredictable world we can be certain of one thing: the CIA won't try pulling a coup d'état in Belgrade. Any attempt at interference, even if sorely needed, is against the current principles of the American public."

Alexander has never set foot in Yugoslavia. He says he would visit there if invited and if there were no attempts to interpret the visit as an acceptance of the status quo on his part. He recalls that in 1958, Tito told King Paul of Greece on a state visit to Yugoslavia: "Alexander should learn our language and customs, and then . . . and then who knows?"

Alexander's mother tongue is English, and though he speaks idiomatic French, German, Spanish, Portuguese, and Italian, his Serbo-Croatian still needs improving. He and his wife, whose mother tongue is Brazilian Portuguese, study Serbo-Croatian one evening a week. "We both love the language," Alexander says. "It's great fun to learn it."

Alexander received initial instruction in Serbo-Croatian in Switzerland, where he attended high school. He is taking his graduate training in Chicago, where a professor from the University of Illinois, a Yugoslav who left his native land in the 1950s, has devoted himself to teaching the language to the princely couple.

He points out that unlike other Balkan dynasties imported from Germany or Denmark, his is a native dynasty: his great-great-great-grandfather was a Serbian chieftain called George Petrovitch and nicknamed Kara (or black) George after his jet black hair and moustache—hence the dynastic name of Karageorgevitch. Karageorge's forces wrested independence from the Ottoman Empire, and he became the prince of Serbia in 1804. But a rival clan, the Obrenovitch, disputed Karageorge's claim and took over after Karageorge's assassination in 1817. In the nineteenth century, the Karageorgevitch dynasty was in exile for more than sixty years. Karageorge's grandson, the fiercely-moustachiod Peter I, returned to Serbia in 1903 and became the first king of the Serbs, Croats, and Slovenes, after the Allied victory in 1918. It was Peter I who declared, "My grandfather was of peasant stock and I am prouder of that than of my throne. Crowns are lost, but the pure blood of those who loved the earth does not die." His son, Alexander I, was declared the first king of Yugoslavia in 1929, and he was the first Karageorgevitch to take a wife from the family of European royalty: Princess Marie, whose mother was queen of Romania and whose great-grandmother was Queen Victoria of England. Prince Alexander, his grandson, is named after him. Alexander has done well in addressing Serbian émigrés in Chicago, and he is planning a tour of émigré communities in such far-flung places as Australia and Latin America. He is a Serbian. Orthodox, and the Karageorgevitch dynasty is Serbian while committed to a Yugoslav or South Slav federation. Dona Maria has remained Roman Catholic (Alexander does not believe in "religious transformation for the sake of convenience") and she has been well-received among Catholic Croatians whose acceptance of a Serbian king has not always been enthusiastic. Their only child, a son named Peter who was born in 1980, was christened as a Serbian Orthodox. But a sly wink from Alexander suggests that in case they have more children, the solution will not be an automatic embrace of Orthodoxy.

When addressing Yugoslav émigrés, Alexander's theme is always unity. He dwells on the heritage of Yugoslavia and avoids saying anything negative. He is staunchly opposed to the Serbian-Croatian cleavage which is even more pronounced among the 300,000 émigrés than in Yugoslavia itself. "Yugoslavia must live as one country," Alexander often declares. "We can survive only as one country, with each national group enjoying its full political and religious rights. Croatia cannot survive by itself, nor can Serbia. We need each other."

But conventional Balkan wisdom has it that the Croatians will not accept a Serbian dynasty again—they did after World War I only because the Serbs were victorious over the Austro-Hungarian monarchy and they liberated Croatia. But if it ever came to a choice between a united Yugoslavia and a Serbian monarchy, even Serbs would go for unity.

Alexander is careful to refrain from condemning Tito. "Tito kept our country together," Alexander says. "He was harsh with opponents, but it was to his credit that Yugoslavia has survived as one since World War II." Tito, Alexander argues, implemented the federation plan of his grandfather, King Alexander, whose asassination in 1934 in Marseilles by a Croatian separatist trained by Italian Fascists is sometimes called the curtain-raiser of World War II. Twenty years earlier, World War I began with the assassination of Archduke Franz Ferdinand by a South Slav nationalist encouraged by what was then the kingdom of Serbia.

Alexander's cautious praise of Tito is unusual. Yugoslav émigrés, who have not stopped fighting the battles of the 1940s, cannot bring themselves to say much that is positive about Tito, whom they suspect was an agent for Russia, if not a Russian by birth. Emigrés cite a strange accent Tito had in the 1940s in his supposedly native language, Croatian, and the official reticence about Tito's parents beyond the standard Communist description of them as honest, toiling people of peasant stock. One unverifiable rumor claims that Tito was the illegitimate son of an Austrian aristocrat, which would explain his stay in Vienna prior to World War I, his ability to play the piano, and his fondness for precious stones and white silk suits. "He knew who he was," Alexander says portentously. "But he was not what everyone thought he was." Alexander would say no more.

From the partisan commander whose forces engaged 600,000 Nazi soldiers and whose hideouts included one across the street from the German military headquarters in Belgrade, Tito rose to become the only world leader who successfully defied Stalin. After Tito's break with Moscow in 1948, aspiring nationalist Communists in Eastern Europe looked to Tito for inspiration. Following Nikita Khrushchev's 1955 pilgrimage to Belgrade—the only time the Kremlin ever said "sorry"—Tito again became the model, this time for those in the East and West who looked for an alternative approach to the Russians and the Cold War. Tito's powers of persuasion got Yugoslavia accepted in the Afro-Asian club. He became a friend and an advisor to Nasser and Nehru, Sukarno and Nkrumah. Nasserism, Nehruism, Sukarnoism, and Nkrumaism are all gone, unlamented and unremembered. But Titoism lives.

Titoism is the one thriving postwar "ism" in the wreckage of political ideologies discarded by East and West, North and South. It is Leninism de-Stalinized; Gaullism without anti-American truculence and Gallic chauvinism; neutralism with an army as self-confident as Israel's; fervent South Slav nationalism masked by an internationalism that is self-righteous and self-promoting.

Stalin was right in elevating Titoism to the rank of the major Communist heresy. That arch-paranoid had a real enemy in Tito, a rival more dangerous than Trotsky, because Tito had a nation behind him.

According to Béla Király, chairman of the Hungarian revolutionary military council in 1956 and now a history professor at Brooklyn College, Stalin ordered the general staffs of East European armies to prepare a detailed plan for the invasion of Yugoslavia. Hungary, Romania, Bulgaria, and Albania were to provide the frontline troops; the Red Army was to have the glory of liberating Belgrade. The soldiers were indoctrinated: they were to rid Yugoslavia's honest working people of Titoist treason. The armies were to be ready for war by the summer of 1950. But, Király says, U.S. resistance in Korea suggested to Stalin the probability of a similar reaction in the Balkan, and he scuttled the invasion plan.

Most Yugoslavs believe, as they are taught to believe, that Stalin did not attack because he feared Yugoslavia's tough army. But in his book *Conversations with Stalin*, Milovan Djilas tells how drained of strength and equipment the Yugoslav army was after World War II. Stalin knew this well because he demanded and received complete reports from the Yugoslav high command.

Tito was the only original East European Communist leader besides Stalin; he was the most successful Balkan head of state in centuries. Yugoslavia is an artificial federation with a bloody history of ethnic strife. Yet under Tito it became one state with a genuinely egalitarian nationality policy. World War I started there, and Yugoslavia has the unique distinction of having defeated both Hitler and Stalin. Yet Tito's theme was stability and co-operation, and Yugoslavia is one European country which did not change its leader for thirty-eight years.

Tito came to power at the age of fifty-one, so he could not beat Emperor Franz Josef's record reign of sixty-eight years. Yugoslavs called him King Tito; his photographs were in shop windows, on office walls, even in private homes. Tito was the last Habsburg, not as a descendant (every large Central European city has its quota of families claiming descent from one enterprising archduke or another) but as an apostolic successor excelling in the traditional Habsburg exercise of maintaining a balance between rival power centers and having his country serve as a standard for normalcy.

Alexander admires Tito's diplomacy. "His policy of nonalignment was brilliant," he says. "I'd keep the same policy."

In the late 1950s, Alexander applied for British citizenship. The request reached Foreign Minister Selwyn Lloyd whose main concern was "no unpleasantness" and who expressed his preference for a simple, nonpolitical solution. Properly instructed, his aides unearthed a law, dating back to an Act of Parliament in the year of 1789, which specified that any descendant of the electress of Hanover is eligible for British citizenship (it was to the electress, granddaughter of James I through her mother, that the British Parliament of 1701, searching for a Protestant sovereign, turned; her son, George, who never learned to speak English, filled the bill).

Thus qualified, Alexander was able to embark on a military career which, he thought, was in consonance with the traditions he had inherited. He enrolled in Mons Military Academy, a sister school of Sandhurst, and eventually joined the Queen's Royal Lancers, whose colonel in chief was Queen Elizabeth. One of her predecessors on that post was Alfonso XIII, king of Spain. "We Royal Lancers," Alexander explains with gusto, "have the unusual privilege of being allowed to stay on our bottoms during the singing of *both* British and Spanish national anthems. It's because we demonstrate our loyalty on the field of battle. We also wear our Sam Brown belts back to front, because Alfonso XIII once visited the Lancers wearing his belt that way, and it has become the right way for us as far as we are concerned. Well, the British are tolerant."

A broad smile settles on Alexander's face. It is clear that he liked soldiering. It was during Alexander's seven years in the British army—most of it spent in Germany with the 16th tank division—that King Peter died. As a captain and professional soldier in the service of Her Britannic Majesty, Alexander was unwilling to assume his father's title and to become Alexander II—advice from Yugoslav monarchists notwithstanding. His diffident disclaimers at the time suggested to Yugoslavs that he had become a Britisher and did not care for the Yugoslav throne to which he had an indisputable claim. Alexander now dismisses these émigré impressions as misinformed rumors.

Emigrés contend that Alexander became interested in his royal inheritance only after he moved to Chicago and had contacts with the Yugoslav community there. "Our realness hit him," one émigré comments. "He now knows that we are not phantoms. He even sends us Christmas cards in Serbo-Croatian and greets people who go to the Serbian church."

Or, perhaps, age has had something to do with it. Alexander is now thirty-four, a time when horizons begin to narrow and the past takes on an importance unforeseen in youth.

"My being a claimant to the Yugoslav throne is a going concern, definitely," Alexander says, and he dismisses a suggestion that the pretension—the weight of the past, of the dynasty—may be a burden. "To the contrary, because of the traditional background of my family, I don't want to get rid of that claim. If I tried to say no— go to hell, I am not interested, I have other things to do—I would be condemned, and rightly so, for the rest of my life. I know that my well-being is linked to the well-being of my people. I got this message since I was born. I couldn't help being thrown into this."

Dona Maria does not disagree. "As you say, dear," she says, putting her arm around his shoulders and giving him a light kiss on the cheek. "We won't give up," she says to me with the smile of a schoolgirl facing a tough test. "But in Brazil, I must tell you, people don't care about royalty. That's how I was brought up. Sure, I am descended from the great Pedro II, who liberated the slaves, but so what, people say. We have to prove ourselves."

"I have to make it on my own," Alexander says, as if to himself, suddenly very serious. "I welcome that."

He makes a face when discussing the two million dollars Peter reportedly deposited in a Swiss bank at the time of his flight to Britain. The deposit was made in the name of the king of Yugoslavia, and the bank refused to let the money be withdrawn after he lost his throne. Newspaper accounts and law suits notwithstanding, Alexander does not believe that the two million dollars ever existed. He argues that the kings of Yugoslavia were never rich, and were, in fact, usually short of cash. He tells the story of how one year his grandfather King Alexander stopped paying his life insurance premium because he needed the money to buy some special gold-mining equipment from an American firm.

"The year he did not pay the premium was the year he was killed," Alexander says, "so Lloyds of London was under no obligation to pay."

Alexander believes that the two million dollars was one of the many fantasies people around his father invented to keep the king going. "It was totally irresponsible," Alexander says, and I cannot tell if it is the son of a tragic father or a sober businessman speaking. He cites another wild goose chase of his father's advisors: they traced a Rembrandt painting, which the royal family had indeed owned, to Australia. The painting, originally stolen by the Nazis, was never recovered.

A strange aspect of his parents' lifestyle was that they always stayed in the most elegant hotels, but apparently could not afford to buy a house and were always in financial difficulties. Alexander does not know if his parents ever paid their hotel bills. "One thing is definite," Alexander says with a grimace, "I inherited no wealth from my father." For the one time in our conversation, his face flushes with pride as he declares: "That means I have to earn my living like anyone else."

"I am so glad," says Dona Maria, "I wouldn't have married you if you had two million dollars. You would have been spoiled. Who wants a rich prince?"

"But two million dollars is not such a lot of money," Alexander teases.

"Oh yes it is," she responds earnestly. "When I was a student in Paris, I didn't have money left for coffee by the end of the month. I know what it means not to have money. Don't I save money now, too?"

"Yes," Alexander replies, "of course you do. And I appreciate it."

Was theirs an arranged marriage?

"Oh no," Alexander says, "I hate those arranged meetings, and I would not have accepted anyone's suggestion as to whom I should marry. Those days are past."

Dona Maria, beaming like a bride, explains that their meeting was "a total accident." They met in Portugal, at a party in Estoril given by her aunt, the countess of Paris. They fell in love immediately. They were married in Seville, Spain, in 1972, in the first non-Catholic ceremony permitted under Francisco Franco's rule. They are both proud of having set such a precedent. Juan Carlos, cousin to both, was at their wedding, as were King Umberto of Italy—their Uncle Beppo—and Dom Duarte João, now the pretender to the throne of Portugal, who is Dona Maria's first cousin. But the most noteworthy among the seventy-odd royalty present was Princess Anne of Britain.

Alexander is one nonreigning colleague that British royalty seem to favor. "It's because I went to school with Charles, the prince of Wales," Alexander explains, "or perhaps because Queen Elizabeth was my godmother, and her father, George VI, was my father's godfather. All I can say is that they have always been very kind to me."

There may be some guilt as well. British royalty have long enough memories to recall that His Majesty's government edged Peter II out of his kingdom and that British officials encouraged him just enough (and it didn't take much) to keep him believing that he still had a chance, when in fact everything had been agreed upon with Tito long before. "Until the day he died," Alexander says, shaking his head incredulously, "my father thought that he would return to Yugoslavia because the people there loved him and the democracies would eventually help him in his just cause. He had tremendous hope."

Peter wanted to be parachuted into Yugoslavia to take command of the anti-Nazi resistance. Churchill and Roosevelt both opposed the idea, for fear of his getting killed, they said. As usual, Peter accepted their counsel.

But had he ignored his friends and allies and acted upon his youthful impulse, he might have saved his throne. Bold action was what the monarchy needed at home and abroad to counteract the Tito myth, and to overshadow the interminable arguments among royalists in London. Peter might not have been able to make peace between the warring resistance factions—nothing could have achieved that miracle—but what a luminous legend, what an apparition from history he would have been in a land haunted by reckless rebels and martyrs engaged in hopeless defiance of mighty invaders.

That would have been a royal decision, a stroke of sovereign folly that no accountant computing actuarial tables or apparatchik believing in Marxist dialectic would dare suggest. Yet it is the stuff of folksongs and epics, magnificent even if ending in defeat.

Does Alexander have such spirit in him? Or will he merely wait for that call from Belgrade that, as far as one can reasonably predict, will never come? Will he accept the verdict of history and stick to computing the probabilities of group insurance?

"If my father had disobeyed Churchill and Roosevelt now and then, he might have had a chance to reclaim his rights," Alexander says, his calculation as coldly realistic as ever. "But of course it is more than likely that he would have been captured or killed if he had tried returning to Yugoslavia during the war."

A few hours later, Alexander again addresses himself to his father's contemplated parachute jump. "Yes, he ought to have done it," he whispers, his voice as soft as the night is still. "It's not enough to be a good ally, and it doesn't pay to be too good an ally, particularly to a superpower. My father was abandoned and swindled. No, you have to take risks and play games. Just like Tito."

Son of the Eagle
Leka

Go, gentlemen, every man unto his charge:
Let not our babbling dreams affright our souls;
Conscience is but a word cowards use,
Devis'd at first to keep the strong in awe:
Our strong arms be our conscience, swords our law.
March on, join bravely, let us to't pell-mell;
If not to heaven, then hand in hand to hell

King Richard III

Leka is king of the Albanians, or, as the Albanian phrase goes, Chief of the Sons of the Eagle. He is also chairman of the Council for the Liberation of Ethnic Albania—a region that includes large chunks of Yugoslavia and Greece as well—and the commander in chief of the armed forces under that council's authority. At forty, he is the only revolutionary activist among claimants to European thrones, and his court prints its own Royal Albanian passport that Leka claims is accepted in a large number of countries.

Leka is 6'9"—a giant of a man married to a slim 5'2" Australian heiress, Susan Cullen-Ward. His face recalls Troy Donohue, an American teenage idol of the 1950s.

He is an eighth cousin of Richard Nixon through his maternal grandmother, a New York socialite. A frequent visitor to the United States, he raises funds among Albanian-Americans for his army and meets with politicians. Among the gifts he has sent in appreciation for hospitality is a baby elephant, which he presented to Ronald Reagan, then governor of California.

He is an international arms merchant specializing in Chinese and Russian weapons. The Kalatchnikoff rifle is the most sought-after item on his list; his primary supply source is Thailand, and prominent among his clients are Arab revolutionaries and smaller insurgent groups in Southeast Asia.

According to knowledgable Washington sources, Leka was on the CIA payroll in the late 1960s and early '70s. American intelligence enlisted his help in obtaining a wide range of Chinese army equipment as well as military information on troop movements in Southwest China. He purchased the equipment and the information from Shan tribesmen who have a centuries-old reputation for carrying out the toughest military and intelligence assignments. During the Vietnam war, the CIA made payments to the Shans and other tribesmen in the region, sometimes to encourage them to defy the Viet Cong, but often merely to keep them from joining the Communist side. In these operations, Leka is said to have subcontracted for the CIA.

Leka denies any connection to any branch of the U.S. government, and blames the CIA for his arrest in 1977 in Thailand, on charges of arms smuggling. The CIA did play a role in his arrest, sources in Washington say. They add that both the CIA, which no longer needed his services in Southeast Asia, and the State Department, which was moving toward a normalization of relations with Albania, had a hand in his sudden expulsion from Spain in February 1979.

The official Spanish charge was that Leka had kept a large arsenal hidden in his home outside Madrid, but that fact had been known to Spanish authorities for a long time. (Leka had lived in Spain for fifteen years; originally he was invited by Francisco Franco.) Leka claimed that he needed the arms for his own protection: besides Albanian agents, there was now a Maoist terrorist group of Spaniards called FRAP, with members trained in Albania, the last citadel of unreconstructed Stalinists and sentimental Maoists. When Spanish police threatened to confiscate his arsenal, Leka and his retinue of sixteen left on a chartered jet. He had hand grenades hooked on his belt, and his wife Susan toted a submachine gun. They reportedly left behind debts totaling seventeen million dollars.

At first, Leka said he might go to Morocco—whose King Hassan II he counts among his friends—or to Argentina, where there is a small but influential Albanian community. But the party landed in Gabon, on the western coast of Central Africa. Gabon officials refused to permit Leka to leave the plane. After a few hours of fruitless negotiations, Leka ordered the plane to take off and to cross the continent, to Rhodesia.

A student of guerrilla warfare, Leka had been a frequent visitor and observer of the fighting in Rhodesia, as well as in Angola and

Mozambique during the Portuguese rule. In Rhodesia, Leka had many highly placed friends.

But Rhodesia was a temporary asylum, and Leka contacted friends in other countries. He tried to set up camp in one of the Arab sheikdoms, and in the spring of 1979, he cabled the sheikh of Sarjah, in the United Arab Emirates, to request his "brother ruler" special VIP treatment. Leka said he was on his way to Saudi Arabia and asked to be received. Sheikh Sultan Al-Qasimi did not respond to the cable. In 1980, Leka was granted asylum in Egypt, and President Anwar Sadat received him.

Leka is a Moslem; Arabic is one of the half-dozen languages he speaks. He appeals for Islamic solidarity. He tells conservative Moslem rulers that he is determined to liberate Albania, the only European country with a Moslem majority, but one that, in 1967, shut down all mosques (and churches), declaring itself "the world's first atheist state."

He leaves visitors with the impression that the secret military training camps he says he maintains are in various Arab states. Emigrés, however, suggest that Leka is referring to his loyal followers among an Albanian diaspora of some three million souls, close to 250,000 of them in North America. Albanians are natural soldiers, émigrés add, and Leka's loyalists are led by old tribal retainers who have done surprisingly well in the New World as restaurant owners and real estate speculators. Leka often visits them. On his most recent North American tour, in the winter of 1978, he was arrested in Canada for a brief time for carrying a concealed weapon; like most Albanians, Leka is always armed.

In official Washington, a mention of his liberation army raises eyebrows, and his business interests elicit snide comments. "He is selling to everyone," one observer noted, "regardless of race, religion, or sex." "We don't feel we need to follow his activities," a State Department analyst of the Balkan scene remarked.

"But even if you take his liberation threat seriously," another U.S. official reasoned, "no small band of irregulars can succeed against a government anymore. Castro was the last man to pull such a coup."

"Leka" is Albanian for "Alexander," a name that recalls the greatest conqueror the Balkan peninsula has produced, Macedonia's Alexander the Great. The name "Leka" is also a version of "Skander," Albania's national hero who defeated the Turks in the fifteenth century. Leka is the only son and undisputed heir of King Zog, born Ahmed Zogolli, whose grandfather, Djellal Pasha, was a general in the Turkish imperial army.

Ahmed Zogolli was nothing more than a tribal chieftain when the European powers, negotiating the dismemberment of the Ottomans' Balkan empire for a century, declared Albania's independence last, just before World War I. The Europeans also supplied a king, a thirty-five-year-old Prussian army officer and a Lutheran—one religion not represented in Albania—named Prince Wilhelm zu Wied, whose only connection with the Balkan was through the queen of Romania, his aunt. After six months of battling anarchy in his Massachusetts-size realm, prim and proper Wilhelm left in disgust. He was unable to contain bloody tribal feuds or to obtain bank credit to modernize his backward kingdom, the most primitive and isolated country in Europe.

During World War I, Ahmed Zogolli dropped from his name the Turkish ending "olli" (meaning "son of") and became Zogu, an Albanian word that means bird. A graduate of a military school in Istanbul, he joined the Austro-Hungarian army and served as a major. He was not sent into combat. His commission was a sophisticated Austro-Hungarian device used to keep him in honorable captivity and to prevent his enlistment with the Allies. Zogu loved wearing a uniform and impressed Viennese society as a tall, dapper, mysterious officer—an exotic apparition from the Balkan mountains and the Moslem East. He had bright red hair— reputedly dyed with henna—a voluptuary's drooping eyelids and a highly waxed moustache that the painter Salvador Dali later copied (they resembled each other even without the moustache). He was a passionate, high-stakes gambler and had a way with women.

In the first Albanian republic, declared in 1920, Zogu was his tribe's representative in the National Assembly; then he became minister of the interior, later minister of war, and, finally, at the age of twenty-seven, prime minister. But too many blood feuds were declared against him, and he found it wise to cross the northern border into Yugoslavia. A year later he returned, occupying the capital Tirana with a cavalry of several hundred White Russians, Serbians, and Albanians—a mercenary army paid by Yugoslavia. In 1925, Zogu had himself elected president of the Republic. In 1928, he became Zog I, king of the Albanians, the first ruler of the House of Zogu, thus replacing the hapless Wilhelm who continued to claim the throne from nearby Romania and in the pages of the *Almanach de Gotha*.

When informed of Zog's declaration, fellow-strongman Kemal Atatürk, the heir of the Ottoman sultans, told the Albanian ambassador in Ankara, "Zog goes backwards. Why should he in this day and age become king?"

King Zog tried to play Yugoslavia against Italy, both covetous of Albania. He encouraged the investment of Italian capital in Albania; he established a bank and a radio station, schools, and roads. By the standards of the region, he was a liberal king who tried hard to move his country out of its Ottoman torpor. But he was also a capricious, dissolute Balkan chieftain, always surrounded by his retainers, spending his days feasting, hunting, and swapping stories. He gambled every day of his life; he and his court frequently visited Monte Carlo.

He was an only son preceded by some half-dozen sisters who spoiled him. Some of his sisters always accompanied him abroad. In the early 1930s, in a hotel on the Côte d'Azur, three of them found themselves in the same elevator with Otto von Habsburg. Otto bowed and wished them a good morning, but the princesses turned their heads. "Why didn't you accept the archduke's greeting?" asked their companion, an Albanian diplomat. "He has fallen," the eldest sister responded with a contempt that only a new—or a very old—dynasty could muster.

Zog remained unmarried until his forties. According to one legend, in his youth he pledged never to marry after his first love, the beautiful daughter of a rival chieftain, was killed by her own father, who objected to Zog; the liegemen Zog sent to abduct the girl returned with her dead body.

But dynastic considerations demanded an heir. When the Greek royal family declined to supply a princess, Zog was introduced to Countess Geraldine Apponyi, a celebrated beauty called the White Rose of Hungary. Her mother was socialite Gladys Stewart of New York and her paternal uncle was Hungary's foreign minister and silver-tongued spokesman at the League of Nations. A romance followed, a diversion from the tragic events of the mid-1930s. But one year after a wedding ceremony of resplendent white uniforms, acres of silk, and forests of long-stemmed roses, Fascist Italy attacked Albania. Europe's newest royalty had to flee Benito Mussolini's Roman legions. Leka was two days old, and his mother, who had had a complicated delivery, nearly bled to death during the escape through the mountains.

The day Italy struck, Zog addressed the nation on radio: he was born in the mountains, he would fight in the mountains, he would die in the mountains. Next day he left for Greece. No explanation, no instructions for his army of 5,000 men. His flight abroad was a shock that is still remembered and held against the monarchy.

Unlike other exiled kings in wartime Britain, Zog did not organize a liberation movement, nor did he raise his voice against fascism and nazism. Britain and the United States did not recognize him as head of a government-in-exile and refused to drop arms to his followers in northern Albania. But London police tolerated his wild poker parties. He reportedly lost tens of thousands of pounds sterling in a single night.

He had fled with a part of the gold reserves of the national bank (half of the bank was Italian property) and a bucket of rubies, emeralds, and other precious stones that he had had the foresight to collect—total wealth estimated at ten million dollars. Zog bought real estate on the Riviera and Long Island, and made investments in other countries as well. He did not like anyone to know what he had in his highly diversified portfolio. His closest political and financial advisor was his wife, Queen Geraldine, who had learned Albanian during her one year in Albania and who earned the admiration of her husband's numerous retainers and old associates.

After World War II ended and the French-educated school teacher Enver Hoxha set up a Communist people's republic in Albania, King Faruk, himself of Albanian descent, invited Zog to settle in Egypt. In Alexandria, next door to King Victor Emmanuel whose forces had driven him out of Albania, Zog set up an export-import business and began manufacturing and selling small arms. According to one story, he sold arms to both sides in the first Arab-Israeli war of 1947-48.

But the regime of Gamal Abdul Nasser soon made Zog feel unwelcome in Egypt. Among other harassments, it insisted that he pay taxes. Zog argued that as king, he could not be taxed by another sovereign entity. Nasser's ·men got testy; Zog abandoned his thriving business and moved to his twenty-room villa in Cannes, where he died at the age of sixty-six in 1961. A few weeks later, monarchist émigrés gathered at the Hotel Bristol in Paris and declared Leka king.

Leka had gone to high school in Alexandria, Egypt, and at Phillips Academy in Andover, Massachusetts. He had studied economics at the University of Geneva in Switzerland and at the Sorbonne, and had attended the British military academy Sandhurst.

Leka is his father's son: a born adventurer, a shrewd businessman, a professional soldier. Of all the pretenders to European thrones, Leka has the strongest claim to the primeval essence of kingship—the mighty warrior leading his tribe into battle. His is the youngest royal house in Europe, a mere half-century; no dynastic wisdom mitigates his desire to conquer. Fellow émigrés discount his claims as exaggerated, and his army and his plans as phantasmagoric—a blend of *A Thousand and One Arabian Nights* and James Bond.

"If it's true what Leka is saying about his preparations for liberation," one skeptic argues, "wouldn't it be wise to keep quiet about it? He is a young man; he has a lot to learn. It's not that simple to liberate a country, even a country as small and without Great Power allies such as our Albania. In the 1950s, the CIA tried but failed miserably. If Leka can do it, more power to him. I wish him well. But these days it isn't enough anymore to be a leader and say 'follow me.' A leader must have a political and social program as well. Leka is trying to butter up people, and usually the wrong people, by giving them military decorations—the Order of Skanderbeg, the medal of God knows what. He is courting everybody, including those who collaborated with the Fascists."

Leka has no patience for émigré politics or for people on the sidelines. For him—as for Mao Tse-tung in the caves of Yen-an or for Fidel Castro in Oriente Province—men count only as soldiers, and nothing but revolution is worth living, or dying, for.

"He is a fake and a buffoon, and his pronouncements are a lot of hot air," declares one émigré leader who asked not to be mentioned by name. "His so-called liberation army is a cover for his arms business. Anyone in the business of buying and selling arms needs protection."

In November 1978, I visited Leka's headquarters, about ten miles outside of Madrid, off the paved road that leads to the village of Pozuelo and nestled among eroded hills covered with wheatfields and orchards. His compound of several acres was surrounded by an eight-foot chainlink fence topped with barbed wire. Fastened to the gate was a meter-high Albanian coat of arms, a black double-headed eagle against a red background.

The cab driver, who had received phone instructions on how to find the place, stopped his banter and looked apprehensively at the uniformed, heavily armed guards, and the two huge bulldogs that jumped at the fence and barked furiously. He did not wait for me to make sure that we were in the right place; as soon as I closed the door, he made a sharp U-turn and drove off.

I find no common language with the guards, one a swarthy, mustachioed Albanian and the other a wiry little Shan. Using signs, I explain that I spoke on the telephone to the big man with the crown on his head and that he is waiting to talk to me. By the time they understand, Leka appears. He shouts two words; the gate flies open. The two bulldogs lunge at me—and lick my face and ears. "They are not always that friendly," Leka says, unsmiling, as he shakes my hand, "they know whom to attack."

"It looks like a military camp," I observe as we walk across a yard of crushed stone.

"It *is* a military camp," he snaps. "Military discipline is the only way to impress on people the need for action."

Leka is a tower of a man with a bulging middle, the deliberate swagger of John Wayne, and the innocent eyes of an English schoolboy. He wears clean, freshly ironed green army fatigues, well-shined black combat boots, and a pistol strapped to his belt. He explains that the insignias on his jacket denote his specialties: guerrilla warfare, commando operations, armaments expertise, marksmanship. The patch of a crowned double-headed eagle makes the outfit an Albanian uniform; his cap badge identifies him as the commander in chief.

"Our units penetrated Albania for the first time in 1975," Leka begins. "Each of our teams is named after a hero in Albanian history, a martyr of independence. The assignment we gave to our first units was to find out if the climate for liberation was ripe. Our units came back with the report that the climate was indeed ripe. Since then, we have been sending in leaflets fairly constantly; we drop them from balloons or float them down rivers in plastic bags. We also plant mines, organize sabotage. Nasty little things."

"Could you be more specific?" I ask.

"No. There are certain things I cannot clarify. Security is most important."

Leka cites reports in the European press: these past two years his liberation front has blown up telephone and telex cables between Albania and Italy, and has staged a rocket attack on the Albanian embassy in Paris. The objective was a demonstration of the military capability of the resistance movement. "There were no casualties, nor was anyone caught," Leka adds, "which was according to our plans." He won't say how many people he has under his command or where he trains his men—he does not want the enemy to know, and he is wary of embarrassing friendly governments.

Leka speaks in the tough, no-nonsense style of military spokesmen. His English is fluent and idiomatic; his accent and choice of words are those of a G.I. "I have had many American friends," he explains. Hollywood's influence seems equally likely.

He sits behind a shoddy wooden desk that takes up most of the space in his office, a room about ten-by-ten feet. The office is in a prefab barrack, the floor is linoleum, and the ceiling has acoustic tiles. On the walls are photographs, inscribed and inexpensively framed, of King Juan Carlos and Queen Sophia of Spain, King Hussein of Jordan, the shah of Iran and the Empress Farah, King Hassan of Morocco, and the late King Faisal of Saudi Arabia. Facing his desk is a large photograph of King Zog wearing a resplendent military uniform.

In the room adjacent to his office, Leka shows me a wall-size map of Albania and a McNally world map with green pins representing Albanian communities of 100 or more families. "There are more than 5.5 million Albanians scattered throughout the world," Leka declares with pride. "In addition to 2.5 million in Albania proper, there are 2 million in Yugoslavia, 400,000 in Greece, 120,000 in the United States, 100,000 in Italy, 34,000 in Australia and New Zealand, and another 10,000 in various Middle Eastern and West European countries. For the past 500 years, there have also been Albanian communities in Calabria and Sicily, now numbering 350,000, many of whom live in isolated mountain villages and speak no Italian. Some 100,000 of these people have emigrated to the United States, most of them living in Louisiana."

Leka travels several months a year to look after his business interests which, he says, go "hand in hand" with his political alliances. He also travels to observe guerrilla warfare. In the late 1960s, he visited Vietnam many times; he has also been a frequent visitor to African countries waging wars in the bush. "I go where the action is," he says, "and I go right into the areas where fighting takes place. That's how I pick up tips. I am an expert in guerrilla warfare and counterinsurgency techniques. I read absolutely everything that's published on the subject of guerrilla war." (The only other kind of book he reads these days is science fiction.)

He travels extensively in the Moslem world. "I am grateful for the political, moral, and financial support from Moslem countries," he states. "They recognize that Albania is a Moslem country and that we have a just cause."

Leka has developed a special relationship with Buddhist Thailand. Originally, Thailand was merely a convenient stopover on his way to the important Albanian community in Australia. But gradually he made friends with Thai officials, both political and military.

"I am extremely well-connected in Thailand," he says. "I went that far in search of an ally because I didn't want a country where there can be a clash of interests. This way, our military secrets cannot be given over to the enemy. The country we rely on must be far from Albania. We cannot get involved with someone closer. And we must have the same enemy ideologically."

Leka will not discuss details but acknowledges that he acquires arms from the Thais on very favorable terms. "One good anti-Communist helps another," he says with a hint of a smile.

"We must use the same weapons as the enemy," he explains. "For instance, what use would an M-16 rifle be for us if we cannot be sure of a supply of spare parts and ammunition? We cannot afford to become dependent on the United States. But for a Kalatchnikoff, Russian or Chinese, I can get all the parts and all the ammunition I want, and in many areas of the world.

"Excuse me," Leka says suddenly, looking at his watch. "I have to call my mother." He dials. "Hi Mom," he says in a cheerful American way. "How's everything?" After a brief chat, they agree that he and Susan will have Sunday lunch in Madrid, at mother's.

"She is a great lady," he says, "you ought to meet my mother."

We return to business with his quick dismissal of his 1977 arrest in a remote corner of Thailand. "It took my friends in Bangkok six days to secure my release," he says, "because it took my agents that long to get hold of a key cabinet member. I explained that I was buying arms to liberate my homeland. Of course I was acquitted."

The story found its way into the international press. Reporters picked up two explanations. One: Leka is a leading arms merchant, and the area he visited—the confluence of China, Burma, and Laos—is an excellent source for all kinds of arms. Two: Leka was buying opium, the most famous product of the Thai hills.

Leka blames the CIA for plotting his arrest. The objective? To discredit him with Albanians at home and in exile. The drug charge? "Rubbish," he says, "another CIA concoction. The easiest charge to make. So primitive. I don't need that kind of business. I get funds from Albanian communities and from my friends. I was buying arms, not opium.

"The jail was not pleasant, but I did learn some things there. When I got home, a letter was waiting for me from my friend, Tunisian President Habib Bourguiba. 'Congratulations,' he wrote. Bourguiba spent many years in French jails. 'Imprisonment is an essential experience for a leader; you are now on your way!'"

Leka laughs joylessly.

He is lyrical when talking abut the Shan tribesmen of Burma and northern Thailand, among whom he spends several weeks every year. "Like the Albanians, the Shans are tough mountain people," he says, "and they have been fighting their neighbors for many centuries. Our customs and mentality are similar, astonishingly so. We don't want mercenaries, but we need people who speak the same language politically and ideologically as we do. The Shans we hire as trainers for our troops learn the Albanian language and take up Albanian citizenship. We give them Royal Albanian passports. Of course we don't force them; they do all these things at their own initiative.

"For example, the commander of one of our units is a Shan prince, the grandson of a Shan ruler. He, too, has become an Albanian. But we don't get involved in their local politics. We stay out of Burmese and Thai affairs, or the activities of the Kuomintang troops in the region. Or Spanish politics. We have our own job cut out for us, and not an easy job.

"The Council for the Liberation of Ethnic Albania was formed in 1975. I have the honor to be the chairman. Council members are by no means all monarchists, and in that group, I am only the leader, not the king. After liberation, we'll decide on the form of government best for Albania. I am content to wait. The council has members from different political parties, including Communists who disagree with the Hoxha regime. In the army, we don't look at their ideological credentials as long as they share our goal of liberation."

"Have you been in Albania yourself?" I ask.

"No, but I will be, in the very near future. I have every intention to land in Albania soon. More I cannot tell you."

Leka cites a report in an Italian newsmagazine on the existence of three dissident groups in Albania: followers of the so-called Titoist faction of Koce Xoxe eliminated in a show trial of 1949, those who sided with Minister of Defense Bellegu, who was executed as a traitor in 1975, and, lastly, the monarchists.

Leka explains that penetration of Albania from land is difficult because both neighboring governments are hostile to his aspirations. "With Greece, we have been at war since 1949," he points out, "and we could make life unpleasant for them if we wanted to. But we haven't done that. Yugoslavia of course has long been interested in swallowing up all of Albania, and it is worried about the loyalties of two million Albanians living in Yugoslavia. None of our neighbors is friendly to us, and they have always been eager to annex as much of Albania as they could."

Albania's government has no Great Power protector since the break with China, which surprised the world in 1978. According to Leka's analysis, the Hoxha regime broke with Peking because it could not accept the argument that China needs to befriend the West; nor could it allow any lifting of the old Stalinist restrictions. The Albanian leadership fears that any thaw could lead to a repetition of the 1956 Hungarian scenario: reform, once permitted, invariably gets out of hand. And as far as the Chinese were concerned, Yugoslavia was a better bulwark against Russian expansionism than tiny, isolated Albania. Since the break, Albania has been trying to build up economic ties with the West, beginning with Greece, Turkey, West Germany, Italy, and Austria. Albania may have significant mineral deposits, and an approach has been made to Sweden to develop and sell chrome.

Albania-watchers have no argument with Leka's analysis of Albania's military strength. Albania's army, 48,000 strong, is supplied with Russian and Chinese arms—all rapidly becoming obsolete, and there is no immediate prospect of replacement. The most sophisticated weapon they have is a ground-to-air anti-aircraft rocket system. They have seventy-five planes—MIG 17s and 19s. Egypt may possibly sell them spare parts but no one else seems interested in doing it. Albania is vulnerable.

Leka has a smirk on his face when discussing a landing in Albania that the CIA organized in the early 1950s. "It was another Bay of Pigs fiasco. Kim Philby was responsible for the planning, and now we know that he was a Russian agent, not the mastermind of British intelligence. Philby betrayed the operation, and instead of a linkup of liberation forces and resistance elements in Albania, the Communists caught lots of good Albanians. But I do not believe that the United States ever seriously contemplated the liberation of Albania. The Americans have always been worried about Yugoslavia, a much bigger country, and the Americans are smart enough to know that any new regime in Albania would have to insist on taking the ethnic Albanian region of Kosovo from Yugoslavia. What's more, the Americans are interested in Greece. During and after World War II, Winston Churchill demanded that Albania stay with the West, but the United States decided to fight for Greece only, and left Albania in a lurch."

Leka is contemptuous of the West, which, he says bitterly, is against his program of liberation because of the fear that any radical change in the Balkan means destabilization, and could have worldwide repercussions. "We have three cards to play," he sums up. "First, Albania's strategic significance—a country on the Adriatic coast, near Italy, in the Balkan. Second, friendly population on the borders, although that factor is nearly canceled out by the hostility of neighboring governments. Third, Albania is not in direct territorial contact with any Moscow-controlled country, so Albania need not fear Russian tanks when it frees itself from communism.

"Unfortunately, Albanians in exile are not totally united, as they should be," Leka says grimly. "It has taken me a long time to get as far as I have gotten. But I still have a long way to go. Then, Albania has one of the toughest Communist regimes, with the worst concentration camps. You don't build an underground movement in one day. If you could do it, a lot of governments would be sorry. It takes a lot of finance, which is not always easy to obtain. We don't have unlimited resources. All we can afford to do at the moment is to snipe at the enemy. But that we do.

"My concern has been to get through to our people, to prove to them that I am not only my father's son but a leader capable of leading the liberation movement myself. Then I have had to fight divergent views and to form a coalition with other parties. I organized the first meeting of all Albanian political factions in Madrid in 1972. We agreed on one thing: a united national front. But the various factions are still *discussing* that national front.

"I have come to two conclusions. One, it is our duty to liberate ethnic Albania. Two, we must bring about a truly democratic regime. There should be a plurality of parties and not necessarily a monarchy. I personally believe that monarchy is a stabilizing factor, and that a monarchy is a better system of government. But I intend to leave the choice of monarch or republic to the people. When I swore allegiance to the throne in 1961, I declared: the day Albanians are free to decide, there will be a referendum on the form of government.

"In the army, I don't stress that I am the king. I am the commander in chief. Being king helps with certain countries. But not stressing that point is helpful in gaining recruits from all colors of the Albanian ideological spectrum."

What does he do in his off hours?

"What off hours?" he exclaims. "I join the boys in their training exercises. We do unarmed combat. We have a range here, and we do much target practice. I have no leisure time. Information piles up on my desk, and it must be analyzed fast. We cannot fall behind developments. We work around the clock here. We have people throughout the world who phone us at odd hours. We must always stay awake. Someone must man our radio and telephone communications systems. If something happens, we must be aware of it right away.

"We monitor all radio communications in Albania, and we occasionally use our own system that we can activate from here whenever we want it. But we don't use it all the time. It's dicey. Friends and enemies alike would like to know the locations of our training camps, which can be pinpointed by zeroing in on our signals.

"The problem is that Albania is too ripe for a revolution. Someone else, a neighbor for instance, could exploit the situation and step in. The people may not resist. What's brewing in Albania is not necessarily the internal combustion Poland and Hungary experienced in 1956. Albanians are so desperate that they are prepared to take almost anything to replace the system they hate.

"Tito is eighty-five. My most urgent problem is to decide whether to act before or after he goes. We have eight contingency plans. But we have not decided which one to put into effect."

After the interview, conducted like a military briefing, Leka invites me for a drink. We cross an area covered with crushed stone. Leka exchanges salutes with two men dressed in the same uniform as he. There is a sign—in Albanian, Spanish, and English—that says: "Do not take photographs."

His suburban ranch house is fifty feet from the prefab barracks. I am introduced to Leka's wife, Susan Cullen-Ward—trim, petite, and in her early thirties. She is the daughter of a wealthy Australian sheep rancher, a divorcée and a keen sportswoman. They married in 1975. Officiating at the wedding were a Moslem ulema, a Protestant pastor (Susan is Episcopalian), and a Roman Catholic priest (Queen Geraldine is Catholic). Susan apologizes for her appearance—she is dressed in black slacks and a gray sweater—she did not expect a guest.

On the floor, there are a few choice Oriental carpets. The furniture is modern and undistinguished, vaguely Scandinavian. The walls are covered with spears and shields from Iran, Saudi Arabia, and various parts of Africa; some are tourist souvenirs, but most of them are fine antiques. Old rifles and daggers, most from the Middle East, are everywhere.

A Shan woman serves us drinks: a pitcher-size glass with Scotch-and-soda for Leka, Scotches in tall water glasses for his wife and me. We talk about Albanian and Scottish highland customs, the institution of High King in Celtic and Albanian cultures, the jungles and palaces of Southeast Asia, World War II, and the Hungarian revolution of 1956—of arms and men.

Leka is confident that Spain will survive as a democratic monarchy, despite the fact that a policeman gets killed every day. It's getting tough; under Franco there were no influences to worry about. But a democracy is a democracy.

He talks about the United States—"Big Brother Who Is Not Watching." He tells a story of how half-a-dozen American agents who infiltrated Albania during World War II eventually sided with the Communists, who then proceeded to drag the agents' bodies behind trucks through the streets of Albanian villages and towns as a demonstration of Communist power against the forces of reaction.

"Americans are such amateurs abroad," Leka says, "so easily tricked and led astray, so afraid of anything that they think is tribal, feudal, reactionary, so eager to join those they think are progressive. So they misunderstand traditional societies.

"All this is off the record," Leka adds, with a faint smile.

"Milord," Susan joins in, "you should not be so hard on journalists."

"Okay, so it's not off the record," Leka says with a grimace. "Tell me," he says, "tell me why is it that journalists must have someone bumped off, and preferably a lot of people, before they choose to write about a political movement? Look, I spent a lot of time and energy so in our tactical operations no one would get killed. Believe me, saving lives is not easy, and we could get a lot more accomplished if we were not so damned careful. It's because I don't want to shed more blood than absolutely necessary, and I don't want to alienate Albanians. Tell me, what must happen before we are noticed in the world press?"

Leka tries to understand my explanation about the exigencies of the profession, the need for specific and reliable details, the audience, but he gets furious.

"Security is more important than publicity," he hisses. "I've got a big job ahead of me. I've got to liberate my country."

I suggest that he try to contact a reporter he trusts to accompany his forces on one of their commando operations.

"How can I trust such a fellow," Leka retorts. "My people would shoot him like a dog if he made any suspicious move—that's how they are trained. *Then* I'd be in real trouble. I just can't let some idiot of a reporter gum up a carefully planned operation we work on for months and months, and spend our money on."

There is a second round of drinks. By the time I get to the bottom of my glass, I have accepted Leka's invitation to cover a commando operation in Albania, and we drink to the day in the not-too-distant future when I accompany His Royal Highness, the Chief of the Sons of the Eagle, on his return to his homeland.

How I would love, in covering the event, to be able to use the line: "The Eagle has landed."

A Gallery of **Romanoffs**

Unthread the rude eye of rebellion,
And welcome home again discarded faith

King John

The lanky youth wearing around his neck a three-inch silver cross
was billed as the voice of the new Russia. Some twenty émigrés,
scholars, federal employees, and their spouses gathered to hear him
in the house of Prince David Chavchavadze, a fifty-five-year-old
leader in Washington's Russian-American community. They were
in for a shock: the newcomer fresh out of Leningrad was kind of a
hippy. His avant-garde poetry alternated pornographic images with
patriotic ones.

Prince Chavchavadze, a genial host, protected his guest from
criticism by taking him on a tour of the library and living room. The
youth was impressed with the icons and the cameos, the pre-
Bolshevik revolution leather-bound books, the sentimental paintings of the Russian countryside, the old silver-framed family
photographs on coffee tables and bookshelves.

"That's the last czar, isn't it?" he asked, pointing to a faded
photograph.

"Yes," said Chavchavadze, who is a second cousin to Nicholas II.

The youth grabbed the picture and kissed it three times. "A
martyr," he cried in a choked voice, "a martyr of our people."

To Chavchavadze, a retired CIA officer whose mother was a
Romanoff princess, the story illustrates the unpredictability of
Russia's future. He recalls that in the 1940s and 50s, when he was a
U.S. Army officer in charge of the liaison with the Russian army in
Germany, he never met a Russian who had a kind word for the
Romanoff dynasty. He spoke with hundreds of officers and enlisted
men, trying to define the so-called New Socialist Man produced by
the country that his ancestors had ruled and which he had never
seen. He felt no animosity toward the soldiers of the regime that
had executed his two grandfathers and driven his parents into exile.

"I spent my free time making friends with Russian soldiers," he
remembers. "We visited one another, talked far into the night, got

247

drunk together. Much to my surprise, they accepted me despite my ancestry. They were not interested in the czars, or in the past.

"Only once did a Soviet insult me. He was a secret police type, and I met him at a party given by Marshal Sokholovsky in Potsdam, in the old royal palace of Cecilienhof, where my cousin Louis Ferdinand had lived as a child. The fellow told the soldiers I was with that I was an enemy of the people and that my father had oppressed the peasants working on his thousands of acres of land and that we had nothing in common except the language.

"The soldiers said nothing, and I didn't challenge him. But the incident has been on my mind. In retrospect, I should have asked for the fellow's name, rank, and serial number, and reported him to our host, his superior. Instead, I simply got up and left.

"In those days of the alliance with the Soviet Union, and later in the 1950s, when I joined the CIA, I didn't give much thought to the Romanoffs, and even less to the chances of their restoration. The monarchy was the past, I concluded. Finished, dead. After 1917, an entirely new Russia emerged, and I didn't think that a Romanoff could be a factor in any new upheaval that might come about.

"But in the 1970s, I am not so sure. When I visited Russia for the first time in my life, in 1976, I found people interested in tradition, searching for continuity, roots. Official guides and Russian tourists spoke of the czars with respect and pride, and, sometimes, with affection. On one occasion, I heard a museum official describe Nicholas II as 'the bestially murdered czar.' Among intellectuals, the imperial past is being reexamined, and the tendency is to excuse the faults of the monarchy.

"Among the new émigrés, there are quite a few with monarchist sentiments. I've even met Jews who favor monarchy. Only a Soviet regime could make a monarchist out of a Russian Jew. The Russians are a people inclined to adulate the head of state. They want to be ruled by someone strong, and they can forgive the excesses of a strong leader. There were, and still are, Russians (including non-Communists) who truly admired Stalin.

"Then there is the phenomenon of anti-Sovietism taking the form of traditionalism, and some of the traditionalists turn to the monarchy. Although Alexander Solzhenitsyn has not declared himself a monarchist—and he despises the last czar—he belongs to the deeply conservative, nationalist line of thought monarchists come from.

"I can imagine a pro-monarchy movement in a post-Communist Russia. Russians may go back to the tradition of electing a czar—the way the first Romanoff, Michael, was elected in 1613. Or, they may turn to one of the Romanoffs, perhaps even to the pretender, Wladimir."

At first glance, he is an English country squire: he is dressed in an old double-breasted blue blazer, a beige turtleneck sweater, gray flannel trousers, and suede shoes. A slim six-footer, he has the baggy, watery blue eyes of his great-grandmother, Queen Victoria of England, and the long nose and thin lips of his second cousin, the duke of Windsor, who was once Edward VIII. His courtesy is casually understated; the suggestion is that he is ever so slightly bored. He is keen on sailing, plays bridge, admires Somerset Maugham, and devours murder mysteries.

But then one notices that embossed on his blazer's brass buttons is the Russian imperial coat of arms, that his smooth English has crackling, explosive Russian "r"s and that his bearing is just a bit too stiff even for a Briton. He declares rather than comments; his predilection is for a swift, sweeping statement. He believes in discipline. If he could, he would crush his opponents. As a czar he would make an autocrat.

His Imperial Highness Grand Duke Wladimir has been the head of the House of Romanoff and the pretender to the Russian throne since the death, in 1938, of his father, Cyril, who was the grandson of Czar Alexander II, liberator of the serfs, and first cousin to Nicholas II, the last reigning czar. According to Wladimir's account, in the spring of 1917, with Russia still at war but the czar confined to his St. Petersburg palace, naval officer Cyril Romanoff asked liberal Prime Minister Alexander Kerensky for permission to leave the country. Permission was granted. With Bolshevik units pursuing him, Cyril fled across the ice to Finland with his wife, Grand Duchess Victoria, and their two small daughters. Three months later, Victoria gave birth to Wladimir in the village of Borgo, near Helsinki. In 1918, after the Bolsheviks executed Nicholas II, his wife Alexandra, and their five children, Grand Duke Cyril became head of the House of Romanoff and assumed the title Guardian of the Throne of Russia. When the murder of Nicholas's family was established beyond a doubt in 1924, Cyril issued a manifesto declaring himself Cyril I, Emperor and Autocrat of All the

Russias. Following stopovers in Germany, Switzerland, and at the Côte d'Azur, he settled in 1927 in the small, isolated Breton fishing village of St. Briac, recommended by British relatives as an ideal place to raise a family.

Fellow exiles have another view of Cyril's accession. They accuse him of violating his oath as an officer of the czar—the commander of the Marine Guards in St. Petersburg—when he pledged (with "unseemly haste") loyalty to Kerensky's so-called Provisional Government. They hurl at Cyril the charge of high treason, commencing with his collaboration with the enemy prior to his flight abroad. "Cyril wore the red star," respectable White Russians have testified. "He tried to gain the favor of the Bolsheviks." Others have argued that Cyril's mother was not Orthodox at the time of his birth, making him, according to the law, ineligible to inherit the throne. But even those members of the imperial family who raised no objections to Cyril's mother were angered by his disregard for an agreement among grand dukes not to press claims to the imperial title as long as the Dowager Empress Maria, mother of Nicholas II, was still alive (she died in 1928).

Many of the monarchists who refused to acknowledge Cyril as head of the House of Romanoff rallied round Grand Duke Nicholas, the incompetent but genial former commander in chief of the army. Cyril's supporters came from among his colleagues in the navy. Factionalism is the law of émigré politics; no legislative program or political strategy exists to inspire coalitions and alliances. There are no pay-offs, no opportunities for statesmanship. In the émigrés' world, nothing is forgotten; there is no forgiveness or grace.

When it comes to Cyril, émigré malice has a lot to build on. During World War I, his wife, Grand Duchess Victoria—an ambitious, strong-willed German princess like her rival, Empress Alexandra—maligned Nicholas II as weak and vaccilating, and contrasted him to the tough and manly Cyril. In exile, it was Victoria who persuaded her husband to declare himself czar and to exercise such prerogatives of the sovereign as granting titles, promotions, and medals. Returning in the early 1920s to her native town of Coburg, now in northern Bavaria, Victoria openly supported Germany's extreme Right, including the then insignificant movement of Adolf Hitler. She believed, along with her mother-in-law (yet another German princess of firm views and great ambitions) that only a strong Germany rising from the debacle of World War I could defeat Bolshevism and restore the monarchy in Russia. Cyril was in complete agreement with the women in his family, which gave rise to the accusation, widespread among White Russians, that "he thought and felt like a German." They point out that Wladimir's name is spelled in the German way, with a "w" instead of the conventional transliteration with a "v". After a few months in Coburg, German authorities told Cyril to desist from political activities, and the couple left the country in a huff.

His enemies describe Cyril as having waited in vain for a call from Hitler—not an unreasonable conjecture. Cyril might well have been prepared to become Russia's führer, but, apparently, he considered it beneath his dignity to initiate contact. Hitler, who courted Hohenzollerns and Habsburgs, was wary of the Romanoffs, and never approached the czar of St. Briac.

St. Briac was the phantom capital of an invisible empire where Cyril lived a life of "sustained pathos," wrote Grand Duke Alexander in his 1933 book, *Always a Grand Duke.* "Under the circumstances, his sovereignty has to be enforced solely by mail . . . Each morning, the robust sunburned postman of the village of St. Briac appears on the threshold of the improvised Imperial Palace, puffing and panting under the weight of batches of letters which carry the stamps of almost every country under the sun. The foreign representatives of the Shadow Emperor of Russia keep him posted daily on the physical welfare and the morale of his far-away subjects." From America, a letter marked "extremely important" suggests that "a word or two of Monarchical Encouragement would be greatly appreciated by the impoverished Russian colony in Harlem." A former captain of the guards, now a dishwasher in a self-service cafeteria in the Middle West, is hurt because he has not been promoted though friends of his who had left Russia as mere lieutenants have been made colonels. Former Russian army officers in Manchuria, a Cossack in Bolivia, and a general in India request imperial guidance on the propriety and wisdom of protecting their new masters from their rebellious subjects. A former Supreme Court justice from Moscow, now a factory hand in Canada, wants it to be understood in St. Briac that a certain young Russian employed in a Montreal bakery is "a very dangerous radical who should not be permitted to return to Russia when the monarchy is restored."

Then, as now, St. Briac was a calm, neat, prosperous village of farmers and fishermen, sailors and retirees on France's windswept northwestern seacoast, about two hours from Paris or London on the World War I aircraft that plies the route once a day. In centuries gone by, the region supplied pirates; at the turn of this century it became a popular summer resort frequented by Britons. In the fall, St. Briac is a study in grays: gray-blue pines, gray-brown granite, gray-green seas, pearl-gray skies. The architecture is an eclectic mix of classical French and Victorian English, with squat Breton stone houses providing both backdrop and contrast.

The house in St. Briac is the least elegant of three residences maintained by Wladimir and his wife Leonida, born Princess Bagration-Moukhransky. Their apartment in Paris is currently occupied by their only child Maria, who is married to Prince Franz Wilhelm of Prussia, great-grandson of Kaiser Wilhelm II and great-great-great-grandson of Queen Victoria. The third residence is a sumptuous villa in Madrid, where Wladimir and Leonida live during the winter.

Grand Duchess Leonida is a descendant of the Georgian royal house which outclasses European royalty in being able to trace its origins to the sixth century. Leonida is wealthy. After the Bolshevik revolution, her family was able to spirit out some of its riches; control over such matters in the distant Caucasus was not as rigid as in the Russian heartland. Leonida later inherited the estate of her first husband, American millionaire Sumner Moore Kirby, who died in a Nazi concentration camp in 1945. Industrialist Kirby, born in Wilkes-Barre, Pennsylvania, owned part of the Woolworth chain and was a benefactor of civil rights causes to the tune of hundreds of thousands of dollars in the 1930s. He stayed in France during World War II and the Nazis deported him because, according to one account, he helped Jews.

Until Wladimir married Leonida, in 1948 in Switzerland, his circumstances were modest. His parents had escaped with nothing more than their clothes and the jewels they hid in their clothes. "There was absolutely no secret Romanoff account to draw upon," Wladimir says. "The Romanoff treasure in the Bank of England is as phony a story as Anastasia's. I am sorry to say that there is no truth to either.

"Our British cousins didn't engage in any direct charity. Queen Mary, whose husband George V was my mother's first cousin, purchased my mother's jewelry, and my father invested that money."

Wladimir does not wish to discuss family finances, nor does he like to talk about the sensitive issue of relations between Windsors and Romanoffs. His cousins however are outspoken. They tell the story of the Dowager Empress Maria, returning in the early 1920s after a half-century of absence to her native Denmark as wife of Czar Alexander III and mother of Nicholas II, who asked her nephew George V to sell the jewels she succeeded in rescuing from Russia. George V dispatched a courier, who was later put in charge of investing the surprisingly small sum of 10,000 pounds sterling that the jewels brought.

It did not take long to discover where Queen Mary's new jewels had come from, and it soon became clear that most, if not all of the Dowager Empress's jewels had been purchased by her English cousins. "Queen Elizabeth is wearing those jewels today," I heard several Romanoffs say with the same inflection of polite disgust. More ironic is the fact that the man George V entrusted with the transaction, Count Vladimir Kleinmichel, received in the 1960s the coveted title Commander of the Royal Victorian Order, given for services rendered to the English royal family.

The immense pre-World War I wealth of the Romanoffs consisted of land, railroads, steel works, and gold mines. As for foreign bank accounts, as soon as World War I broke, Nicholas II instructed his minister of finance to transfer to domestic banks all Romanoff money abroad. "Thus for perfectly good patriotic reasons, the Romanoffs lost all their money in the revolution," explains Ivan Bilibin, the seventy-one-year-old head of Wladimir's Imperial Chancellery. "For Cyril and his family, the jewels realized just about enough money to scrape by."

Wladimir was offered a scholarship to Winchester, the oldest English public school, but his mother vetoed the plan, fearing that the experience might transform him into an Englishman. Private tutors instructed him in English, German, and French, as well as diplomatic history and what was referred to in those days as "the military arts." His father taught him Russian. Wladimir later went to the Russian high school in Paris and attended the London School of Economics. Except for a stint he did in 1939 as a mechanic in Peterborough, England, Wladimir has not been employed. The name he assumed in Peterborough was Mikhailoff, the same name his ancestor Peter the Great used two centuries earlier as an apprentice shipwright in England and the Netherlands.

He considers his position as head of the Imperial Family of Russia a full-time job. But he does not like to be called a pretender. "One pretends to nothing," he is in the habit of saying. "One happens to be born in a certain position." He is patiently waiting for the fall of the Communist system, he says, and he is absolutely certain that it is at hand. He stresses the "moral authority" of monarchy, and his standard adjective for the Communist regime is "bankrupt"—the same adjective used by the opponents of the czar for close to a century before the 1917 revolution.

The grand duke and the grand duchess live off investments and contributions from White Russian communities. Several times a year, a plate is passed around for "The Grand Duke's Fund" in many Russian Orthodox churches, though principally in Argentina, France, and Australia. An estimated 10,000 Russian émigré monarchists pledge loyalty to Wladimir.

The mansion in St. Briac, built by a retired Breton seaman in the 1880s, is a masterpiece of local architecture: the masonry is granite and the woodwork is pine, stained dark. The furniture is also locally made; some pieces are simple, others elaborately carved, a few two to three centuries old.

Two rooms on the ground floor serve as a Romanoff museum. On display are pieces of the original imperial china, ornate regimental cups and gilded commemorative plates, painted Easter eggs from the last empress and military decorations going back to the Crimean War of 1854. A silk handkerchief from the turn of the century proclaims in two languages the eternity of the Franco-Russian alliance; jewel-encrusted silver daggers once signaled the allegiance of Caucasian chieftains to the imperial family. Among the bronze busts, paintings, etchings, and photographs the one haunting presence is that of Nicholas II, the doomed czar. His sad eyes have a dreamy glow in *tableaux vivantes* with Queen Victoria and Edward VII and Kaiser Wilhelm, and with officers aboard battleships, and in many official Romanoff photographs ("Playing Croquet with Children of the Imperial Family", "Checking War Plans with Commanders of the Army").

"The collapse of the monarchy in 1917 is pretty much constantly on my mind," Wladimir says. "No single factor or person was at fault. Any revolutionary upheaval builds up over time and is based on an infinity of small factors that accumulate until they reach their final, culminating point: an explosion."

Wladimir disagrees with those who argue that Nicholas II was weak or that Empress Alexandra was a bad influence or that cabinet ministers were incompetent or that the Russian proletariat lived under exceptionally harsh conditions. He points out that Russia had the smallest proletariat among major European powers and that the unrest of industrial workers was limited to St. Petersburg. "The disorders there could have been snuffed out," Wladimir says, and it is clear that this is what he would have done. "But either no one realized what was happening or no one had the courage to take drastic measures. We were too busy fighting a war.

"World War I itself was unfortunate because we were insufficiently prepared. And of course it was a tragedy that countries, in reality friendly with one another, decided to go to war. There was no natural alliance between Austro-Hungary and Germany; nor did we form with Britain and France a logical bloc. All the monarchs took their roles seriously and they tried to avoid war. But the monarch does not make decisions by himself even if his rule is absolute by law.

"The war weakened Russia, accentuated our inherent weaknesses and gave a coup de grace to the monarchy. After the war, an entirely different equilibrium emerged. But of course one cannot talk about an equilibrium. It is more correct to talk about a change in the center of gravity. Communism has passed its apogee. In every sense, it is now declining. How fast that decline will be is hard to tell. But the decline itself is a definite fact."

Wladimir reads the newspapers and meets with people who come from the homeland, but the Soviet Union he attacks is still the monster borne by the Bolshevik revolution. What Wladimir and his generation of émigrés cannot quite accept is that the regime's utopian rage petered out long ago and that stolidly rational calculation has replaced murderous paranoia. These past few years, for instance, emigration passports and expulsion decrees have become a hard currency of detente. The Kremlin now has a bourse responding to Western demands for liberalization, accepted as part of the price to be paid for U.S. credit and technology in addition to checking domestic dissent. The bourgeois art of compromise is again a basic strategy of the Russian way of life. As before the

Bolshevik revolution, the dissidents form a contemptible, small yet closely watched minority.

Each émigré lives in hatred of the regime that banished him; in his memory, that regime is preserved like an old shoe in a shark's belly. It does not greatly matter to him that the original traitors of the motherland, the companions of Lenin, were purged by Stalin, who was in turn denounced by Nikita Khrushchev, who was then booted out by Leonid Brezhnev.

Successive waves of political refugees from communism do not recognize their kinship. Those who escaped from the Bolshevik terror do not easily embrace the generation of émigrés whose acquisition of legal exit permits the West considers a fundamental human right, and whose appreciation sometimes extends to "liberal" Communists. Refugees of the Cold War are baffled by new tactics: why doesn't the KGB simply liquidate critics of the regime? How is it possible that mere harassment now follows the publication of a dissident's anti-Communist tract instead of forced labor camps or execution? Older émigrés even darkly suspect that the celebrated dissenters of our day—often second-generation Bolsheviks—are in fact part of the Communist system.

Wladimir considers it "a truly historic development" that the West, after decades of closing its ears to news of *gulag*, is now listening to the horror stories of the Soviet labor camps. He finds Solzhenitsyn "most valuable because he was the first Russian to get through to the West." But he is furious with Solzhenitsyn for "presenting an inaccurate picture of World War I, and one hostile to the monarchy. He simply doesn't know the facts. Those of us who grew up with memories of that war know that he is wrong. Very wrong indeed."

Wladimir has firm views on the responsibilities of the writer. "A writer must pursue truth," he declaims, his "r"s exploding. But by pursuing his own version of truth, Solzhenitsyn would be no more welcome in Wladimir's regime than in Stalin's or Brezhnev's. Wladimir dismisses the contention, put forth by fellow exiles, that Solzhenitsyn is a monarchist. "We have heard," Wladimir says, "that Solzhenitsyn has some vague monarchist sympathies, but we don't consider those sentiments worthy of note.

"It is not impossible that if things change in Russia, the country may return to some sort of monarchist government. I personally think the reason is very simple: most people capable of thinking conclude that in the past the monarchy worked reasonably well in Russia, while all other forms of government—Kerensky's democratic regime and the various Communist dictatorships—have only brought about disappointment. In addition, those who once hoped for some sympathy or at least understanding from Western powers now realize that the West is in fact completely allied to the forces which are in power in Russia today. National socialism, too, failed to liberate Russia. Thus all other systems failed miserably."

Wladimir spent most of World War II in France. "In 1944, the Germans forced me to pack up and leave St. Briac, where I had been under surveillance, and I found myself in Germany in August. The Germans did not behave incorrectly. They fetched me in an embassy car and asked me where I preferred to reside. I chose to stay with my older sister Maria, married to a German, the prince of Leiningen.

"The German officer in charge of my surveillance was from the old Prussian army. He was a decent fellow who had spent time in the Coburg garrison and had good memories of the duchess of Coburg, my grandmother. He told me confidentially that he had received orders not to let me fall alive into the hands of the Allies.

"The Germans had no particular reason to treat me as a prisoner and no particular reason to consider me an ally. They could not suspect me of approving their policies in Russia. It is obvious to me why they never approached me with any sort of political plan: they wanted to make Russia a German province, and they knew that they could not obtain my support for such a scheme."

In John J. Stephan's 1978 book *The Russian Fascists*, Cyril and his wife Victoria are mentioned as sympathizers with nazism, but there is no reference to Wladimir. By the time Cyril died in 1938, Russian émigrés turning to nazism and fascism might have been monarchists as well, but their leaders came from classes other than royalty. According to Stephan, the Russian extreme Right contrasted the moribund Romanoff monarchism with the vitality of German, Italian, and Japanese dictatorships. And the Romanoffs themselves realized that a lower-class dictator such as Hitler or Mussolini had no reason to be interested in restoring an ancient dynasty.

In the spring of 1945, with German forces collapsing, Wladimir went to Austria, with hopes of reaching neutral Switzerland. But he was stranded in Austrian Feldkirchen for seventeen months. "I got out thanks to a French officer who advised me not to return to France but to go to Spain, where I stayed with my mother's sister Beatrice. I owe Franco a debt of gratitude. He was most helpful. He was a great personality and achieved much as head of a relatively small country. Even if his rule was basically a dictatorship, it was an extremely mild one. I returned to France in 1950. I was lucky that nothing happened to me during World War II, and I consider that God protected me in those troubled times."

Some Russian soldiers who deserted the Red Army and offered to fight alongside the Germans contacted Wladimir and asked for his counsel. "I advised them to be extremely careful," Wladimir says, "but I could not tell them not to fight."

Was Wladimir ever a Nazi? These days, the label is quickly affixed. During World War II, however, the issue was to be for or against Hitler. Wladimir did not collaborate; in fact, American intelligence received word that Wladimir had "told the Germans off."

Two salient facts need to be recalled. First, many anti-Communist Russians reckoned that Germany was the only force capable of destroying communism. Second, Hitler was determined to annex Russia to his Reich, and thus he wanted no Russian nationalist revival. He vetoed suggestions to exploit anti-Communist sentiment in Russia, and he did not see the great potential in those units of the Red Army which offered to fight communism alongside the *Wehrmacht*. Whatever ideological and emotional base there might have been for an alliance with anti-Communist Russians, Hitler's obsession with total conquest and his thirst for mass slaughter precluded such a possibility.

World War II was not Wladimir's war. He had no opportunity for political gain, and neither Hitler's madness nor the despair of his victims moved him. It was all someone else's nightmare.

As isolated as he was in occupied France, Wladimir still received word about the German atrocities in Russia a few weeks after they began. "But even before that," Wladimir says, "I had not thought that the Germans would help me to return to Russia. There never was one time when chances of a restoration seemed more likely than at other times. In my lifetime, restoration has always been a fairly remote possibility. We have of course always hoped for the fall of the Communist regime, but that fall and monarchist restoration are two very different things."

Wladimir does not like to explain. He is impatient with mere words; he is a thwarted man of action. But on the subject of the exile's duty he addresses his subjects, the world.

"There is only one thing we exiles can do and that is to behave in a manner proposed by the boy scout motto: Be prepared! To my way of thinking, the only way of justifying our existence lies in being ready to serve our country and to do our duty if one day called upon to do so."

Wladimir doesn't like the word "restoration" because it sounds like going back to something. "One can never go back in life to anything. Rather, I would say: forward to monarchy! While in my opinion all nonreigning European royalty have equally remote chances, it must be said that monarchy is holding its own in Europe. It is a most convenient form of government, infinitely adaptable. It can accommodate every system, from complete dictatorial absolutism to extreme democracy.

"When it comes to Russia, everything depends on the circumstances of the change. Perhaps democracy would be a good idea, though not for the start. After a firm system of government, one would have to adopt another firm system of government, at least for the beginning, until new conditions emerge. A monarchy of the future would have to be different from what we had in 1905 or 1917. It's the principle that counts, not the form.

"The great advantage of monarchy is its guarantee of continuity. It seems to me that if you can have a different president every four years, why not a different flag every four years? But if there is indeed a good reason to keep the same design and colors for the flag, why shouldn't there be a head of state, a king, who stays the same?"

Wladimir's favorite monarchs are Peter the Great (Wladimir admires Peter's strength and determination although finds him "too hasty as an innovator") Nicholas I ("a no-nonsense czar, three-fourths of what a monarch ought to be like"), and Alexander I, who first worshipped and then fought Napoleon ("a great ruler although a romantic").

For Wladimir and Leonida, exile is not a bad life. They shuttle between France and Spain, using a stateless travel document recognized by the U.N. ("For us, it is pretty well impossible to take up a foreign nationality," Wladimir explains. "We can't very well be someone else's subjects.") They used to go to the south of France but they find that it has become terribly crowded, loud, and modern. They prefer quiet St. Briac where they play bridge, go for rides in their flashy Alfa Romeo or neat little Austin, and have dinner in one of the superb seafood restaurants in the nearby towns of Saint-Malo or Dinard. Wladimir sails in the choppy bay and plays tennis in a local club. Leonida grew up in Madrid, and they have many friends among Spanish aristocracy and exiled royalty. They enjoy Spain because it is still traditional Europe, a bit like Old Russia.

Once a year, they take a longer trip. They frequently visit White Russian communities in South America. (In Buenos Aires, monarchism is particularly strong, and they are feted as czar and czarina.) They have attended ceremonial functions such as the hundredth anniversary of the U.S. purchase of Alaska from Czar Alexander II, Wladimir's great-grandfather. (As guests of the governor of Alaska, they were wined and dined and toasted, but they were saddened by the complete Americanization of a land that was once Russian.) They have cruised to such places as Japan and South Africa. But no matter how isolated the places they visit, they run into White Russians.

Then there are plenty of royal and aristocratic weddings, christenings, and funerals to attend. British cousins do not usually invite them, but Wladimir and Leonida did have an opportunity to present their daughter Maria, a student at Oxford, to Queen Elizabeth at a tea in Buckingham Palace.

The world offers the Romanoffs recognition, deference, even adulation. They are living metaphors for vanished splendor, for barbaric power, for mystery and tragedy. People throughout the world—including people who otherwise have nothing to do with Russia—cannot bring themselves to believe that the Bolsheviks wiped out the last czar's entire family. The myth of Anastasia is built on a rock of faith.

Not even Communists—heirs to the revolutionaries who shattered and burned priceless czarist treasures—are free of the thrall of the Romanoff legend. In the 1970s, a Soviet official attending a Washington party awash with vodka and good will was astonished to discover that the American to whom he had been speaking was a descendant of Czar Alexander II. "I am proud that you are a man and not a degenerate," the Soviet burst out, embracing the Romanoff. "I want to be proud of the men whose ancestors ruled over my ancestors for 300 years. You have given us greatness."

Family feuding has forced Wladimir to avoid other Romanoffs. He has disowned them; they have disowned him. As far as he is concerned, there can be no negotiations; there is nothing to talk about. Error has no rights; it must be shorn of any hint of legitimacy. The feud is as serious as any dynastic crisis in Russian history.

Wladimir lives a life of passionless ease, without the stresses and dangers earlier Romanoffs endured. Idleness does not seem to bother him; he is capable of spending hours in contemplation. For him the past is full of glory; the present is bland and insubstantial. Perhaps more than any of his nonreigning colleagues, Wladimir misses not being able to rule. King Umberto and Prince Louis Ferdinand have their many friends; Archduke Otto busies himself with the cause of European unity; Henri, the count of Paris, and Louis-Napoleon, the prince imperial, live the life of rich Frenchmen; King Michael has his memories of royal courage and his machine shop; King Simeon, Prince Alexander, and Dom Duarte João are young men with projects; King Leka has his guns and soldiers and fantasies; King Constantine plays golf and waits for that call from Athens. Wladimir seems to be the most repressed among them: a brooding prisoner of his ambitions and his resentments. He has allowed himself only one great passion: contempt for his opponents. Perhaps more than any of his royal colleagues, he has let his life be filled with the echoes of other lives.

Over a lunch of delicate *brochette d'agneau* flanked by robust, Russian-style red cabbage, conversation fluctuates between Russia and France. Wladimir does not see much of a difference between royal France and republican France, and he never rooted for Henri, the Bourbon pretender, or bothered to meet Louis-Napoleon, the Bonaparte prince. Grand Duchess Leonida proudly describes Georgians as the most independent people of the Romanoff empire. She points out that the Russians subjugated Georgia only in the early nineteenth century and mentions that her brother, Prince Irakly Bagration, is the claimant to the throne of Georgia. "Separatism is a problem," Wladimir notes with a grim look on his face. One imagines that Georgian separatism is *his* problem.

Leonida is friendly and voluble. Born in Tbilisi, near the Caspian Sea, in 1914, she has dark hair, olive skin, round features, and lustrous brown eyes.

"I will tell you a little story you will like," she tells me as the Breton maid in a starched uniform serves *tartes aux fruits*. "A true story."

She then proceeds to tell me that toward the second part of the nineteenth century in Georgia, her grandmother, Princess Bagration, hired a washerwoman. She was a healthy, nice-looking villager. She always came on time and her wash was spotless. Every year she got pregnant, but she kept losing the baby. Princess Bagration felt sorry for her and asked why she was having problems. The washerwoman explained that she had a good-for-nothing cobbler for a husband. He beat her up when he drank too much, which happened often and particularly when she was pregnant.

You ought to go to the priest, the princess said, he will tell you what to do.

The washerwoman went to the priest, who suggested that the next time she got pregnant, she should offer the child to God. The child will be a boy, the priest said, and he will live, but you must make absolutely certain that he will become a priest, a man of God, because if he doesn't, not only your family will suffer grievously for generations, but terrible calamities will befall Georgia, Russia, and in fact the whole world.

The washerwoman went home. Sure enough, she got pregnant again. Although her husband beat her as before, she delivered a healthy baby. It was a boy, of course, and in due time he was sent to the seminary to become a priest. He was a good student, but he left before his ordination. He became a troublemaker, a revolutionary, an outlaw. We all know him: He was Iosif Dzhugashvili, later called Stalin.

Wladimir's lips, pressed tightly together, make it clear that he does not like the story. A hint of imperial censorship floats across the embroidered roses of the tablecloth.

Wladimir's face is tense when discussing family matters. He defends his father's decision to assume the title czar "as a way of making absolutely clear the succession, a step necessary in those confused times." Wladimir did not follow his father's example, however, because he thought it was "not necessary."

"Now my daughter Maria is the heiress presumptive," Wladimir declares. "There can be no doubt about that. Our laws of succession are perfectly simple. Males inherit first, then females. But since my cousins married morganatically and without my permission, they have disqualified themselves. I don't condemn those who marry morganatically. But they are not suited to lead. Marrying within one's class is a matter of self-discipline, and if a person is conscious of one's duty, there is no absolute obstacle to finding a suitable mate."

Maria, born in 1953 in Madrid, is a beauty who inherited her mother's soft Middle Eastern features and her father's blue eyes and high forehead. She was educated at home, then in the English high school in Madrid, and finally at Oxford, where she took courses in French and Spanish as well as in Russian literature and history. "We taught her from the very beginning her duty to her country and family," Wladimir notes, "and she has lived up to our expectations."

"**W**ladimir is an ungracious scoundrel, and his behavior is unmonarchic—against the Romanoff family and against the Russian people," roars Prince Vasili Romanoff, seventy-two, in an interview in New York. Vasili is one of the three surviving male members of the imperial family born in Russia before the abdication of Nicholas II. In 1976, he was one of five senior Romanoff princes who signed a statement, published in the Russian émigré press, condemning Wladimir's "willful unwarranted act" of granting his new son-in-law, Prince Wilhelm Franz of Prussia, "the illegal title of a Russian grand duke." The statement also protested Wladimir's earlier action of declaring his daughter Maria "the sole Heiress to the Throne, foreseeing the beginning of a new dynasty of Hohenzollern-Romanoff." Vasili explains that except for Wladimir, the Romanoff family accepts the abdication of the last czar. "Thus there is no more Romanoff *dynasty*. However, we continue as a *family*.

"None of us is entitled to give out honors and titles and medals as Wladimir and his father Cyril have done. It was nonsense for Cyril to declare himself czar, and it is outrageous for Wladimir to claim that his son-in-law—my second cousin, it so happens—is now Orthodox and to give him the Russian name Mihail and to make him a grand duke. Wladimir has created a new family as if we, the rest of the Romanoff family, did not exist. From our point of view, Wladimir does not exist and never existed!

"The whole world knows that neither Wladimir's mother nor Cyril's mother converted to Orthodoxy at the time their sons were born, which means that according to our law of the imperial family, neither of them is eligible to occupy the throne.

"But none of us can rightfully claim the throne. The monarchy is no more. If Russia wants to become a monarchy again, it is up to the Russian people or its elected representatives to choose a new czar, as they did in 1613 when they elected the first Romanoff. It is unseemly for any of us Romanoffs to push ourselves forward and say 'I am your ruler.' The Russian people may want a republic, or perhaps they are accustomed to their horrible socialist state. But there has to be an election."

"The quarrel with Wladimir is most unfortunate," says Prince Nikita Romanoff, fifty-six, an historian whose 1975 book *Ivan the Terrible* won critical acclaim. "We cannot talk to Wladimir. He will not speak with any Romanoff unless that Romanoff recognizes his daughter's right to the throne first."

British-born Nikita lives in Manhattan's Upper East Side and was educated in England and at Berkeley. He is an American citizen and has visited Russia in 1963 and in 1971 to do historical research. He found Soviet officials polite and the Communist regime much weaker than in previous decades. A grand-nephew to Nicholas II, he is diffident and bears a striking resemblance to the actor Peter O'Toole.

Nikita defends the czars in the cadences of an Oxford don. "Consider not only what my ancestors did but also what they could have done yet didn't. They were autocrats, but, except for Peter the Great, they acted within the law. They were like the sultans—there was nothing to hold them back."

Nikita disputes the view that Russia was a prisonhouse of nations and points out that the British Empire did not enjoy the consent of its constituent parts. He thinks it is unfair to compare Russia with other European countries; Russia is farther to the East, and so much bigger, and reforms take much more time to take root. "The czars had no evil intent," he says, sipping his tea and reaching tentatively for a small English biscuit. "But they were unable to cope quickly with a situation. People got exasperated because some things didn't function like clockwork. Still, there would have been no Bolshevik revolution if not for World War I."

Nikita believes that monarchy may stage its comeback in the future and that people may come to recognize monarchy's usefulness when it is a last resort. The danger of monarchy, he cautions, is a deification of the monarch. He thinks that the majority of Russian monarchists living in exile recognize either Wladimir, or Nicholas, the other candidate suggested by imperial law. In his opinion, very few would be prepared to recognize Maria. He backs Nicholas.

Prince Nicholas Romanoff, fifty-six, is the son of Prince Roman, who was the Elder of the Family—a purely ceremonial title—until his death in 1978. Nicholas's grandmother was a sister to Queen Helena, wife of Victor Emmanuel III, king of Italy until 1946.

Nicholas is well over six feet tall, barrel-chested, boisterous. He receives me in Rome, in a spacious, sunlit apartment filled with Italian Renaissance furniture, paintings from the past five centuries, and rare books.

"I feel sorry for Wladimir," Nicholas says. "He inherited his isolation from his father and he chose to perpetuate it. He is all alone, estranged from the rest of the Romanoff family. Perhaps it's too late for a reconciliation, but I want to say that I respect him as a Romanoff, and, as far as I am concerned, he is number one among us. But that doesn't mean that he is the czar, only that he is the head of the family.

"I must respect him even though he is dead wrong when he insults and ignores the rest of us Romanoffs. He thinks of himself as the czar. He thinks he is doing his duty; I accept that. But what I object to—and object strenuously—is his insistence on the rights of a reigning sovereign. For instance, he demands that we ask for his permission to marry. Must a Romanoff who lives, say, in Australia, write to Wladimir for his permission? And must we all marry royalty? My God, what rubbish! Believe me, a nice little German princess is hard to find these days. I myself married an Italian countess and I didn't think of asking Wladimir for his permission. So Wladimir disowns me.

"He also claims the right to tell us what names we may have. He says we ought to call ourselves Romanovski, not Romanoff, because we have forfeited our membership in the Romanoff family.

What gall! I shall not speak to him or write to him unless he calls me by my name.

"I have no interest in being a prince. I don't care for all that princely stuff and nonsense. Call me *Principe*, if you like, or call me Signor Romanoff or call me Nick. Whatever pleases you. But by God, my family name is Romanoff. Nobody can take my name away from me.

"What is important to me is that I am on speaking terms with everyone in the family. Everyone except Wladimir, of course. It's sad how scattered we Romanoffs are. We should be at peace with one another. We have an identity and we should be known for what we are: members of a once-ruling family.

"In the past, we made mistakes, even grievous mistakes, and we paid dearly for those mistakes. But no member of the family could call himself the czar. A pretender, a chargé d'affaires, a viceroy who keeps the throne warm—we simply do not have such things in our family tradition. Politics shouldn't divide us, and we should present ourselves as one family although we have been brought up in different countries. I happen to be stateless; I just don't have enough strength to acquire an Italian nationality. But other Romanoffs have taken up various nationalities. There is nothing wrong with that.

"I was born in the south of France, married a Florentine countess, a marvelous woman, and our three daughters are Italian. They didn't want to learn Russian, and I didn't force them. I don't like to force people against their will. Perhaps if I had a son, somehow I would have found a way to coax him into learning Russian. But daughters? They will not carry the family name. Let them be what they want to be, I thought. So, as a result, I am on excellent terms with them. I am their friend and I am a happy father."

The three daughters, aged between sixteen and twenty-nine, are strikingly beautiful. Their photographs are on all the walls and blend with the oil portraits and pastoral landscapes of earlier centuries. The youngest bursts into the room—like her sisters, she is tall, slim, with long blonde hair—and gives a big kiss and hug to her father. Nicholas delivers a lengthy, complicated telephone message from her boy friend. A squeal of delight, another kiss and a hug, and she runs out to return the phone call.

"My daughters are 100 percent Italian, 100 percent today's young people. I sometimes wish they were less Italian and less modern, and a bit Russian and old-fashioned. But should I have created a piece of Russia in our home? A museum with my family as part of the exhibition? Exiles are such sad people. I avoid pathetic exiles, I prefer those who get ahead and get out of the rut of being in exile. Yes, one should not forget one's Russian soul, but one ought not to exclude everything else.

"I thank God for my wife and daughters. I am surrounded with beauty. I manage my wife's estate near Florence. We have vineyards and cattle on 600 acres. I slipped into a farmer's life some thirty years ago. It's a good life.

"As a teenager I hid from the Germans during occupation. I cannot really say I suffered under a dictatorship but I did witness repression, constriction. Then I spent four lazy years in Egypt, in exile. When we came back to Italy, I went to work for the Americans in Rome. I helped out in the psychological warfare division of the U.S. Army and later I was in charge of typewriters for the USIA [United States Information Agency]. I never finished college, but I have the war and our exile in Egypt as excuses.

"I like the countryside; I go boar hunting. And I am inordinately proud of the beautiful white cattle we raise. It's called Chianiana, and it's the typical cattle of Toscana: big, white, giving excellent lean meat. The best meat in Italy, if not in the world."

Nicholas spends part of the year in Rome and travels abroad at least once a year, usually in the Mediterranean area. "I am a Mediterranean," he declares with a broad smile. "I love this blessed puddle of a sea. I feel like a stranger on any other sea." He collects naval books and paints aquarelles, but only ships and seascapes. He boasts: "I can recite all the names of all the battleships in the Battle of Jutland on May 31, 1916."

He confesses also to being a secret writer; he writes for his drawer, in the grand tradition of Russia. His subject: the Russian Imperial Navy. He has not shown his work to publishers; few people know about it, he says, and he is not at all sure that it is worth publishing. He lets out a big, raucous laugh and downs a glass of brandy. He belongs in a tavern with old chestnut beams and heavy oak chairs.

Nicholas cannot imagine a restoration of the monarchy in Russia. "Many strange things have happened in Russia," he says, shaking his head, "but the strangest would be a return of the monarchy.

"My hope is that one day the Russian people will say: Peter was a great czar, Catherine was a good ruler, Nicholas II was weak, but, on the whole, in its time the empire grew.

"If I am ever permitted to visit Russia, I wouldn't want to see the past. I would want to see the present. I would like to take pride in the present, for which the Russian people paid such an enormous price. History could have taken a different course. But I know that the achievements of the present would not have been possible without the past in which my family was involved.

"There are so many losers, so many sad people among those who fell victim to history. Our older generation of Romanoffs have gone through a lot, and those bloody, murderous conflicts leave a mark. The older generation—the generation of the Civil War—is unforgiving, unchangeable. But for me, it's different: it's against my convictions to see things in black-and-white, or red-and-white. I say we Romanoffs should be the best of the losers."

Yevgeni Vagin calls himself "an esthetic monarchist." He left his native Leningrad in 1977 on an Israeli visa the police suggested he apply for though he is not Jewish. The KGB wanted to be rid of him. Within days, he received his exit permit and went to Rome where he has been living ever since.

Prior to his departure, Vagin spent eight years in Soviet jails and labor camps. He was convicted of having taken part in a clandestine organization which recruited some thirty members between 1964 and 1967, and which planned to overthrow the Communist dictatorship. The group called itself the All-Russian Social-Christian Union for the Liberation of Russia, and it developed an anti-Marxist and non-Western ideology of religious Slavophilism. Unlike the plots and factions unveiled by the show trials of the 1930s and '40s, the Social-Christian Union indeed existed. It printed and distributed anti-Communist literature and was astonishingly successful in enlisting members, most of them intellectuals and many of them from prominent Communist families.

A soft-spoken, frail man of forty, Vagin has a scraggly reddish-brown beard and wide-set, china-blue eyes. He is a writer, a journalist, and is currently employed by the Italian radio. At Leningrad University he studied literature and planned to specialize in Dostoyevsky—the novelist who began as a revolutionary and ended up as a monarchist. Vagin looks like a Russian revolutionary; not the grim, suspicious conspirator slated to take charge of the secret police once the revolution is successful, but the born dissenter who will be the first purge victim of the revolutionary regime.

He characterizes his monarchist sentiments as "vague" and "dreamlike," growing out of an Orthodox faith that was strengthened in the labor camps, and his belief that the past need not be rejected but studied for clues and lessons. Like the American scholar John B. Dunlop, who analyzed the Social-Christian Union in his 1976 book *The New Russian Revolutionaries*, Vagin is reluctant to describe the movement he had taken part in as monarchist, but agrees that its objective was a theocratic state possibly headed by a constitutional monarch, elected by a national assembly and representing national unity, not any party. Vagin, number three leader in the Social-Christian Union, was perhaps the closest among them to the idea of a traditional monarchy, both because of his interest in restoring "lawful authority" and because of his search for "moral authority."

In an interview in his Rome apartment—a typical refugee crash pad where books and folding beds constitute the two main categories of furnishings—Vagin talks about a definite interest in monarchy among intellectuals as well as the masses. "But I know of no monarchist movement or program in Russia," he adds. "The monarchist idea has an attraction although Nicholas II is sharply criticized among neo-Slavophiles as responsible for the descent into the hell of communism." He reports a strange cult of the last czar: large numbers of people have been going on pilgrimages to the site where he and his family were murdered; several articles in *samizdat* publications have dealt with him; books on his life written in Western languages are smuggled into Russia, copied and circulated; there is often applause when Communist propaganda films show old clips of him; new official documents and Marxist studies of his reign are published and snapped up; old books with his picture fetch high black market prices; young intellectuals display his picture in their apartments.

"But the Communists of today or yesterday are not going to be the monarchists of tomorrow," he cautions. Vagin no longer believes that ex-Communists such as Hungary's Imre Nagy or Czechoslovakia's Alexander Dubcek can bring about a true transformation of Communist society. Ten years ago, he thought that a Czech liberalization or even a Hungarian revolution could take place in Russia and be successful. Now his faith is not in disillusioned Communists—or their secret sympathizers in high positions—but in young people "unblemished by communism." To him, a religious awakening is the key to radical change in Russia. He thinks that such a change is slowly taking place: a rejection of materialism, a renaissance of the soul.

I am taking a walk with émigré writers in Venice, an incomparable city built on shifting sands by refugees who sought sanctuary from the Huns some 1,500 years ago. Someone quotes Dante, banished from his native Florence: "How salt is the taste of another's bread, and how hard a path it is to go up and down another's stairs." Did Dante support the pope or the emperor? No one in our group is sure if Dante was a Guelf or a Ghibelline.

The eminent Russian poet Joseph Brodsky declares mournfully that the Soviet Union is indeed the future because bureaucratic rule and oppression are in store for the West as well. He says regimentation is inevitable because of the pressures of overpopulation, rising consumer demands and the exigencies of a technological society. But Brodsky's poetry reflects a newly found religious faith; critics see him as an ally of Solzhenitsyn and a mystic.

Eduard Goldstuecker, head of the Czech Writers' Union during the Prague spring of 1968 and an old underground Communist, calls Slavic revivalism reactionary, atavistic, and out of tune with the twentieth century. "There can be no return to the times of Peter the Great," he thunders, "there can be no return to the past. History marches forward!"

"The Russians come from darkness and they love darkness," whispers novelist Arnost Lustig, another supporter of Dubcek's. "Russian émigrés brought their darkness with them to the West. Of course they suffered most of all—more than anyone else in Eastern Europe. But they never understood and still don't understand those who are not Russian. They want to save us one more time."

We agree that the Communist regime cannot last. The people are opposed to it; reason rebels against it; dissent is spreading. Where will the fire be next time? In tense Poland? In stolid, furtive Bulgaria? Why not in Russia itself?

If the regime collapses—in Hungary in 1956, it took less than forty-eight hours—what will be left? Is there a legacy worth saving, a concept of justice, a moral or philosophical principle, a style of living?

Who will lament the passing of the politburo? Will the world be a poorer place to live without it? And after bonfires have turned all the propaganda brochures and police files into cinders, who will look back lovingly at the times of Stalin, Khruschev, and Brezhnev?

It is dawn, and the light is iridescent, refracted by the sea and the pink marble of the Doge's Palace. The exiles disperse; it is time to surrender to sleep.

There is a recurrent refugee dream of going back home and not being able to get out again. Children born in exile disappear, and beloved friends in the old houses are stony-faced, hostile. There are refugees who never stop running for their lives: the fires burn, the killing continues, the enemy cannot be vanquished.

Will the day come when an émigré, now brooding over the deep Russian past or weighing the meaning of true liberalization, follows Lenin's footsteps in taking a train from Germany to St. Petersburg to save Russia and to redeem the world?

The Monarchist Hour

Heaven and earth conspire that everything which has been, be rooted and reduced to dust. Only the dreamers, who dream while awake, call back the shadows of the past and braid nets from unspun threads.

Isaac Bashevis Singer,
The Spinoza of Market Street

I am a monarchist when the sun goes down, and the scarlets and golds give way to an egalitarian darkness. It is a setting that inspires me to dismiss the insistent present and wander backward—to reflect, to revise, perhaps to regret. It is a time to remember a waltz, a quatrain of long ago, and to recall a lost kingdom.

It is an hour when I, a moralist, am moved listening to a friend, a well-adjusted housewife with fine children, talking about her first boyfriend. He was the best dancer in high school, and she is still in love with him. He lives on another continent—émigrés have conquered the world—but they see each other secretly, once every five years or so. He is now a balding, ulcerous business executive, and she is no more that lithe girl who knew by heart Tatiana's letter to Onegin. But for those few hurried hours in a hotel, the everyday world disappears and everything is as perfect as it was when they were eighteen.

Sunset is a time when I feel an urge for the touch of a silver goblet, and I like to be mystified by a coat of arms with lions and roses, swords and stars. I think of the distant secrets of my ancestry, and I try to decipher the handwriting of fate in the succession of Miguels and Manuels in Portugal. I lament our estrangement from the past. I search for permanence and applaud loyalty as the highest form of passion. I am inclined to forget that monarchy was once absolute and that under its aegis dissent was equated with treason, and injustice and brutality flourished.

The Third World is going through its revolutions of 1649, 1789, and 1917 now. In the past two decades, monarchs were deposed in Iran, Laos, Ethiopia, Afghanistan, Cambodia, Libya, Yemen,

Zanzibar, and Iraq; the kings of Jordan and Morocco have lived through a series of assassination attempts. Asia has twelve monarchies: Bahrein, Bhutan, Japan, Jordan, Kuwait, Malaysia, Nepal, Oman, Qatar, Saudi Arabia, Thailand, and the United Arab Emirates. In Africa, Lesotho and Swaziland are ruled by tribal kings; Morocco's monarch is a descendant of the Prophet Mohammed; in 1976, an army chief of staff declared himself Bokassa I, emperor of Central Africa, but was overthrown three years later. Tonga's monarchy and Europe's ten make the world total 26.

Among Europe's non-reigning royalty, there was much sympathy for the shah of Iran—the most powerful post-World War I monarch. They recognize that the bell that tolls for one king tolls for all. That the shah was mere second-generation royalty did not lessen their concern. A king is a king is a king, and there are fewer and fewer of them on thrones. Just as the coronation of Spain's Juan Carlos raised royalist expectations throughout Europe, the shah's fall diminished hopes of restoration—a hope that no pretender ever surrenders.

The shah was unbeloved. He erred, his family stole, his men murdered. No tribe, army regiment or party apparatus could be relied upon to save him and to suppress the rest of the nation. Suddenly, his time was up; his good deeds were forgotten. The King of Kings had to go.

The temptation is irresistible: deposing a king is high drama, and the measure of exultation the righteous are entitled to feel rises in direct proportion to the power he arrogated. But when a monarchy is gone, and the crowned head rests on the sandy ground of the executioner's pit or on a Côte d'Azur beach, there is a sudden emptiness, an eerie silence. Then the void is filled with new lies, cheap bombast, and the clamor of politicians from whom only a strongman can rescue us: a chairman of a new revolution, a low-born despot, an ersatz king.

There are no more crowned heads in the ancient realms between the Volga and the Rhine; no courts in the peasant lands of the Balkan. In France and Italy, royalty no longer set standards for elegance, or centralize administration.

An age of fable has ended. The world has gotten old; skepticism is our wisdom. We do not believe in the magic of pedigree, and we expect the son not to take up his father's role. There are no more once-and-future kings foretold and prayed for; no secret sons and false pretenders; no royal pathos of trust and betrayal. We have canceled faith, the gold standard of monarchy, as well as "the Pleasure of His Majesty," once the common currency.

Republican accountability requires a pursuit of the rational. Citizens bow to the technician whose presumption is efficiency and whose excuse is science. He knows all about systems, and "functional" is his highest praise.

Kings appear so much more benign now than at the time they wielded the power of life and death, and chose between peace and war. Compared to the dictators who followed them, their faults seem eminently forgivable; their folly is ever so human.

There is no question that under the czar, conditions in courts, jails, and villages of exile were more humane than under the dictatorship of the proletariat. Escapes were common, and revolutionaries wrote their best books and pamphlets while in detention. But the argument favoring decadent caprice over scientific ruthlessness is good only for idle chatter. Nostalgia for royalty is not a potent political force; it cannot send people out into the street to demonstrate. Monarchism has become a mood rather than a movement—a longing for another century, a way of expressing a sense of loss, an argument with time.

Of my meetings with nonreigning royalty, the one with Otto von Habsburg came closest to a reunion. It was like a conversation with my favorite high school teacher, the one who taught me his love of history. We cited the same prime ministers and poets; we shared references to rebellions and invasions. He has come to respect those who manned the barricades of 1848, and I no longer despise the Habsburgs whom my great-grandfathers fought.

Now that we are older and I, too, have been tested in what Central Europeans call "the School of Life," we can agree fully on one subject: the brutal unfairness of history. But Otto has too strong a sense of the "ought to be" to shrug his shoulders, accept defeat or come to terms with the way things are. What holds him back is an exalted view of man, rather than pride in who he is. He is too dedicated a pedagogue to give up correcting reality.

But he now concedes that the rebuffs he receives baffle him.

I found myself reluctant to remind him of the obvious: that the Habsburgs' subject nations objected to serving as units in a multi-national empire under Austrian administration and that his ancestors were, for the most part, incompetent and unpopular.

The distinction between teacher and student will not and perhaps cannot disappear. He was once a star student, but, as a teacher, he cannot become one of the boys. I was not a bad student, but I can never be his teacher. We both insist on a wall to separate us and appreciate all the more those choice moments of sharing history lessons that suspend our basic, unchangeable difference in position and purpose. We remain teacher and student, royalty and subject. We are loyalists of the past, partners in the same illusion.

Nonreigning monarchs are refugees from the mobs of modernity, superseded by the fickle moods of democracy and the reptilian immobility of totalitarianism. Measured against the gray of republican rectitude, monarchy is the splendid diversion, the nostalgia option, the purple possibility.

Perhaps a king is an exile in time. Perhaps he belongs with knights in shining armor and damsels in distress—if not with fauns and naiads.

But is history as irreversible and as obedient to immutable laws as Hegel and Marx, Spengler and Toynbee tell us? Is it a preposterous notion to believe that time is not a one-way street without detours and bends and alternate routes?

Desperation and daring are two factors that skew the rational calculation of politicians. They may claim that the future belongs to them, but they cannot predict—and much less control—people who, certain that they have nothing to lose but their chains, take to the streets.

No revolution follows a master plan; it is the momentum that is unstoppable. There is a subterranean compulsion to live up to historic ideals. Fighting Hitler and Stalin, Tito cited Karageorge's war against the sultan; the Paris Commune of 1871 marched under the slogans of 1789. A lost cause is equally powerful: the Hungarian rebels of 1956 claimed the inheritance of the 1848 revolution.

There is a peculiar strength that flows from recurrence and remembrance. It is a kind of magic—for magic is the power released when elements seemingly disparate or long ignored are joined. And what a glorious defiance it is to rebel against those hypocrites who call themselves the vanguard of progress and presume to own history!

Regardless of his personal imperfections, a monarch represents the majesty of history. He is an heir—a link in a chain that leads to the Middle Ages that in turn connects to antiquity and beyond, to the beginning of measured time when the first hero slew the dragon of disorder and established the rule of law.

The moon rises, the patron of lovers and plotters. I survey a moonlit garden—the natural habitat for conspiracy. Every shadow and scent is an accomplice.

The failures of squabbling parliamentarians and dull apparatchiks alike can result in new types of revolutionary upheavals. (Who could have predicted an alliance in Iran between Marxists marching forward and Muslim fundamentalists determined to undo the twentieth century?) Then, luck and youthful folly, surprise and timing can bring about a restoration.

There is no formula for second youth. But take a measure each of King Michael's thoughtful courage, or Commander Leka's entrepreneurial recklessness, and Henri Bourbon-Orléans's eloquence, or King Umberto's operatic performance, and it requires only a modest dose of whimsy to imagine that a prince, too, could pull off a coup, and more successfully than King Constantine. And who knows, we might be around, incredulous but grinning, when he does.

BIBLIOGRAPHY

Alexander, Grand Duke of Russia. *Always a Grand Duke*. New York: Farrar and Rinehart, 1933.

Barzini, Luigi. *From Caesar to the Mafia*. New York: The Library Press, 1971.

Bocca, Geoffrey. *Kings Without Thrones*. New York: The Dial Press, 1959.

Burke's Royal Families of the World. London: Burke's Peerage Ltd., 1977.

da Costa, Sergio Correa. *Every Inch a King*. London: Robert Hale, 1950.

Crankshaw, Edward. *The Habsburgs*. New York: The Viking Press, 1971.

Curley, Walter J. P., Jr. *Monarchs-in-Waiting*. New York: Dodd, Mead and Company, 1973.

de Diesbach, Ghislain. *Secrets of the Gotha*. New York: Meredith Press, 1968.

Dunlop, John B. *The New Russian Revolutionaries*. Belmont, Mass.: Nordland, 1976.

Franck, Nicolette. *La Roumania dans l'Engrenage*. Paris: Elsevier Sequoia, 1977.

Goldner, Franz. *Austrian Emigration 1938-1945*. New York: Frederick Ungar, 1979.

de Gramont, Sanche. *Epitaph for Kings*. New York: Putnam, 1967.

von Habsburg, Otto. *Charles V*. New York: Praeger Publishers, 1970.

Henri, Comte de Paris. *Mémoires d'Exil et de Combats*. Paris: Atelier Marcel Jullian, 1979.

Henry, Walter. *The Soldier Kings*. New York: G. P. Putnam, 1970.

Isabelle, Comtesse de Paris. *Tout M'est Bonheur*. Paris: Robert Laffont, 1978.

Le Livre de la Famille Impériale. Paris: Librairie Académique Perrin, 1969.

Louis Ferdinand, Prince of Prussia. *The Rebel Prince*. Chicago: Henry Regnery, 1952.

Maurois, André. *A History of France*. New York: Farrar, Straus and Cudahy, 1956.

Nowell, Charles E. *A History of Portugal*. Princeton: D. Van Nostrand, 1952.

Peter II. *A King's Heritage*. London: Cassell and Company Ltd., 1955.

Seton-Watson, Hugh. *The East European Revolution*. New York: Frederick A. Praeger, 1951.

_____ . *Eastern Europe Between the Wars, 1918-1941*. Cambridge, 1945.

Stavrianos, L. S. *The Balkans Since 1453*. New York: Holt, Rinehart and Winston, 1965.

Stephan, John J. *The Russian Fascists*. New York: Harper & Row, 1978.

Vasari, Emilio. *Dr. Otto von Habsburg oder die Leidenschaft für Politik*. Wien-München: Verlag Herold, 1972.

Vodopivec, Alexander. *Die Balkanisierung Österreichs*. Wien: Verlag Fritz Molden, 1966.